Hangin' with Winners

Hangin' with WINNERS

A LIFETIME OF CONNECTIONS, ANECDOTES AND LESSONS LEARNED

BY RAY COLE WITH ROB GRAY

bpc

ISBN-13: 978-1-950790-08-1
Library of Congress Control Number: 2021914915
Business Publications Corporation Inc., Des Moines, IA

Business Publications Corporation Inc.
The Depot at Fourth
100 4th Street
Des Moines, Iowa 50309
(515) 288-3336

To Jackson, Addison, Grayson, Kaden and Hayes:

You have given your Grammy Susan and me boundless joy, and shown us how being a grandparent is one of the few things in life that's not overrated. We will love you always.

CONTENTS

FOREWORD
BY ROB GRAY

"Ray Cole is a force of nature. He is about the most friendly, optimistic man I've ever met. He really is. He's so excited about life and politics and media and his family and friends. And that enthusiasm is infectious. ... He's so direct and without guile. That makes you do what he wants you to do, which I think is kind of the secret of his success."

George Stephanopoulos to Rob Gray (Feb. 26, 2020)

A big orange "X" is carefully scrawled across the interview transcript I sought to excavate in order to form the framework for this foreword.

The wise words I wanted to find lurked within one of many de facto no-go zones among my 60-plus interviews for this book, which co-author — and whether he likes it or not, star of the show — Ray Cole gently decreed is not, and absolutely cannot, be about him.

I ignored the "X." I dug deeper into my interview with the great Iowa-based writer and biographer Chuck Offenburger and discovered exactly what Ray seemingly hoped I wouldn't.

It was — gasp! — about him. A man from tiny Kingsley, Iowa, who became perhaps the most influential person at ABC, ESPN and Disney that no one really knows.

Shhh, he'd say. But it's still true.

"He's obviously struck them as somebody who is genuine," Chuck said when asked why so many famous people would agree to an interview with me — a relatively unknown sports reporter/columnist for Iowa State fan site *CycloneFanatic.com* — and first-time co-author. "If you can just act like you are genuinely interested in this person's story, it's like they can't resist telling you. They're just going to spill their guts. And when you get good at that — and Ray is — people will probably wonder later why the hell they told him as much as they did. ... It's pretty remarkable how he's been able to do that."

It's not an act — as Chuck obviously knows. Ray is deeply interested in everyone's stories. He's developed deep bonds with both the famous and anonymous precisely because he truly cares about where they came from, what they're about and where they're going.

"I feel like I'm a younger version of Ray," said former NCAA and NBA basketball star Jay Williams, who has turned personal tragedy into a tremendous career in broadcasting and media. "He struck me right from the beginning of our relationship as a person who encapsulates my business and life philosophies. In order for that to make sense, you have to understand its context and know about something that happened to me in my life. After almost passing away at age 21 and then spending years trying to make a professional basketball comeback, I had someone close to me say something that set the precedent for my life. It was, 'Hey, this is business. This isn't personal.' That statement reverberated badly because every time I had done business up to that point, it was also personal. To me, making it personal was not only the best way to conduct business, it also produced the strongest relationships. So, from the beginning, we just hit the ground running. Ray later asked me to come out to Iowa for a Variety - the Children's Charity dinner. We became family around that event, going out there and meeting his wife (Susan) and spending time with them. There is always an energy that Ray carries with him, and I carry it the same."

That energy led many to type a phrase that became something of a mantra for this project: "Anything for Ray."

I wouldn't have fully understood these three words if I hadn't already met Ray for the first time a few months earlier for a buffet lunch at the Des Moines Golf and Country Club.

He pitched the book. Said someone had recommended me for the project. Asked if I would be interested. I didn't hesitate. "Yes, of course," I said. The "anything for Ray" bug had struck me — but only because I knew I would gain something meaningful from our association.

For one, I had never written a book. I probably should have, but was deathly afraid of taking that step in my writing career. The fear of never being "good enough" is strong in me. It's real and scary. Meeting Ray made that momentarily melt away. Where others see a zero sum game, or so-called give-and-take relationship, he always envisions a win-win scenario. It's a unique trait and one that reverberates throughout the pages of this book. Ray is a rare person. There's no affect. Only empathy. I cannot emphasize this enough.

So, "anything for Ray," it was — and is. With gusto.

"I first met Ray Cole at a (ABC) board of governors meeting long ago and I felt exactly what the world does on meeting him, which is, 'Have I known you forever?'" said legendary journalist Diane Sawyer. "'Because it feels as if your warmth and your high wattage should have been in my life.' There is such enthusiasm, though I think it is too ordinary a word for what he has. (There's) a powerful combination of curiosity and eagerness to learn and (an) absolute conviction that if we do it together the world can be a better place."

That's not a pie in the sky proposition. Really, if it were, would Sawyer buy into it? No, Ray has struck that rare balance between success and compassion; of giving and taking — but mostly giving.

I became convinced of this during a one-hour lunch. Then I dug into a project that mushroomed well beyond what we discussed and adjusted accordingly. *Anything for Ray* should have been the title of this book. I feel it. More than 60 other people interviewed herein — and countless others outside of our purview — do, too.

"Ray Cole is exceptionally engaging not based so much on what he says, which is always thoughtful, but how he says it," former ESPN talent development executive Gerry Matalon said. "It's how he engages in such a warm, others-oriented tone of speaking where he puts you at ease and makes you feel like you've known him forever. That kind of interaction is what makes him stand out and I think it's just organic to him. Ray makes people feel significant, he makes them feel valued and he makes them feel appreciated. Those are three core things that every person needs to feel."

I know I did. Ray pushed me past my self-imposed limits. He did so gently, even at times when I'd guess he was troubled by my slow pace.

That's one of many reasons why I'd do "anything for Ray." And I hope once you've read this book you'll honor him the same way by pushing past perceived limits, embracing the win-win scenarios and treating everyone with kindness and respect.

"Ray's social intelligence is off the charts," said Martha Raddatz, ABC News' chief global affairs correspondent. "You're drawn to Ray and he's just a natural. And you know what else about Ray? As in your life he comes, you never feel like he just wants to use you. Ray genuinely cares about you. It's like everybody who meets Ray remembers him and I just think it's because he is kind and curious with a capital 'C' underlined. He's always the optimist in the room."

Take note: It *is* about him.

And no big orange "X" will ever change that. For me, or for anyone else whose life he's touched.

"Ray's approach to business is sort of what author Malcolm Gladwell wrote about in his book, *The Tipping Point: How Little Things Make a Difference*," former ABC News, ABC Network and Disney executive Ben Sherwood told me. "Ray may be the ultimate example of the 'connectors' that Gladwell talked about in that book. Through one avenue or another, he has forged relationships with countless 'winners' and has built an incredible network. And that network really has been productive for him and helped him succeed as he deployed it whenever he had a business or personal challenge. It's all a part of the 'winning' strategy executed by this otherwise ordinary guy from Iowa."

ACKNOWLEDGMENTS

BY RAY COLE

It's not possible to thank and acknowledge by name all the people who have enriched my career over the past 40-plus years. But it is important to recognize a few of the people who have blessed my life along the way, and whose support and encouragement have made all the difference.

It all starts with family. My wife, Susan, and I were both raised in Kingsley, Iowa, where for years the sign on the entrance to town read, "Welcome to Kingsley. Some bigger, none better." Golfing legend Arnold Palmer once said, "Your hometown is not where you're from. It's who you are." Susan and I were fortunate to grow up in a small town where the default setting was almost always set to "friendly" in most folks. It was there that our parents showed us by example the joy that comes from hard work and community service, and how love of family comes above all else.

We are proud of our daughter, Kristy Latta, her husband, Jeff, and their kids Jackson and Addison; our daughter, Brittney Johnson, her husband, Kane, and their boys Grayson, Kaden and Hayes; and our son, Brandon, and his girlfriend, Jessica McNamara. Susan's love, in particular, has always meant the world to me. As I said while accepting the Robert D. Ray Pillar of Character Award in July 2019, she has contributed mightily to any of my character strengths while, at the same time, patiently tolerating my many character flaws!

I owe much to the many colleagues it was my privilege to work with from the outset of my television career as an intern at KCAU-TV in Sioux

City, Iowa, in March 1976. My first mentor was Clair Giles who had, in fact, signed and filed the original license application with the Federal Communication Commission to put the station on the air in 1953 with its original call letters, KVTV. Upon graduation from Briar Cliff College (now University) the following year, I accepted a full-time position at KCAU and succeeded Clair following his retirement. My new boss, and second mentor, was Bill Turner, who was an established community and industry leader. At the time, Bill was serving as chairman of the ABC-TV Affiliates Association's board of governors; it was especially gratifying for me to be elected to serve in the same capacity some 30 years later.

In 1985, my career and life was changed in immeasurable ways when Philip J. "Phil" Lombardo and his then-fledgling Citadel Communications Company purchased KCAU-TV. Phil was an experienced broadcaster with a burning entrepreneurial spirit in his soul. He also had a well-deserved reputation for being a tough and demanding taskmaster! From our first dinner meeting until this day, it's impossible to quantify the amount that I've learned from Phil and adequately describe the diverse experiences we've shared together. He has been the mentor of all mentors.

Over the past 35 years, our family has developed close relationships with Phil and his wife, Kim. The personal nature of these connections has often transcended the business ones. Ditto for longtime Citadel colleagues like Colleen Liebre, Dan Ackerman, Andrea Capodanno, Teresa Fuquey, Roger Moody, Marshall Porter, the late Tony McMahon, Russ Hamilton, Charlie Cusimano, Ray Johnson, Randy Shelton, John Walters, Brad Edwards, Erin Nanke, Tim Seaman, Danielle Feenstra, J.D. Walls, Rod Fowler, Jeff Swanson, Kay Wunderlich, Lanise Ethen, Ken Bell, John DeLuca, Bill Lancaster and so many others to whom I'm forever indebted. We certainly had our challenges and experienced many frustrations but one thing is certain: It was never boring! These broadcasting professionals understood what it meant to operate "in the public interest, convenience and necessity." They also recognized that being a leader was about much more than whatever title they held and demonstrated the kind of "winning" qualities and attributes discussed throughout this book. Simply put, they made my career rewarding and more fulfilling.

I'd also like to extend a special word of appreciation to all those who have corresponded with or spent time with me in years past, and/or took time out of their busy schedules in the midst of a pandemic to be formally interviewed for this project:

- Dr. Jennifer Ashton (ABC News chief health and medical correspondent)
- Chris Berman (ESPN studio host and former *SportsCenter* anchor)
- George Bodenheimer (Co-chair of the Disney Media Networks, president of ESPN and cable industry pioneer, retired)
- Bob Bowlsby (Commissioner of the Big 12 Conference and former director of athletics at the University of Iowa and Stanford University)
- Terry E. Branstad (Former governor of Iowa and U.S ambassador to China)
- Susan Braun (CEO of The V Foundation, retired)
- John Buccigross (ESPN *SportsCenter* anchor)
- Chris Bury (Senior journalist in residence at DePaul University and former ABC News *Nightline* national correspondent)
- David Chalian (CNN vice president and political director)
- Rece Davis (ESPN *College GameDay* host and play-by-play commentator)
- Chris Fowler (ESPN college football and tennis commentator)
- Fran Fraschilla (ESPN college basketball analyst)
- Mike Greenberg (ESPN *Get Up!* co-host and radio host)
- Fred Hoiberg (University of Nebraska head basketball coach, former Chicago Bulls head coach, former Iowa State University head coach, former NBA player and former Iowa State player aka "The Mayor")
- Dan Houston (Chairman, president and CEO of the Principal Financial Group)
- Bob Iger (Executive chairman of The Walt Disney Company, former chairman and CEO of The Walt Disney Company, and author of *The Ride of a Lifetime*)
- Ben Jacobson (University of Northern Iowa head basketball coach)
- Aaron Kampman (Aplington-Parkersburg High School, University of Iowa and Green Bay Packers All-Pro NFL defensive end, retired)
- Jon Karl (ABC News chief Washington correspondent, former chief White House correspondent and co-host of *This Week with George Stephanopoulos*)
- Jimmy Kimmel (Host, *Jimmy Kimmel Live!*)

- Rick Klein (ABC News political director)
- Bill Knapp (Chairman emeritus of Knapp Properties, Iowa business legend and philanthropist)
- Ted Koppel (Iconic journalist and founding anchor of ABC News *Nightline*)
- Lisa Kovlakas (ESPN corporate citizenship manager)
- Jack Lashier (Director of the Iowa Hall of Pride, retired)
- Gerry Matalon (Founder of Matalon Media and former ESPN media talent executive and performance coach)
- Kenny Mayne (Former ESPN *SportsCenter* anchor)
- Sean McDonough (ESPN play-by-play commentator)
- Sheri McMichael (Executive director of Variety - the Children's Charity of Iowa)
- Zubin Mehenti (ESPN *Keyshawn, JWill & Zubin* co-host and radio host)
- Rob Mills (ABC-TV Entertainment senior VP of Alternative Series, Specials and Late Night Programming)
- David Muir (ABC News anchor and managing editor of *World News Tonight*)
- Kevin Negandhi (ESPN *SportsCenter* anchor and college football studio host)
- Chuck Offenburger (Longtime "Iowa Boy" columnist for *The Des Moines Register* and author, retired)
- Bill O'Shaughnessy (President of Whitney Global Media)
- Daphne Oz (Nutrition author and former *The Chew* television host)
- Dr. Mehmet Oz (Cardiothoracic surgeon, professor and *The Dr. Oz Show* television host)
- Jamie Pollard (Director of athletics at Iowa State University)
- Dr. Jerry Punch (Former ESPN motorsports and college football commentator)
- Ben Pyne (Former president of Disney/ABC Television global distribution)
- Martha Raddatz (ABC News chief global affairs correspondent and co-host of *This Week with George Stephanopoulos*)
- Suku Radia (CEO and president of Bankers Trust Company, retired)
- Scott Raecker (Executive director of the Robert D. and Billie Ray Center)

- Paul Rhoads (Ohio State University football defensive analyst and former head football coach at Iowa State University)
- Robin Roberts (ABC News co-anchor of *Good Morning America* and founder of Rock'n Robin Productions)
- John Rouse (ABC-TV executive VP for Affiliate Relations and Marketing)
- Bernie Saggau (Executive secretary of the Iowa High School Athletic Association and former president of the National Federation of State High School Associations, retired)
- Diane Sawyer (ABC News anchor of primetime specials, former co-anchor of *Good Morning America* and anchor of *World News Tonight*)
- Jeremy Schaap (ESPN *E:60* and *Outside the Lines* host)
- Connor Schell (Former ESPN executive VP for content and executive producer of the *O.J.: Made in America* and *The Last Dance* documentaries)
- Tim Seaman (KCAU-TV news anchor)
- Ben Sherwood (Founder and CEO of Mojo, former president of ABC News, former co-chairman of the Disney Media Networks and president of the Disney-ABC Television Group)
- John Skipper (Founder of Meadowlark Media, former executive chairman of DAZN Group and former co-chairman of the Disney Media Networks and president of ESPN)
- Robin Sproul (Executive vice president of Javelin and former ABC News vice president and Washington, D.C. bureau chief)
- David Stark (President and CEO of UnityPoint Health-Des Moines and former president of Blank Children's Hospital)
- George Stephanopoulos (ABC News co-anchor of *Good Morning America* and host of *This Week with George Stephanopoulos*)
- Anne Sweeney (Former co-chair of the Disney Media Networks and president of the Disney-ABC Television Group)
- Jake Tapper (CNN lead Washington anchor, host of *The Lead* and *State of the Union* and former ABC News chief White House correspondent)
- Aaron Thomas (Principal and head basketball coach at Aplington-Parkersburg, Iowa, High School and 2010 Arthur Ashe Courage Award honoree)

- Gary Thompson (The "Roland Rocket" and two-sport All-American at Iowa State University)
- Lesley Visser (Pioneering female sports journalist and 2020 Sports Emmy Lifetime Achievement Award recipient)
- Dick Vitale (ESPN college basketball analyst and Naismith Memorial Basketball Hall of Fame inductee)
- Rusty Wallace (Former ESPN auto racing analyst and NASCAR Hall of Fame inductee)
- Rich Waller (President, CEO and chairman of Security National Bank, retired and 2016 recipient of the W. Edwards Deming Business Leadership and Entrepreneurial Excellence Award)
- John Walters (Radio "Voice of the Cyclones" and former sports director at WOI-TV)
- David Westin (Anchor at Bloomberg Television and former president of ABC News)
- John Wildhack (Director of athletics at Syracuse University and former ESPN Executive VP of programming and production)
- Jay Williams (ESPN *Keyshawn, JWill & Zubin* co-host, radio host, and NBA analyst)
- Bob Woodruff (ABC News correspondent and co-founder of the Bob Woodruff Foundation)

And finally, a huge thank you to Rob Gray who has served as a superb writing partner and with whom I've developed a lasting friendship. Rob worked for more than 10 years as a reporter for *The Des Moines Register*, and is now a senior writer for CycloneFanatic.com — a website devoted to covering Iowa State University athletics. I've learned the irrefutable lesson that writing a book is a lot more work than it is fun, but with Rob's collaboration the challenging task became both doable and enjoyable.

The encouragement to write this book came from many places. My daughter Brittney once worked as an account executive at our Des Moines station and has always been a cheerleader for the television business. There were also many former industry colleagues who reached out in September 2019 in the immediate wake of the sale of our last two ABC stations in Providence, Rhode Island and Lincoln, Nebraska. John Wildhack, the director of athletics at Syracuse University and former ESPN executive, dropped me a note and said, "Yours is a phenomenal story and history with ABC. Seriously, you should write a book. What you saw and what you were a huge part of is truly amazing." David Westin, the former president of ABC News, wrote to say, "You were more than 'associated with' ABC, you were a good part of what made ABC what it was." A brief note from David Muir, anchor of *World News Tonight*, was perhaps the most touching of all: "You will always be family."

But the one person who pushed me the strongest and longest to undertake this challenge was Scott Raecker. Working with the late Governor Robert D. Ray, he helped found the *Character Counts!* program which later led to the formation of The Robert D. and Billie Ray Center at Drake University. Scott commented often about the extent to which my career was very much about making connections and building relationships. In an interview for this project, he told Rob Gray: "I encouraged Ray to write this book not for the entertainment value, but for the motivational value. I look at it from the point of view of somebody reading it and saying, 'Hey, I could do that. I know somebody who knows somebody of prominence that I could get connected with and they might be able to help.' That's the story of Ray's life, and what 'winning' means to him. We're not talking about X's and O's. We're not talking about win and loss records. We're talking about living a life of significance and having a positive impact, transforming the lives of others and strengthening the communities that you are involved with."

Many of the people we interviewed for this book have undertaken similar writing projects of their own. We consequently received some helpful advice — and empathy! — along the way. For example, we talked with Jon Karl, chief Washington correspondent for ABC News, the very same week that his best-selling book *Front Row at the Trump Show* was published. He said, "The most important thing that I learned from the process of writing (my book) is how important it was to take a step back and look at the events that I've experienced from a perspective gained with a little bit of time … to go back and try to make sense of what happened. I have learned so much more about the events I've experienced that I had no idea (about) at the time." Jon was spot on, as much of the research and recollections gathered for this book yielded new perspectives that I hadn't considered before.

Jimmy Kimmel published *The Serious Goose* in 2019 and it hit No. 1 on the children's picture book list. He said at the time that the writing and illustration process was "tortuous" and my own experience has given me a new appreciation for that description! It was heartwarming when Jimmy sent me a copy of a letter dated Feb. 28, 2020 that he had overnighted to Blank Children's Hospital. He wrote, "As I believe my friend Ray Cole mentioned, in December of last year, I released a picture book titled *The Serious Goose* and promised to donate all my profits to children's hospitals around the country. Enclosed please find a check (and a book) to support Blank Children's Hospital. Our son Billy is alive and well thanks to hospitals like yours and we are forever grateful for what you do for families in Des Moines." Any amount of angst experienced by Jimmy while writing and illustrating his book was well worth it: The check made payable to Blank Children's Hospital, and included with his letter, was for $10,000.

Emmy-winning TV host and author of several health/fitness books Daphne Oz told us what she learned in the process of writing a book is that you often feel as though you have a cross to bear. Amen to that! Daphne talked candidly about being the overweight kid in a family full of health nuts. She then went on to describe the need to overcome the inevitable frustration that comes with writing — and to find a path to work through it — so you're able to share valuable insights with others who might find some benefit in them. Daphne said the experience "became my calling as it gave me a lens and a filter, and a new perspective. It allowed me to speak about health and wellness."

Daphne's famous dad, Dr. Mehmet Oz, offered generous praise and his own encouragement to me as well when telling Rob Gray, "Ray Cole is one of the most honest, honorable and powerful people in the television business. He's just the kind of person you want to do business with. It is the goal of life to find people who are ready to bring joy and share what they did to find success. This book will show how Ray lives the joy trait and knows the importance of sharing the reasons he's succeeded with others. That's what makes *him* a 'winner.'" No matter how much frustration or impatience I felt along the way, it was impossible for me to even think about turning back after reading those words.

So again, thank you to my family, friends, colleagues and the countless "winners" like John Wildhack, David Westin, David Muir,

Jon Karl, Jimmy Kimmel, Daphne Oz, Mehmet Oz and Scott Raecker, who have loved, guided, supported and/or inspired me.

Ben Sherwood, another former colleague on my "winners" list, spoke about the relationships forged and network formed, through one avenue or another, during the course of my career. Ben said, "It's all a part of the 'winning' strategy executed by this otherwise ordinary guy from Iowa."

Ben's kind words are as humbling as they are personally meaningful. To whatever extent they may hold up, my purpose in writing this book is not to dispense or dole out advice per se as much as it is to simply share stories that flow from a variety of those diverse connections. More importantly, it is to pass along some insights into a few of the "winners" who have graced my life.

It is my sincere hope that the anecdotes and lessons they reveal will enlighten and serve as inspiration to others in the same way that all those mentioned in this book have inspired me.

PROLOGUE:
"WINNING"

*"You've got to get to the stage in life
where going for it is more important
than winning or losing."*

Arthur Ashe, tennis star and humanitarian

What does it mean to "win?" Textbook definitions refer to goals achieved and/or gains obtained by effort or fortune. Should it more broadly encompass a "life is about more than W's" interpretation? To my way of thinking, the answer is unequivocally yes. We should consider the connections created and causes advanced as a reflection of our success, no matter how big or small. The key to such an approach: relationships.

It's as amazing as it is humbling to reflect on my myriad relationships with "winners" that were forged over the course of an otherwise average broadcasting career now spanning six decades. They involve fellow station employees, network colleagues, syndicated programming executives and other vendors, broadcast industry leaders and trade association board members, politicians, and community leaders, organizations and events. Looking back and recalling where I have been and what I have done, I realize how those connections have produced cherished memories like the one involving a private meeting with Arthur Ashe in Howard Cosell's office in January 1985 (see the Howard Cosell profile later in Chapter

Three). They have also yielded many heretofore untold anecdotes and, most importantly, countless lessons learned. It occurred to me that there might be some value in sharing a few of them.

Our company owned KLKN-TV in Lincoln, Nebraska, from 1996 to 2019. During my frequent station visits, I would often take a walk through the campus of the University of Nebraska. Located just outside the northwest entrance to Memorial Stadium is a statue of legendary football coach Tom Osborne along with a quote from another of the state's favorite sons, William Jennings Bryan. It reads: "Destiny is no matter of chance. It is a matter of choice. It is not a thing to be waited for, it is a thing to be achieved." That message always struck me as simple yet profound. While circumstances often do play a role, it is possible to develop "winning" traits and make choices that give us the best chance to find success and happiness in our lives. As Oprah Winfrey once said, "You are not your circumstances. You are your possibilities. If you know that, you can do anything." So, with that thought in mind, what are some of the qualities and characteristics common to "winners" from all walks of life?

Diane Sawyer, one of the outstanding journalists of our time, made it clear that "winning" is not a word she's given much thought to during her lifetime. She told us, "I think more of the moment when your purpose meets joy. When you feel that you've really delivered on something you care about. Where you get to wake up every day and the thing you want to do is the thing that you get to do. And then that somehow makes the world stronger." She then added, "Follow what you are genuinely passionate about and let that guide you to your destination."

Another former *World News Tonight* anchor, Bob Woodruff, told us, "I'm not sure there are any secrets or guaranteed blueprints that lead you to being a 'winner.' I think everybody has a different definition of what that is. I think people are 'winners' when they feel satisfied with what their life is, with what they are doing, and with the impact they are having on those around them." Bob added that his advice would be to find a way to make yourself happy and satisfied with your life. "That, in your own mind, should amount to success," he said.

To be clear, no one with aspirations to ascend to the top of their profession, as Diane Sawyer or Bob Woodruff have, should ever care or think for even a second about putting the word "winner" on a résumé or in their bio. But it can be instructive to learn from the experiences and insights of others to help guide us on our own individual journeys. It's worth remembering that Diane delivered the weather at WLKY in Louisville, Kentucky at the outset of her career. "Yes," she said. "I ended up being a weather girl for a while — maybe the most disastrous weather girl in the history of television — but scrambled to shore."

As for Bob, he studied to become a lawyer in part "because my father said, 'Please don't become a lawyer.'" Always itching to be on the road to find something new, Bob would travel to places in the Middle East and Southeast Asia on adventures between commitments to university studies or jobs. He was teaching young Chinese students about law when the infamous Tiananmen Square protests took place in 1989. Bob Simon, the venerable CBS News correspondent, hired him to get his crew around town as a fixer. It was that experience around a huge story in our world's history that persuaded Bob to pursue a career in journalism.

Diane and Bob are only two of the dozens of "winners" profiled or mentioned in this book whose careers personify the kind of "chance versus choice" destiny that William Jennings Bryan spoke of. Bob Iger, executive chairman of The Walt Disney Company, is another. His career got off to a start similar to Diane's by doing the weather at a cable TV station in Ithaca, New York. In reference to that experience, Bob has said, "I began as a weatherman, and I learned very quickly I wasn't very good at it." Diane made the point to us in an interview for this book about how a company is often molded by the enthusiasm of the person at the top. She then added, "Bob Iger is singular in that he is the most towering combination of creativity, confidence and clarity. His enthusiasms are vast and deep, and always seeking to ennoble the world."

That's pretty high praise from one former weather person to another! But I couldn't agree more with Diane. I've known Bob since the mid 1980's when he was working for legendary sports producer and executive, Roone Arledge. His leadership as a forward-thinking and visionary CEO from 2005 to 2020 was nothing less than transformative for The Walt Disney Company.

Other examples of "winning" executives who rose to the top after unassuming, if not humble, beginnings quickly come to mind. George

Bodenheimer and Anne Sweeney at one time served together as co-chairs of the Disney Media Networks. Their responsibilities included oversight of ESPN and ABC-TV, respectively. It was my privilege to work closely with both of them throughout their time in those roles.

George was someone who had worked his way up the ESPN ladder, literally, from the mailroom to the boardroom. One of his earliest duties involved being a driver for Dick Vitale, another "winner" who is profiled later in this book. Dick loves telling, whenever and wherever he can, how "George used to be my driver and then he became my boss. But he always treated me the same — great!"

Anne's career path was no less extraordinary. She started as a page at ABC during her senior year of college. "Who knew in the fall of 1978 that my first job in television would lead to a career in television?" Anne said. "I'll never forget the feeling of it. I thought to myself, 'I don't know what it is that I want to do here, but this is the kind of place I want to be at.'"

There's an old Chinese proverb that tells us, "Pearls don't lie on the seashore. If you want one, you must dive for it." That kind of mindset is second nature to most all the "winners" with whom I've crossed paths. They understand the importance of having a dream, of "diving" in and then working hard in pursuit of it.

Peggy Whitson, a native of Mount Ayr, Iowa, personifies that proverb's deep meaning. What was her dream as a young girl? To be an astronaut. Peggy saw Neil Armstrong walk on the moon and her mother, Beth, told Jack Lashier in an interview for the Iowa Hall of Pride how Peggy said, "Mom, I'm going to do that someday." Now retired, Peggy was eventually promoted to the position of NASA's chief astronaut. She holds the records for the oldest woman to walk in space and for the most time spent in space (665 days!) by any American. Ever. Jack Lashier said it perfectly: "There were probably a lot of kids that thought that same thing after seeing Armstrong walk on the moon, but Peggy followed through and did what was necessary to make it happen." In other words, she dove in.

You will hopefully learn something new about successful people — some famous and many not so famous — whose friendship has blessed my life. It was a pleasant, eye-opening surprise to see how, in many of our interviews, they opened up about themselves and/or pointed to "winners" in their own lives.

Lesley Visser is a pioneering sports reporter and one of the most highly-acclaimed sportscasters of all time. She shared this heartwarming story with us: "I was 10 years old when my mom, a teacher, said to me, 'What do you think you might want to be when you grow up?' I told her how I wanted to be a sportswriter, which was insane in 1963. Instead of saying girls grow up to be teachers or housekeepers or nurses — the choices weren't that wide back then — she said, 'That's great.' And then she added, 'Sometimes you have to cross when it says don't walk.'"

A short time prior to our interview with Lesley, it was announced that she would become the first woman to receive the Lifetime Achievement Award at the Sports Emmys. Yes, it can sometimes pay off to cross when the sign — or someone else! — says don't walk.

The very same Lifetime Achievement Award was presented to Dick Vitale just one year earlier at the Sports Emmys. Lesley serves on the board of The V Foundation with Dick and Robin Roberts, and considers both of them to be "winners" in every respect. Lesley said, "Robin Roberts has done so much for so many, and so much for The V Foundation. She is one of those people who possesses the grace of Maya Angelou and the chops of Diane Sawyer. Robin is really rare. Rare and dignified and honorable and a giver. As for Dick Vitale? I mean there just are not enough words. I think Dick is the leader of the band at The V Foundation." It's an honor to count Robin and Dick among the "winners" profiled later in this book.

George Stephanopoulos, who works alongside Robin Roberts as co-anchor of *Good Morning America*, is another special person. We share an occasional golfing companion, Michael J. Fox. While George enjoys a much closer relationship and personal friendship with him than I do, there are few life experiences that bring more joy than a round of golf with Michael. He will be the first to tell you that he's a horrible golfer. In reference to his game, Michael has said, "I've been so lucky to be celebrated for what I do and really kind of humbled about that. It's great to do something where I really suck!"

After accepting an invitation to play with me in the 2009 Principal Charity Classic Pro-Am, Michael said, "I am committed to showing that people with challenges can lead an active life." The tournament put out a release prior to his appearance that said, "Michael J. Fox is an inspiration to millions of people around the world. His optimism, generosity and dedication to helping others demonstrate the spirit of The Principal Charity Classic." George, in an interview for this book, said, "I hate golfing with Michael because, even with everything he's dealing with, on three out of five holes he beats me!"

As for George, I've watched him evolve from White House senior advisor to ABC News political analyst to ABC News anchor. His work ethic is extraordinary. So much so that it once prompted the concern expressed in the following email exchange from December 2011:

> Ray to George: *"You've become a good friend and I'm one of your biggest cheerleaders. With that in mind, I have something I'd like to tell you. I've always looked at one's personal life and one's professional life as being two halves of the same sphere. When we talked around the debate in Iowa this past weekend, I asked Ben (Sherwood) to make sure that this 'GMA/This Week' arrangement allowed for the proper balance in your life. Those little girls of yours will grow up faster than you can ever imagine — having just married off my youngest daughter in Napa Valley in October allows me to know how true a statement that is! Your work ethic is off the charts. But find the right balance for you and your family in all this. If anyone can do just that, it's you."*

> George to Ray: *"You just made me tear up, Ray. I'll treasure this note."*

Looking back, it was as presumptuous as it was naïve of me to think there was anything to worry about when it came to George's work/life balance. That became especially evident when George shared with us the valuable and lasting advice he received on the evening in November 1992 when Bill Clinton won the presidency. He told us, "I called my parents and my dad said, 'Remember the myth of Icarus (whose father warned him about complacency and hubris ... and to not fly too close to the sun). Make sure you keep your balance.' I've always held that close to my heart and mind."

At the conclusion of our interview, George offered a simple and poignant definition of what "winning" means to him: "It's about having a life that includes a lot of love. Valuable relationships. Worthy work. And some broader and deeper sense of purpose. It's not defined by where you end up, but by how you go about trying to achieve all those goals on any given day, in any given moment." There's no doubt that George has kept his balance in a way that would make his father proud.

David Westin previously served as a boss to both Robin Roberts and George during the time he held the position of president of ABC News. He spoke effusively about working for Tom Murphy and Dan Burke back in the Cap Cities/ABC days. Tom was chairman, and Dan was president and COO. David told us, "They ran their company with a special brand of integrity and decency. They were competitive. They could make tough decisions. But you always knew they were doing it for the right reason."

David spoke about another boss, Bob Iger, in similar terms, saying, "Bob is very competitive but he doesn't come across that way. He comes across as very gracious and thoughtful, but there's a steel inside him, without a doubt, or he couldn't have accomplished what he has. And he's accomplished an enormous amount."

But David saved his most generous praise for a former U.S. Supreme Court associate justice, Lewis F. Powell, for whom he worked as a clerk. He talked about Justice Powell's remarkable range of life experiences that included working as an intelligence officer in World War II. David said, "He'd have all these experiences he could draw upon that were extraordinary. But he treated every person as an end, not a means. He always made you feel like he valued who you were. He was exactly the sort of person you would want on the Supreme Court of the United States." David left no doubt that Lewis Powell was a special "winner" in his life, and made clear he would have held the same high regard for Justice Powell even if he had clerked for him as a municipal court judge.

While my earlier thoughts on how our personal and professional lives are two halves of the same sphere did not necessarily apply to George Stephanopoulos, they do warrant some consideration. No one understands this better than Daphne Oz, particularly as it applies to the challenges of parenting today. Her thoughts on this subject were quite striking.

"With grace and faith, we have to accept that our kids come to us fully formed in so many ways," Daphne told us. "The 'nature vs nurture' argument has never been more real than when you're staring your own kids in the face, and seeing parts of yourself reflected along with parts of them that have been there from day one that you've had nothing to do with. We have to take our ego out of it entirely, and see how our job is to polish and burnish as much as we can to make their best selves shine and then get out of the way."

Daphne was just getting started as she dove deeper into this subject, saying, "The astrophysicist, Neil deGrasse Tyson, once told me how everyone is worried about buying their kids the newest toy or putting them in the best school to prepare them for success. He said, 'Let them jump in a puddle! Let them see what happens when gravity and mass displace water and how that happens. Yes, it's going to annoy you because you're gonna have dirty sneakers and pants to clean, but see their brain light up. If you had little electrodes stuck to that brain to see what happens there, you'd know it's so worth that extra load of laundry.'

"My own view of parental success has become much more granular in terms of how it is dated day to day," Daphne continued. "I don't set big, lofty goals a year out, two years out or more. I think what matters most for children are the everyday moments, and just because they happen all the time or might feel small it doesn't make them any less significant. I just really focus on putting one foot in front of the other and try to teach my kids to do the same." What a refreshing, thought-provoking and "winning" approach to parenting — and contentment.

John Skipper, the former executive chairman of DAZN and former president of ESPN, was among those who reflected on the "winning" traits of those they have crossed paths with throughout their career. About his predecessor at ESPN, John said, "George Bodenheimer was among the most balanced human beings I've ever seen; he cared dramatically about performing well but always wanted to do the right thing." He also talked about his admiration for fellow University of North Carolina alum, Michael Jordan, partly because "he's a Tar Heel" but also stemming from the fact that "he was all about working the competition and winning." It was clear from his comments that John was a big fan of the NBA's Adam Silver ("He's done a spectacular job and he, too, cares a great deal about success while always doing things the right way") and MLS's Don Garber ("He's done a great job building a new league, and I regard him as a role model and friend of mine").

Some of Skipper's most effusive praise was, however, reserved for legendary basketball coaches like John Wooden, Pat Summitt, Geno Auriemma and Dean Smith. When it came to the latter, he said," I don't know that anybody personified graciousness the way Dean Smith did. As a fan it was sometimes difficult because he only wanted to win if you could do it the right way. Dean didn't believe, for example, in calling timeouts to stop an opposing team's run. He believed in playing in a certain way — with grace and class. He was a great 'winner.'"

In much the same way that Pat Summitt impressed John Skipper, the iconic women's basketball coach also made a lasting impact on Robin Roberts. In an interview I conducted with Robin on the *Good Morning America* set in 2016, we discussed the second cancer diagnosis she received in 2012. Robin told me, "So going through it the second time you kind of have an idea about what to expect, but it doesn't make it any easier. There's a little anger. There's never a thought of 'Why me?' No one is deserving of a second diagnosis or any diagnosis for that matter, and you just think of all the many, many people who are in the same situation that you are. You just do whatever you have to do to keep moving forward. As the great Pat Summitt told me, 'Left foot, right foot, breathe. Left foot, right foot, breathe.' And you just keep moving forward."

Pat Summitt once talked about "winning" in a way that adds even greater nuance to Robin's reference to her close friend and legendary coach's encouraging words:

> *"Winning is fun ... sure. But winning is not the point. Wanting to win is the point. Not giving up is the point. Never letting up is the point. Never being satisfied with what you've done is the point."*

It is noteworthy how, when contemplating what "winning" meant to them, several people brought up the name of Stuart Scott. A longtime sportscaster at ESPN known for his hip-hop style and many catchphrases, Stuart tragically passed away from cancer in 2015 at age 49. Gerry "GMAT" Matalon, a former ESPN talent executive, talked with us for some time about Stuart. GMAT told us that when it came to the topic of "winners" and "losers" his colleague and friend would always say, "Losers worry about failure while winners worry about regret."

GMAT added that what most often drove Stuart was not worrying about falling short of others' expectations but being regretful about falling short of his own. "Stuart also felt an enormous responsibility to everyone who depended on him to inform, educate and engage them, and (to those) whose vocations were affected by his performance," GMAT said. "Our conversations were less about content, and more about community — our work community — and how we serve others in a manner that benefits all."

Longtime ESPN anchor and show host Rece Davis talked about how remarkable it was to witness the way Stuart willingly opened up to let people see his fight and resiliency. Rece talked about seeing him do *SportsCenter* shows when he was thoroughly exhausted, and when most others wouldn't have. Rece said, "Maybe people who were watching at home didn't necessarily see that part of the fight, but the people in the building did and it was inspirational to them as well. They saw what it meant to Stuart — how he was going to be courageous in the battle knowing all of those things might well be very impactful on people, whether it was helping them from a mental standpoint in dealing with the adversity or illness that they face, or whether it's motivating others to give time, resources, finances or whatever it might be to be able to contribute in some small way." Stuart was presented the Jimmy V Award for Perseverance at the ESPYS in July 2014 only months before his death.

We were the beneficiary of the deeply compelling thoughts of many other current and former ESPN employees as well. Chris Fowler told us, "There are so many different people you come in contact with, and there are so many different qualities and characteristics of those people that you admire. I was just thinking about John Saunders the other day and posted a video about him. He was a mentor to me and I don't use that word loosely. He was older and wiser and more experienced than I was when I was coming up, and he was generous with his time with me and I learned lots of things from him."

Longtime programming executive Connor Schell, who shortly after our interview announced his departure from ESPN to form his own production company, said, "(Winning) starts with hard work, and I would say I learned that from both my parents who are really smart people but always worked hard. They were never satisfied with mediocrity. So, that's a fairly important characteristic (which underscores) that nothing comes easy, you have to work for success and you have to be patient."

ESPN personalities Sean McDonough and Jeremy Schaap grew up, quite literally, in the business. They, too, talked about the influence their famous dads, Will McDonough and Dick Schaap, had on them.

Sean said, "My dad had an amazing work ethic. You don't get all those scoops that he had without working hard to cultivate relationships and gather the information. He set a great example, not only with the way he conducted his professional life, but also with the way he treated other people."

It was much the same for Jeremy who told us, "Growing up in the business, I was fortunate to be around people who were very talented and very committed to their work; many were the best at what they did in this field. My father, of course, was foremost among them but also many of his colleagues and friends. So I got to see from a very young age this business at some of its highest levels. My father was a guy who did it the right way, and I'd like to think through exposure alone some of that rubbed off."

Sean McDonough and Jeremy Schaap are apples that most definitely didn't fall far from the tree.

And then there was ESPN *SportsCenter* anchor Kevin Negandhi who said, "For me, 'winners' are truth seekers. There's really no sense of 'winner' in the singular sense from playing in one event or doing one thing. Because 'winner' is plural in that there's always a new challenge in front of you. If you settle for things in a 'one and done' way, then you're not going to get better. I think the best way to describe a 'winner' is a person who's continually striving to be better and better every single day."

Kevin also shared his family's story, telling us, "My parents were immigrants that came from India, and I was the first person in my family born in America. Convincing them that sports broadcasting is a career that can be sustainable and successful was tough. We didn't have examples of Indian journalists, reporters or anchors on the TV screen or in the newspaper. The best thing that I've always said about my parents is that they never, ever put me in a box. They allowed me, if I wanted to, to search out something or expand on something. All they asked was, 'Whatever you're going to do, just make sure you do it the right way, believe in it, and give it a 100% effort.'" Kevin was the first person of Indian-American descent to serve as an anchor on a national sports network. It has been my great pleasure to get to know Kevin from our time working together in support of the annual Dick Vitale Gala for The V Foundation.

We also talked with Kevin's Indian-American colleague, Zubin Mehenti. He is currently co-host of *Keyshawn, JWill & Zubin*. This weekday morning sports show airs on ESPN Radio and is simulcast on ESPN2. One of the early stops in Zubin's career was spent working as a sports reporter/anchor for me at WOI-TV in Des Moines. Coincidentally, Kevin's first full-time job brought him to Iowa as well, in the Ottumwa, Iowa-Kirksville, Missouri market. I can assure you of this: both Zubin and Kevin are extremely proud of their Indian-American heritage and that fact was driven home in their separate interviews for this book.

It was striking how Zubin's story paralleled that of Kevin's. He talked about his parents and how they had come to this country in 1974 and settled on the East Coast. They'd really never been out to a place like Iowa, and didn't know at first what to think or say when he discussed with them the employment offer from WOI-TV. Zubin recalled, "My dad said to me that if this is what I wanted to do for a living, they were not going to stand in my way. But the story goes much deeper in that what my parents ultimately said to each other was, 'Listen, if this is what he wants to do, we have to let him go do it. It's part of the reason we immigrated to America.'"

On April 25, 2019, the first night of that year's NFL Draft coverage, Kevin Negandhi and Zubin Mehenti were paired up to co-anchor a primetime show together. The following pinned tweet can still be found to this day on Kevin's Twitter feed: "A pic for our immigrant parents. Two Indian-Americans hosting *SportsCenter* tonight. Never thought I'd see this let alone be a part of it. Zubin and I promise to work hard and make our families proud."

Many of the "winners" we talked with pointed to their parents and family as the foundation of their success. Ben Sherwood, a past president of ABC News and the former president of the Disney/ABC Television Group said, "My path is not a linear one. To start, I lucked out being born into a family where there was so much love and a big emphasis on doing something with one's life that was purposeful. I feel so fortunate, extremely privileged to be the product of a nurturing family where my parents encouraged me and my big sister all the time to try to reach our full potential."

Paul Rhoads, an Iowa native and former head football coach at Iowa State University, told us, "Any 'winning' traits that I might be blessed with were instilled by my parents. I saw values and character traits instilled every day through dad and mom in how they lived, as much or more as what they talked about. Once those values are set you start to appreciate them, learn even more, and then pass them along to your own children and others." Paul recently joined the football staff at The Ohio State University.

Former University of Iowa and Green Bay Packers football standout Aaron Kampman echoed similar thoughts saying, "I grew up in a faith-based home where I saw the principles of a Christian life modeled in my parents, in their marriage to one another and in how they interacted in life. They knew how to work very, very hard and put in an honest day's work. I would say those two traits, the service orientation of my parents and the hard work, were qualities that really helped shape the way that I see the world."

Jon Karl, the intense chief Washington correspondent for ABC News, had just completed his term as president of the White House Correspondents Association and published a best-selling book titled *Front Row at the Trump Show* at the time we spoke with him. He talked lovingly about his stepfather who was a "total self-made guy" with "impeccable integrity" who had a big influence on him. Jon also talked about an anthropology professor who challenged him as a college student. That professor, Walter Fairservis, was rumored to be the inspiration for the "Indiana Jones" character. The influences on our lives can emanate from so many different people and places, and manifest themselves years later in peculiar ways.

Like Jon Karl, Jake Tapper also once served as chief White House correspondent for ABC News. Now a lead anchor at CNN, Jake said, "My mom and dad influenced me the most. Qualities they had like working hard and not having a defeatist attitude have gotten me where I am today. I learned similar lessons from Peter Jennings and Diane Sawyer: the idea of working hard, doing your best, and showing up every day."

In the same way Jake Tapper did, many of the television news people we talked with reflected back on the outstanding journalists they grew up watching and/or had the opportunity to work with at ABC News. Role models and mentors like Peter Jennings, Cokie Roberts, Ted Koppel, Charlie Gibson and Diane Sawyer.

Chris Bury, the senior journalist in residence at DePaul University and former ABC News *Nightline* national correspondent, told us about the "leadership by example" standard exemplified by Ted Koppel. "Ted would never ask you to do anything that he wouldn't do himself," Chris said. He then shared a detailed story to prove his point.

"So when the Iraq War broke out in 2003, Ted didn't sit in the studio," Bury said. "Instead, he became embedded with the U.S. Army's 3rd Infantry Division where he was with Major General Buford "Buff" Blount III. As such, he was part of the first wave of American journalists embedded with the U.S. military who broadcast live the moment when the 3rd Infantry Division moved across into Iraqi territory on the way to taking Baghdad. It was a dangerous assignment for Ted, as two other American journalists assigned as imbeds to the same unit died. Michael Kelly of the *Atlantic Monthly* was the first American journalist killed in Iraq. David Blume, a correspondent with NBC News, died a short time later after a deep vein thrombosis became a pulmonary embolism attributed to the cramped conditions of the vehicle he was traveling in and reporting from. Clearly, this was a very dangerous assignment for Ted. He's the anchor at this point. He's famous, he's made millions of dollars and is widely respected. Ted didn't have to take such a risk, and yet in doing so demonstrated the style of leadership that was uniquely his."

In the case of Martha Raddatz, she talked with us about how tough and demanding the late Peter Jennings could be as a mentor. That was especially true for new correspondents he didn't know well, and for whom he often had a raised eyebrow.

"I know exactly when it was that I finally cut through with Peter," Martha said. "He would be tough and just test you, test you, test you. It was a ritual of his that someone dubbed 'stump the correspondents' that he'd always call and inquire about what question you wanted to be asked. You'd tell him and then, of course, he would ask you something entirely different. And one day it dawned on me. So when he asked, 'What do you want to talk about?' I said, 'Peter, you can ask me anything you want.' Smiling, he said to the show producer, 'Hummm ... she's finally figured it out. I want her to know everything.' But that was Peter. He was going to put you through your paces and the more you knew, the better. That was his mentoring style. You're not going to find anybody who would say they are not a better reporter because of him."

David Muir also shared an especially poignant anecdote about the "fatherly nature" and "calming influence" of longtime ABC News correspondent and anchor, Charlie Gibson. Recalling the time in 2006 when he was about to file a report from the Israeli-Lebanon border during Israel's war with Hezbollah in 2006, David told us, "The editing system crashed moments before *World News Tonight* was to go on the air. The executive producer was in my ear, far more frantic than Charlie who was also suddenly in my ear. This was just before we went on the air and he said to me, 'David, we're just going to have a conversation right off the top of the broadcast. And you will, through a series of questions from me, tell the audience what it was you were going to tell us in your report.' And then, in so many words, he said, 'Are you ready?' I replied, 'I'm ready.'

"The next thing I heard was the show open in my ear immediately after which Charlie and I proceeded to talk for about two to three minutes," David continued. "I'll never forget that day and how he had a way of putting people at ease. He could slow things down for a moment so that they could be digested not only for the team presenting it but, more importantly, by the audience at home. That was a valuable moment for me because, in the end, what we wound up doing on the air on live television was probably more conversational, more thoughtful and far more impactful." With David Muir now at its helm as anchor, the *World News Tonight* broadcast leads all the networks in evening news viewership.

In addition to their parents, several athletes cited the "winning traits" that were instilled in them by coaches during their playing days. Gary Thompson, a two-sport All-American at Iowa State University, told us that "winning" in many ways relates back to the coaches you had. He said, "I was fortunate to have coaches that were competitive and played by the rules. That's where you build your character."

Another former Iowa State basketball standout, Fred Hoiberg, shared a similar sentiment. He said, "I'm so fortunate to have had coaches that I was able to learn from. I think you learn more from your high school coach than anybody because you're at such an impressionable age. So for me it starts with Wayne Clinton and I'm grateful for how he taught the fundamentals … and (his role) in one of the great moments in my life: winning a state championship during my senior year at Ames High School. I chose to go to Iowa State in the community I grew up in and played for Johnny Orr. He was a larger-than-life figure (and) those are three of the greatest years of my life. Tim Floyd came in for my senior year and he had a very different philosophy than Johnny, but one that was very important in helping me with my career. I don't know if I would have made it to the NBA had I not played for both of those guys."

ESPN basketball analyst and former basketball coach Fran Fraschilla talked in great detail about the valuable lessons to be learned from athletics. Looking back at his own coaching career, he said, "I tried to be a humble winner, but I also tried to be a gracious loser. I tried to impart that on my team like, 'Listen, we're not going to win all the time so when we do lose or win let's figure out what we can learn from these experiences.' So for me, sports are just an incredible metaphor for how life works."

Fran's former boss at ESPN, John Wildhack, is now the director of athletics at Syracuse University. John summed it up this way: "It's about more than just how many games you win or how many championships you claim. It's about competing the right way, conducting yourself the right way, and living your life the right way. I learned during my years at ESPN, but also on my own in terms of collaboration, that those are the keys to being a good leader."

Not everyone we talked with is a household name. Some are very accomplished Iowans who offered their own points of view on "winning" habits.

William "Bill" Knapp's life story is a rags-to-riches one unlike that of any other Iowan. His business achievements and impact on the community and state is truly extraordinary. We talked to Bill on what was the 75th anniversary of the Battle of Okinawa. He told us how he piloted a landing craft that repeatedly hit the beach. "Every time I drove that boat back out and pulled the ramp up, I wondered how many of those soldiers would never come back," Bill somberly told us. "I could get out of there to go back and return with more troops, but after they got dropped off it was war at its very worst. The enemy was in tunnels and we had to use flamethrowers and bomb them ... and when the enemy did finally emerge out of those tunnels it was brutal hand-to-hand combat. It was the bloodiest battle of the Pacific War with over 75,000 American casualties. I was just lucky not to be one of them."

That war experience changed Bill's outlook on life. And while his upbringing on a small Iowa farm taught him a strong work ethic, it also showed him that milking cows twice a day, 365 days a year was probably not the life for him. There was, however, one trait instilled by his father that was key to Bill's later success in business: honesty. He said, "My father told me 'You keep your word if it takes your hide, hair and everything that you have.' And so I've always had this deep sense of trying to be honest and faithful." Now in his 90s, Bill's guiding business influence and philanthropic generosity have had a transformational impact on Central Iowa.

Two of Iowa's most successful and longest-serving politicians are also profiled later in the book: Governors Robert D. Ray and Terry E. Branstad. When talking about public or community service, Governor Ray would often say, "Everyone can do something to make a difference in this world. We might not be able to do it all, but we can do something. And isn't there great satisfaction in that?" His most enduring legacy was the founding of the Institute for Character Development in 1997. Governor Ray believed strongly that good character was something that could be developed and practiced in homes, schools, workplaces and communities across our state.

The *Character Counts!* program actually came about during one of Governor Branstad's terms leading our state. "It's interesting the way that *Character Counts!* got started in Iowa," Branstad told us. "We were getting ready to celebrate the Iowa Sesquicentennial, the 150th anniversary of Iowa becoming a state. Knowing how much Governor Ray loved Iowa — and how much I enjoyed working with him — I asked him to serve as the chair of the Iowa Sesquicentennial committee. We ended up having a wonderful, year-long and statewide celebration.

One of the ideas we had was to sell Sesquicentennial license plates so that counties would have some funding to put events together. Governor Ray also wanted something permanent to come out of the celebrations, and that's where the idea to use the leftover funds to start *Character Counts!* came from." To this day, the program continues to emphasize character development and ethical leadership under the guidance of Scott Raecker as its executive director.

Bernie Saggau and Gary Thompson are two other Iowans who share impressive "winning" accomplishments. Chuck Offenburger, a retired columnist for *The Des Moines Register* and Iowa legend in his own right, authored books about Bernie and Gary. He told us, "Both of the Bernie Saggau and Gary Thompson books had something in common in that I couldn't shut off the interviews. I could probably still be writing the damn things today because one interview would lead to five more. I'd hear all these great stories. I had known that Bernie was probably one of the most prolific speakers in Iowa in terms of high school graduations, athletic banquets, chambers of commerce dinners, and every kind of event like that. He once told me that he had spoken at 24 commencements in one year! I went to a lot of those with him — probably 10 of them over a two-year period — when I was working on the book just to hear and observe him while he was in public. I learned a lot by doing that.

"I did the same thing with Gary Thompson," Offenburger continued. "Besides all of his Iowa State heroism and accomplishments, I dug deeply into his business career. He came out of Iowa State as an All-American and at that time in the late 1950's pro basketball was not nearly what it is today. He played instead for the Phillips 66ers, an AAU basketball team, for five years. He did so because a full-time, year-round job came with it. If he had signed on with an NBA team, it might have been good only for the season and he'd have to go out and find a job after that ... and the salaries were not nearly like they are today."

Offenburger, known as "The Iowa Boy" to his readers, further noted how Bernie and Gary were so well prepared in everything they did. He said, "Whether it was in basketball and Gary's fanatical concentration on the fundamentals of the game, or Bernie's focus on being a great basketball official. They would approach business matters the same way and really do the research before they made any decisions. They became 'winners' because they were hellacious hard workers. They got ready for any kind of competition they were involved with whether it was business or athletic. They had a real knowledge and both of them had incredible success."

Perhaps you may never have heard the names Bill Knapp, Bernie Saggau or Gary Thompson before. But you will want to read their profiles in order to learn about these extraordinary Iowans, and their remarkable and unique "winning" stories.

Several other Iowans made the case that "winning" has less to do with ourselves — and more to do with helping others. David Stark, the CEO of UnityPoint Health-Des Moines said, "The first thing 'winners' have is a will to serve others — and they do it without seeking credit for themselves. I think the second thing they have is the willingness to do things that others can't or won't do. They're the one who runs into the fire. They're the one that gets it done. They're the one to volunteer. They take responsibility. They find the solution. A lot of that comes with a conviction that comes from believing in something or someone or a cause."

Now the radio voice of the Iowa State Cyclones, John Walters once served as the sports director for me at WOI-TV in Des Moines. His thoughts echoed those of Stark's, saying, "There are so many qualities that can lend themselves to being a 'winner.' One of those involves thinking outside the box of 'what's best for me' and thinking about a bigger picture. It's a willingness to put others ahead of yourself (and) do something good with whatever platform you have."

Similarly, the Ray Center's Scott Raecker shared his thinking on the best way we can serve others. He told us, "It's about discovering ways to be a servant-leader … (finding) the inspiration to step out and use your relationships, to maximize the opportunities to do good for others and the community."

Prior to serving in his current position, David Stark was president of Blank Children's Hospital in Des Moines, Iowa. This medical facility's mission is to meet the special health care needs of children by encouraging families to be a part of their child's healing. David told us about its unique history: "The founder, A.H. Blank, made a special trip during World War II to see President Franklin D. Roosevelt. He returned home with the approval for the only civilian hospital to be built in the country during the war. Being in the movie theater business, Mr. Blank also had a personal relationship with Walt Disney who dispatched several of his top artists to Des Moines to paint four original murals on the walls of the new hospital. I'm talking 5 foot tall by 15 feet wide Disney murals featuring Snow White, the Three Little Pigs, Bambi and Pinocchio. We still have these Walt Disney originals from 1944."

As noted earlier, an important aspect of "winning" involves making connections and leveraging them in a positive way. David Stark and I agreed that Blank's Pediatric Emergency Department would benefit greatly from new artwork with more contemporary Disney characters. With this in mind, we reached out to Bob Iger who was still chairman and CEO of The Walt Disney Company at the time. He immediately embraced the historical connection between Blank Children's and Walt Disney himself. Oftentimes timing is everything, and it certainly didn't hurt that Disney had just recently announced an initiative to support children's hospitals around the world!

Bob made a special trip to Des Moines in April 2018 to dedicate a new 110-character Disney mural. With immense pride in his voice, David told us, "No other place in the world has this. It resides in our emergency department, so when kids come in they see Mulan and Moana and Nemo — they see all their favorite Disney characters on a mural that's the whole length of the wall in our emergency department at Blank."

During the dedication ceremony, Bob said, "This is important. I respect history, but live in the present and I know that helping children ... there's probably no greater calling than to do that." Blank Children's Hospital now has a newly established Disney connection some 75 years after the original one was formed. Now that's leveraging a connection to a "winning" outcome!

It's important to note that not all the "winners" found in this book are individuals; many are organizations or events which stand out in their own right: Variety - the Children's Charity of Iowa, the Principal Charity Classic, the Broadcasters Foundation of America, The V Foundation and the ESPY Awards. And in many cases, they are connected in meaningful ways. For example, organizations like Variety - the Children's Charity of Iowa, Blank Children's Hospital and other charitable groups are the beneficiaries of the proceeds from the Principal Charity Classic.

As in business, serving others and doing good works can be greatly enhanced by "winning" relationships. David Stark explained it this way:

"One of the themes you notice with 'winners' is they associate with other 'winners' who are doing good things. They recognize how they can do even bigger and better things by working together. I've had the pleasure of serving on the Principal Charity Classic board for a few years. This event has been a big supporter of ours (Blank Children's Hospital) and a big supporter of Variety. We've been able to connect those two together, so you will see kids that have had a bicycle donated to their family during the golf tournament. Those are our patients at Blank, and Variety is there helping them as the Principal Charity Classic makes that special connection as part of their focus on doing really good things in our community."

The ESPYS is another event profiled in this book and it, too, is one that has many purposeful and consequential connections. While celebrating the emotional connection that fans have to their favorite sports, teams and players, the ESPYS also holds related events that raise funds for The V Foundation.

That aforementioned connection was embodied by the ESPYS longtime executive producer, Maura Mandt, who unexpectedly passed away in February 2020 at the all-too-young age of 53. Connor Schell, her boss at the time, told us, "There is one word that best describes Maura: relentless. She was someone who didn't stop, and it was always in pursuit of making whatever it was she was working on better. Sometimes, even at its most annoying! But you understood that her interests were never compromised. They were always, 'How do we make this one story inspirational? How do we make this one moment more powerful? How do we deliver something that no one's ever seen before? How do we raise more money for The V Foundation?' She just didn't stop.

"The other thing about Maura is that she was one of the great connectors of people that you ever met. She would meet someone, talk to them, and immediately say, 'You should talk to so and so' or, 'Hey, I know someone you would really like' or, 'So and so is working on a project, who do you know that could help?' And then before you knew it, Maura had sent an email or made a phone call and connected two people who otherwise *never* would have come in contact with each other. You put her relentless pursuit with her ability to connect people, and it helps explain why she was so great at her job."

Whether it's the way the Principal Charity Classic fosters relationships to support local charities or the manner in which Maura Mandt built connections to benefit the ESPYS and The V Foundation, all organizations should work to uncover synergy wherever possible and leverage connections to "winning" outcomes.

By listening to "winners" we can stumble across unique ways to learn new lessons about leadership and success. Jamie Pollard, the widely respected director of athletics at Iowa State University posed an interesting question and observation: "Do you know what develops and builds leadership? Failure. I think you learn so much more from 'losing' than you'll ever learn from 'winning' and those that learn the most, and adjust the quickest, from their losses are the ones who will win more often. And you know what else? Disappointment is an awesome motivator." There is much more about "Accepting Failure and Embracing Adversity" among the lessons found in Chapter Seven.

Rob Mills, an ABC Entertainment programming executive with a title as long as his work ethic is deep, told us, "It's through our experiences growing up that we learn 'winning' and 'losing' is very black and white. As you go through life, you learn it is actually more about shades of gray and that there are many ways to describe a 'winner.' It is the knowledge that you've given and done your best, and you've done it with the very best of intentions. That makes you a 'winner' — no matter what the final result may be."

You will hopefully find the profiles in this book to be enlightening, and unearth lessons along the way that are relatable and instructive. There is an abundance of wisdom shared by the diverse group "winners" on the pages that follow, and you will discover how they have been able to develop a set of core competencies and characteristics that are key to success: vision, dedication, optimism and curiosity, passion and enthusiasm, perseverance, sincerity, honesty and integrity, and a generous spirit and willingness to give back.

Most importantly, echoing the words of the late Arthur Ashe, it's my sincere desire that you come away with a clearer understanding of how "going for it is more important than winning or losing."

1.
TELEVISION EXECUTIVES

GEORGE BODENHEIMER

*"George just genuinely cared about everybody who worked
with him and for him. People often talk about ESPN's
culture and how strong it is, but he's the guy who built it
and embodied it. It is a culture of 'we're all in this together'
and ideas can come from anywhere, and everybody in the
organization is valued. That makes ESPN a remarkable
place to work—and that's what made George Bodenheimer
an extraordinary leader and a very special person."*

Connor Schell, Former ESPN executive vice president for
content and executive producer of the *OJ: Made in America* and
The Last Dance documentaries

Collaborative and competitive. Bold and decisive. Innovative and empathetic.

These attributes — and many more — defined the remarkable career
of iconic ESPN executive George Bodenheimer.

And don't just take my word for it. That's how his esteemed colleagues
described his myriad "winning" qualities.

Rece Davis, ESPN anchor and host of *College GameDay*, called
Bodenheimer "eminently approachable."

Chris Fowler, who helmed ESPN's college football studio shows for
25 years, deemed him "calm, decent and classy."

Sean McDonough, longtime ESPN play-by-play announcer, marveled at how George "possessed everything you want a leader to have, including intelligence and great judgment" before adding that "his special gift was his way with people."

John Wildhack, a former top ESPN programming and production executive, extolled the fact that "George never needed to be the loudest guy in the room or say the most in the room. But make no mistake, the vast majority of the time he was the smartest guy in the room. George had an incredible talent for taking a very complex subject or complicated situation and distilling it down in terms that everybody could grasp."

John Skipper, who succeeded Bodenheimer as president of ESPN, summed it up this way: "George is among the most balanced human beings I've ever seen. While caring dramatically about performing well, he always wanted to do the right thing."

The thing is, George almost always did just that. For himself. For his company. For his family and loved ones. Still, an element of luck met his unwavering commitment to success. We don't "win" alone — ever. That's one of the enduring lessons that permeates the pages of this book.

"George encouraged healthy debate around ideas," longtime Disney executive Ben Pyne told us. "He felt the more robust the discussion was, the better the ultimate decision, even if people disagreed with each other — and *especially* if people disagreed with him. He would listen, weigh all the options and, ultimately, make a decision. His openness to creating a culture where people could express themselves, all respectfully, said a lot about his character as a leader."

George would be the first to acknowledge how sometimes in life timing is everything. "I was very fortunate because ESPN was started at a time when the cable industry just exploded in growth with MTV, CNN, HBO, USA — all the networks that came to fore over the last 40 years. ESPN led the way with those networks as our industry exploded and changed the television landscape," he told us. "Sports would never go out of style. It is part of America. ESPN wisely invested from a first-mover advantage in a little old concept called 24-hour-a-day sports."

But George would have to begin his career toiling on ESPN's ground floor — literally. The man who would become the then-fledgling cable sports network's longest-tenured president began his journey in Bristol,

Connecticut as a mailroom clerk. One of his early duties? Picking up renowned ESPN college basketball analyst Dick Vitale at the airport.

Seventeen years later, George became president of the sports world's most powerful company. How'd he do it? By doggedly following a simple but hard-to-follow formula. "If you want to succeed, you outwork your competition, whoever that might be, whether they're in your company or (at) another company," Bodenheimer told us. "That's number one. Number two, I use the expression, 'Every day is a school day.' Never stop learning. You've got to be inquisitive. Working hard and learning, and being able to establish relationships with people, I would say those were the keys to my being able to grow over all those years (with ESPN)."

Those years melded humble beginnings with explosive growth. One notable — and somewhat controversial — move involved the folding of the ABC Sports brand into the broader ESPN portfolio. This significant change occurred in 2006 during my tenure as chairman of the board of governors of the ABC Television Affiliates Association. By then, ESPN had become synonymous with sports. It was truly "the worldwide leader" — and George had the prescience to know that marrying the brands would benefit sports fans and The Walt Disney Company alike.

Quite understandably, many people at the broadcast network and its affiliated stations saw the shift as a slap in the face to what legendary producer turned executive Roone Arledge had built at ABC. Longtime ABC sportscaster Keith Jackson called me to vent his concerns, and then stirred the pot even more by going public and saying, "It was inevitable. When ABC was sold to Capital Cities, and then to Disney, the handwriting was on the wall. A lot of people worked to make ABC what it was, and they deserve more than to have their legacy callously tossed aside."

George had extended the courtesy of calling me in advance of the announcement, and we discussed the predictable negative backlash. To his great credit, George was able to smooth out the criticism by responding to it in a direct and straightforward manner, saying in a statement, "The fact that we're now placing a greater emphasis on ESPN is not intended to convey a lack of respect for what ABC built."

George and his team listened attentively to the concerns and constructive suggestions from members of the affiliate board. They included the placement of a new *ESPN on ABC* graphic during broadcasts on the network to reduce the possibility of confusion among viewers about which platform they were watching. In 2007, George presented credible research to the board of governors showing how viewers desired, and got more enjoyment from, sports programming on ABC that was associated with the ESPN brand.

Big changes like the one mentioned above are often hard to accept. "Winners" like George Bodenheimer shrug off such challenges and focus on solutions. Success doesn't always follow a linear path — occasional missteps should be expected, and even anticipated, so they don't become stumbling blocks.

"Failure is a part of it," George told us.

One such example of "failure" occurred amidst the successful absorption of ABC Sports into the ESPN brand. "When we first introduced ESPN Mobile — and I think it was either 2006 or 2007 — it was not successful after a lot of fanfare," recalled Bodenheimer. "We quickly adjusted our strategy and instead of sitting around and saying, 'Oh, well, that's too bad that didn't work,' we simply revised our strategy and ESPN Mobile — what's now known as the ESPN app — is now the clear leader in digital sports media. But it's often written about as a 'failure.' Well, really, who cares? You lick your wounds for a day and you keep moving. But if you're afraid to fail, you're really not going to go very far. It's definitely a part of 'winning.'"

So is giving back.

Under George's leadership, ESPN's commitment to charitable organizations — most notably, The V Foundation — crystallized. His post-ESPN life has included penning a memoir entitled, *Every Town is a Sports Town: Business Leadership at ESPN, from the Mailroom to the Boardroom*. All the proceeds from the book were donated to The V Foundation, where George serves on the board of directors and chairs a significant fundraising campaign.

"When you bring up George Bodenheimer's name, I think about the leadership of ESPN and how they're so heavily involved with what the company stands for," said Lisa Kovlakas, the network's corporate citizenship manager. "Whether it's The V Foundation, or how we are doing things to help grow youth sports, or the initiatives to change people's lives in different communities through various programs — it all comes down to leadership."

It also stems from collaboration. Decisiveness. Innovative approaches to challenges.

Some succeed. Some fail. "Winners" like George Bodenheimer see past either outcome — and plot a path forward that ensures salutary results outpace mixed or troubling ones.

"Every business has bumps," George said. "Some bigger than others. Setbacks — whether it's hiring people, or creating a budget or launching any business — happen. Nothing goes as planned. What was that great Mike Tyson quote? 'Everybody's got a plan until you get punched in the face.' It's true, and you've got to keep moving forward and figure out how to fix things. That's the true mark of a leader."

That's certainly true for George. Former Disney/ABC executive Ben Pyne said he often referred to ESPN in its early years as "the little engine that could." Collaboration and competition stoked that engine. Bold and decisive maneuvers kept it on track. Innovation and empathy fueled growth and expansion in terms of commercial success and charitable giving.

"Winners," as George pointed out, don't do it by themselves. That's true for him — and anyone else who seeks to build a lasting legacy.

"There aren't a lot of bosses like George Bodenheimer," Rece Davis told us. "I don't mean that as a criticism (of other bosses). I just think that there is so much on the plate of someone who is in a role like that and to have the ability, even if it's for a short moment of time, to make someone feel appreciated and at the same time not make them feel like, 'Yeah, okay, here's the obligatory call … the obligatory 'attaboy' note. You felt like George wanted to take the time. It's a part of who he is, and why I have so much respect for him and the type of person that he is."

Connor Schell conveyed a sentiment similar to Rece Davis's, saying, "George made everyone around him — whether you were in the mailroom or an anchor for *SportsCenter* or a top executive — feel important. He made everyone feel that their opinion mattered, that their voice was heard, and that they were all part of something bigger than themselves. He cultivated this idea of 'we're all in this together' and we're a team. It was remarkable to watch."

George Bodenheimer was a caring and visionary leader, genuine sports television legend and WINNER with whom it was a privilege to work alongside. He was confident and collaborative. He's someone I'll always take great pride in calling my friend.

BOB IGER

"Bob Iger is the rock. He grew up in network television and once ran ABC Entertainment, and really understands it. Bob is the epitome of understanding creativity, creating and producing content, and excellence in how to run a business. In this industry, you can find people who can do one well or the other well, but very few can do both well."

Ben Pyne, Former president of Disney/ABC Television
global distribution

Creativity. Confidence. Clarity.

These are the three words journalism icon Diane Sawyer chose to describe Bob Iger.

Visionary, innovative and bold are a few more words I'd use to help fill out Bob's unique personality profile.

"He always thinks big," former Disney executive Ben Pyne summed up.

Bob, the current executive chairman and former chairman and CEO of The Walt Disney Company, is perhaps the best example of a self-made person I've ever seen. When others hesitate, he pounces. While some fret, he pushes forward. The Walt Disney Company has grown exponentially under his leadership — and largely because when Bob encounters the proverbial "box," he immediately seeks to escape or eliminate it altogether.

"Who would have ever predicted that his first big acquisition would be Pixar?" Pyne asked. "I would often make presentations about The Walt Disney Company to international clients. I would include this powerful slide that showed how when Bob bought Pixar in 2006, there were all these quotes from people saying things like, 'It's the biggest mistake. ... Overpaid. ... I can't believe it. ... Will never make money.' In the wake of the Marvel acquisition in 2009 it was much the same, 'How could you pay $4 billion for cartoon characters?' When it came to Lucasfilm, the analysts were much more positive. What the wonderfully smart people on Wall Street didn't realize is that there was tons of intellectual property, particularly in the case of Marvel, tied up in these assets."

Bob knew. Largely because he always prepared. He'd not only done his homework, but had created his own master class on success, behind the scenes, in his own mind's eye.

"One of the most beautiful qualities of true leaders is giving you courage and, if necessary, holding that courage (for you) until you find it," Diane Sawyer told us. "They see what is possible and are moving you there and strengthening you as you go; giving you the ability to do hard things and giving you the unequalled delight of achieving something. Someone once said that companies are molded by the enthusiasm of the person at the top. Bob Iger's enthusiasms are vast and deep, and always seeking to ennoble the world."

Bob's ability to ascertain the value of various media entities is legendary, but it's his acumen for developing personal relationships and enriching the common good that has most impressed me.

One example: Bob's devotion to charitable causes — all the while building on the Disney legacy. Blank Children's Hospital in Des Moines, Iowa, has a special connection to Walt Disney. The hospital's benefactors, A.H. and Anna Blank, were close friends with Disney's founder, who had some of his top artists contribute artwork to the hospital when it opened in 1944. I spoke with Bob in January 2017 about building upon that 75-year connection by adding new and more contemporary Disney art to the hospital's walls.

"We support numerous hospitals for children, and I am certain we can fulfill this request," Bob wrote to me in an email. "I will have our philanthropy people follow through with you on it."

And so they did.

Over the next year, the Disney Corporate Citizenship and Blank Children's Foundation teams worked diligently to come up with a layout and location for new, original artwork. After considering more than a half-dozen design possibilities, they settled on a silhouette version consisting of 110 characters and objects from the extensive Disney and Pixar catalog: *Dumbo*; *Zootopia*; *The Jungle Book*; *Lady and the Tramp*; *Bambi*; *Mulan*; *Alice in Wonderland*; *Winnie the Pooh*; *Cars*; *A Bug's Life*; *Wreck-It Ralph*; *Tangled*; *Ratatouille*; *Monsters, Inc.*; *Toy Story*; *Pocahontas*; *Finding Nemo*; *The Lion King*; *Lilo & Stitch*; *Big Hero 6*; *Cinderella*; *Brave*; *Hercules*; *The Aristocats*; *The Little Mermaid*; *Frozen*; *Pinocchio*; *Aladdin*; *Up*; *WALL-E*; *Moana*; *Beauty and the Beast*; and *Bolt*. And, of course, Mickey Mouse, Minnie Mouse, Donald Duck, Chip and Dale, Goofy and Pluto were also prominently featured.

Made of adhesive vinyl, the completed artwork measured 46 feet wide and 8 feet tall. For the opposite hallway wall, a similarly sized mural featuring characters from the Disney classic, *Peter Pan*, was created. The final designs far exceeded everyone's expectations. Stephanie Voltz, a longtime executive assistant to Bob, said it perfectly in an email, "Ray, they are fantastic! My jaw dropped when I saw them. Walt Disney would have loved them, and Bob will too! They are very magical and will bring many smiles."

Bob visited Des Moines in April 2018 to tour the hospital, see the original artwork, and personally help unveil and dedicate the new artwork. He was thrilled to see Walt's original murals for the first time, saying, "There's something very vivid about them. The characters pop off the walls."

It was an honor for me to introduce Bob at the dedication ceremony and talk about an initiative he had announced just one month earlier involving The Walt Disney Company's commitment to dedicate $100 million in company resources to children's hospitals around the world over the next five years.

My introduction also provided the opportunity to discuss our long association and friendship, and point to his many accomplishments as steward of one of the world's most well-known, respected and beloved brands. In his dedication remarks, Bob said, "We really have a chance to follow in Walt's actual footsteps to build on something that he himself had a hand in creating and that makes this hospital, this visit and this day very special." He later added, "Being able to bring a little of Disney's values into a hospital where children and families are experiencing times of incredible stress and anxiety is a great thing."

At the conclusion of his formal remarks, Bob surprised the hospital executives, doctors, nurses and other invited guests with an announcement that The Walt Disney Company, in addition to the new artwork and other donated products and services, would be making a cash donation of $100,000 to Blank Children's Hospital. It was a very special day indeed.

"Bob Iger loved the historical connection between Walt and our children's hospital," said David Stark, the chief executive officer for UnityPoint Health-Des Moines, which oversees Blank Children's Hospital. "No other place in the world has anything like this. The new Disney artwork resides in our emergency department, so when kids come in they see Mulan and Moana and Nemo — they see all their favorite Disney characters on a mural that extends the whole length of our emergency department at Blank. During the dedication Bob said, 'This is important. I respect history, but live in the present and I know that we're helping children. There's probably no greater calling than to do that.'"

That's Bob. When it's time to make a difference, he steps up. When it's time to "think outside the box," he obliterates perceived limitations. "One of the things I love about Bob Iger is his ability to attack new subject matter," former Disney executive Anne Sweeney told us. "He's an intense learner, a big reader and is not afraid to share what he knows, what he's learned or the new things he needs to think about. It was amazing to watch him learn all the pieces of his job: television, film, theme parks and everything else that came with it. Bob does fall into the force of nature category for me."

Sweeney was one of several executives who spoke effusively about Iger's leadership abilities "Bob would challenge us in terms of really looking ahead and trying to figure out where the business and the industry were going," said John Wildhack, former ESPN executive and current director of athletics at Syracuse University. "One of his great traits was being such a forward-thinking CEO, and a visionary. Bob is just one of the great CEOs in the history of American business."

Challenges can be daunting for many people. Particularly unforeseen ones, like the COVID-19 crisis. But uncertainty fuels Bob. He finds the silver lining in any situation, then illuminates the upsides to otherwise stressful waypoints.

"Bob would engage on ideas that might seem crazy, and things easily brushed off by other people," longtime ABC Entertainment executive Rob Mills told us. "When others are saying 'Why?' he would often be the one saying 'Why not?' One of Bob's greatest strengths was being able to see past the latest acquisition and into the future, and toward what it should look like. He was a little prescient in that regard and it made all the difference as every one of his acquisitions, and initiatives like Disney+, have been a huge success."

Bob's corporate office is poetically located at The Walt Disney Studios in Burbank, California, a site bought and paid for with revenues from the 1937 release of *Snow White and the Seven Dwarfs*. Walt Disney once said, "Most of my life I have done what I wanted to do. I have had fun on the job." Bob has always maintained a similar philosophy as evidenced by the joy and optimism shown while running the largest media company in the world. He explained it succinctly to me in a March 2019 email: "Being CEO of Disney never gets old!"

Bob Iger is a WINNER whose managerial focus and leadership style built upon the history and heritage of the omnipresent "wonderful" in the Wonderful World of Disney and inspired the continuing sense of "magic" that defines the Magic Kingdom. The challenge of maintaining the creative spirit and legacy of the iconic Walt Disney could not have been placed in better hands.

2.

TELEVISION NEWS

Peter Jennings

"I was always drawn to Peter Jennings as a kid. He had this James Bond globetrotting style, if you will, but it was more than that. It was the conversation he was having with America every night. ... I hope that the conversation we're having with America these days on 'World News Tonight' is a continuation of that conversation I gravitated to as a kid, and one that follows in his great tradition. And I know that I'm just one of the people hoping to emulate the standards set by Peter Jennings along the way."

David Muir, ABC News anchor and managing editor
of *World News Tonight*

Peter Jennings' final sign-off as the revered anchor of ABC's *World News Tonight* on April 5, 2005, included a troubling personal disclosure: He had been diagnosed with lung cancer.

Peter's voice was raspy. He'd been the award-winning anchor of *World News Tonight* for more than two decades. He'd risen to the top of his profession by holding himself — and others — to exacting standards. Yet that day, Peter spoke from a vulnerable part of his heart.

"A journalist who doesn't value deeply the audience's loyalty should be in another line of work," he told his faithful viewers.

Peter passed away three and a half months later, but his legacy permeates television news to this day.

He was the ultimate self-made man. Fearless. Witty. A self-taught impresario with an insatiable curiosity.

"He was as curious a journalist as I've seen," said David Westin, the former president of ABC News. "Peter was always learning things and was impatient with those who weren't. He was very knowledgeable and very worldly because of that voracious curiosity."

Some wondered if Peter ever truly slept. His knowledge of history was only matched by his ability to meet someone precisely where they found themselves in a given moment.

"Working with Peter Jennings adrenalized you, and it was wonderful," Diane Sawyer, who would later sit in the same anchor chair, told us. "Peter didn't just go to the Middle East, he knew every street corner café. He knew the changing face of the region. He knew what had been invested and all the dashed possibilities. It was very rare in our world to find someone who hadn't just reported it, but lived it, grew up with it, cared deeply and let that be his teacher. I think what turned Peter into an extraordinary journalist was being able to understand the essential, deep roadmap of history and human nature."

To care. To listen. To turn up the smallest voice in order to speak truth to power.

"I think everybody at ABC News in that era was very proud to work on his broadcasts because of how he would inspire them," said the former vice president of ABC News, Robin Sproul. "Peter could lead a conversation and inspire you about why we were doing what (it was) we were doing, the importance of what we were doing, and how to get to the story."

Every story mattered. Every sentence spoken mattered. Every newscast amplified facts and doused disinformation.

"He had a firm sense of the nobility of what journalism could be on its best days," added Westin. "And one of the things that has stuck with me more recently was how Peter was the first one to say, 'We're not the story. The story's out there. Don't point the camera at me. Point the camera at the people who are the story.' That's something I fear we may not always respect anymore. Peter did not want to become the story."

Peter could be a taskmaster, too. While style wasn't inconsequential, substance rightfully reigned supreme. But there were no affectations with Peter. He was who you thought he was. Every angle. Every take.

"There's no doubt that Peter Jennings was exacting, and I think he was a perfectionist as well," said David Muir, who currently serves in the anchor role shaped by Jennings and is one of the many journalists influenced by him. "He held himself to a high standard and expected everyone else would perform at that level — and by performing, I mean to be as curious; to understand that there aren't just two sides, there are multiple sides to every story."

"Peter was so tough," said ABC News chief global affairs correspondent Martha Raddatz. "But that was Peter. He was going to put you through your paces and the more you knew, the better. That was his mentoring style. You're not going to find anybody who wouldn't say they were a better reporter because of him."

While he could often be an exhausting taskmaster, Peter could also be a generous and supportive mentor.

"Peter Jennings was just a master in terms of broadcasting abilities," said Jake Tapper, former ABC News correspondent and current CNN anchor. "He took a real interest in making sure that I understood how to broadcast. Peter was always trying to work with me on my tracking — that's the narration — in a way that as I look back on it, is kind of amazing. He was definitely tough and very demanding, but I don't think that's a bad quality. It's good to have somebody who demands a lot for a news broadcast. Peter was very skeptical of people in power and that was refreshing because a lot of broadcast journalists, too often, are too comfy with those in power. He wasn't."

Peter excelled in the field and in the studio. Why? Because he could turn frantic moments into revelatory ones. The surface rarely interested him. He strived to excavate and reveal what existed many layers beneath it.

"The more chaotic things get around me, the calmer I get," Peter once said. John Berman, a CNN anchor who had worked alongside Peter at ABC News, confirmed just how true that statement was. Berman said, "I was his writer for two years, and got to see it firsthand. Peter processing breaking news was like Ted Williams seeing the stitches on the ball when he hit."

Pressure produced insight. Deadlines trained the sharp light onto truth. His leadership brought out the best in harried field reporters.

"He reminded me of a lot of great athletes who are motivated by having a bit of a chip on their shoulder," former ABC News correspondent Chris Bury said. "I watched *The Last Dance* about Michael Jordan (and the Chicago Bulls) and took note of how he would always find a slight or some insult to motivate him in a particularly difficult game or playoff series. (Green Bay Packers star quarterback) Aaron Rodgers is another athlete like that who is still sort of driven, to his core, by not being picked first in the NFL draft. Peter did not finish high school and did not have a college education. He was, in a way, very insecure about that and it drove him to learn about the world with this insatiable curiosity.

"Peter was demanding in his own unique way. He would call you up after a broadcast if he liked your story, but he also never hesitated to call you up if he did not like your story. But when he called to compliment you, you felt like a million dollars."

Peter was as well-read a man as you could find and was always trying to learn more. He mastered French and other languages. His lack of a formal education served not as an impediment, but as a catalyst for discovery.

David Muir absorbed that aspect of Jennings' personality and each night as he begins *World News Tonight*, his words reflect Peter's vision, whether from New York, Washington or somewhere else across the globe.

"I often take *World News Tonight* on the road all over the world," David told us. "Without reflection, perhaps, I would not have noticed this but looking at the kinds of stories that I'm drawn to and the people I'm drawn to, I hope that it follows in that great (Jennings) tradition."

Peter's combination of good looks, grace, class and intelligence contributed to what Ted Koppel, his fellow ABC News anchor, once described as Peter's "animal magnetism." While not necessarily quite sure about that description, I can say that Peter Jennings was as charismatic as anyone I've ever met in my lifetime. It was among the reasons why spending time with him was always particularly memorable.

On one occasion, my family had accompanied me on a trip to Los Angeles for an ABC affiliate meeting. It was during a reception at the Century Plaza Hotel that we turned around only to find Peter off to the side of the room with our 4-year old daughter, Brittney, engaged in a lively conversation. It would have likely continued much longer if not for the commotion caused by the clicking of cameras and bright flashes from several photographers who had also taken notice. Peter would later tell me that his boss, Roone Arledge, insisted he fly home to New York via L.A. from an assignment in Moscow just so he could participate in the news portion of our affiliate meeting the next day. It was obvious that Peter would have preferred to have flown home directly, saying that he was eager to see his own daughter, Elizabeth, and that engaging Brittney in the way he did was the next best thing!

The reason for Roone's insistence on his participation in the meeting became clear the following morning when Peter led the questioning of Vice President George Bush as part of a panel discussion that also included David Brinkley, Sam Donaldson and George Will.

As it would turn out, Peter and Brittney met again on Jan. 25, 2000, in Des Moines. He was in town to anchor ABC News' coverage of the Iowa caucuses the night before. Peter had accepted an invitation to speak to my Breakfast Club, so I invited Brittney, now 15 years old, to join us. On the way to the breakfast venue, he wrote a beautiful note to Brittney on the back of a photo that an ABC photographer had taken at the Century Plaza nearly a dozen years earlier. Peter was warmly received at the breakfast gathering. We agreed beforehand that he would touch only briefly on the previous night's Iowa caucus results, which saw George W. Bush win the Republican vote and Al Gore win the Democratic vote. Peter's remarks focused instead on *ABC 2000 Today*, the incredible millennium eve special that had been broadcast live on the network just a few weeks earlier. The program attracted an audience estimated at 175 million viewers, with Peter serving as the primary anchor for an unprecedented 23 hours straight. The sense of pride and accomplishment he took in that massive undertaking was evident.

Peter Jennings was a WINNER for the remarkable way he inspired and then led those around him, and for how he could assimilate his self-taught intelligence, life experiences, worldly travel, profound sense of history and valuable contacts. On a moment's notice, he could draw on all that knowledge to convey a clear story that his audience could grasp and understand. And then, even in the most chaotic of times — like during the week of 9/11 when he was behind the anchor desk for more than 60 hours — he could do so in a commanding yet calm and reassuring way.

TED KOPPEL

"Aspire to decency. Practice civility toward one another. Admire and emulate ethical behavior wherever you find it. Apply a rigid standard of morality to your lives; and if, periodically, you fail — as you surely will — adjust your lives, not the standards."

Ted Koppel, iconic journalist, founding anchor of ABC News *Nightline* and 25-time Emmy Award recipient

Martha Raddatz's pulse pounded.

The then-chief correspondent at WCVB-TV in Boston feared she might stammer as she reported from the 1988 presidential campaign during her first appearance on ABC News' epochal *Nightline* program.

"Seriously, I had never been so petrified in my life," Raddatz, now ABC's chief global affairs correspondent, told us.

Why?

"Having Ted Koppel talk in your ear was like television nirvana," Raddatz answered. "I remember how I wanted to be accurate and probably was, but likely by just reciting facts or something. But yeah, he was the gold standard."

Ted served as the anchor of *Nightline* from March 1980 until November 2005. So it's perfectly understandable Martha approached her first on-air exchange with him brimming with both apprehension and excitement. The "gold standard" expected your best effort, but only because he never failed to put forth his own.

"In all the years that he was *Nightline* anchor, Ted and his group really were like a separate civilization within the D.C. bureau," recalled longtime ABC News executive Robin Sproul. "Ted was known by every single administration official and every single member of Congress. To get a call from Ted with his deep and beautiful voice, and to know that he's interviewed every major world leader and knows more about foreign policy than you could ever hope to know, could be as intimidating as it was memorable. To have *Nightline* based in Washington, with Ted at the helm of it, brought a real prestige to our bureau. He was an amazing and brilliant talent, and was just really like no one else on television."

Ted was inimitable. Funny. Fearless.

"Ted Koppel was the State Department correspondent when Henry Kissinger was the secretary of state," said David Westin, former president of ABC News. "He took from that a sense of world affairs and the role of a journalist holding government to account. Ted always took that very seriously and did wonderfully well at it. If you wanted credibility, you had to go on *Nightline* and be interviewed by Ted Koppel because there was no substitute."

In October 1993, I was the outgoing chairman of the Siouxland Chamber of Commerce, and Ted graciously agreed to give the keynote address at the annual dinner. He did so as a way of recognizing my longtime support of his program, refusing to even discuss a speaking fee or honorarium of any kind. But breaking news involving a constitutional crisis between the Russian president and Russian parliament almost prevented Ted from attending, until some creative travel arrangements at the 11th hour helped make it happen.

We flew Ted from Florida to Chicago's O'Hare airport on a commercial flight. I talked the airport manager in to meeting Ted's flight at the gate. He boarded the plane, escorted Ted off it, and then drove him across the tarmac in a security vehicle with lights blazing to a private jet, where I was waiting for the short connecting flight to Sioux City. That would never happen in a post-9/11 world! In any event, Ted and I made it to the dinner with 15 minutes to spare. He was, of course, a big hit with the dinner's attendees.

Another story involving a trip with Ted on a private plane is even more memorable.

In April 1994, we worked together on a special edition of *Nightline* with the title *Viewpoint: Whitewater - Overplayed Underplayed?* It was presented on April 19, 1994, across the ABC television network from 10–11 p.m. ET and 11:30 p.m.–1 a.m. ET, originating live from Old Main hall on the campus of Drake University. Bill and Hillary Clinton's real estate investments in the failed Whitewater Development Corporation were a controversial, hot-button topic. As the program's title suggests, we delved into the media coverage and treatment of the story. Guests included longtime Bill Clinton political advisor James Carville, the late talk show host Rush Limbaugh, renowned First Amendment attorney Floyd Abrams and then-ABC News White House correspondent Brit Hume. It was a spirited, informative and highly-rated broadcast.

Now, about that second plane trip ...

Arrangements were made on the day of the broadcast for me to pick up Ted, James and Brit in Washington, D.C. for the trip to Des Moines on a private jet. The on-board conversation was quite cordial until an hour or so into the flight when Ted and Brit began challenging James on how it was that Hillary Clinton had yet to publicly address her role in Whitewater (Ted had tipped me off beforehand that he might try to "rile up James as a bit of foreplay" in advance of that night's program). The plan succeeded as James became, quite literally, spitting mad as he vehemently pushed back with the fact that "no first lady in the history of the Union has ever held a press conference and Hillary won't be the first. It's never happened and never will happen." Brit countered by calmly and respectfully pointing out that no other first lady had ever been on point for her husband's administration in the manner Hillary was on the issue of health care. The hypocrisy was evident and it was clear that it would be "game on" during the broadcast later that evening.

It was even more fascinating to watch what happened later that same week. On April 22, 1994, Hillary Clinton held what later became known as the "Pretty in Pink" press conference, a reference to the hue of her attire. The Q&A lasted 72 minutes and came about months after reporters first called for her to address her role in Whitewater and several highly criticized commodity trades. While it was later learned that the Clintons had, in fact, been considering holding just such a press conference, there's no doubt in my mind it was the *Nightline* special — and to some extent the exchange on the plane with Carville preceding it — that pushed their thinking over the top.

One final postscript to this story: Richard Nixon passed away on April 22, 1994. The media coverage of the historic Hillary Clinton press conference was greatly overshadowed by the news of Nixon's death. The timing was perfect from the Clinton point of view as coverage of the prior day's presser was pushed down in television newscasts and off the front page of newspapers everywhere. There was little doubt that the Clintons and Carville had calculated the likelihood of things playing out exactly the way they did. As Ted would tell me later, "That S.O.B. Carville, he got the last laugh after all!"

In November 2005, Ted departed *Nightline* after 25 years as its anchor and left ABC News after 42 years. The final broadcast could have featured a retrospective on the many interesting subjects and memorable moments over the preceding 25 years: Palestine Liberation Organization (PLO) chief Yassar Arafat, Supreme Court Chief Justice Warren Burger (his first live television interview), Bishop Desmond Tutu, outgoing Philippines President Ferdinand Marcos (and talk of his wife's extensive shoe collection!), Gary Hart (a prelude to the Colorado senator's withdrawal from the 1988 presidential race), Nelson Mandela in a revealing "town hall meeting" format, Madonna (her controversial music video that had been banned by MTV was played in its entirety), Jim and Tammy Faye Bakker (following a sex scandal that brought down his church), and/or the infamous exchange with longtime Los Angeles Dodgers executive Al Campanis (whose unfortunate, racially insensitive comments led to his subsequent firing by the team).

Instead of a walk down memory lane, Ted opted instead to have the final *Nightline* broadcast focus on the extraordinary series of programs he'd presented 10 years earlier about a dying Brandeis University sociology professor, Morrie Schwartz. It was after seeing those interviews with Morrie in 1995 that sports journalist Mitch Albom began making his own regular visits to see Morrie, who had been a favorite professor of his while attending Brandeis. Those weekly conversations became the foundation of *Tuesdays With Morrie*, a best-selling book containing warm and insightful advice about living life and facing death. For the farewell edition of the program he was so instrumental in building, Ted chose to interview Albom about the manner in which the *Nightline* interviews led to him reconnecting with his old professor, and how the powerful lessons contained in *Tuesdays With Morrie* resonated with so many people.

"Having Mitch Albom participate after he had reconnected with Morrie and interviewed him for his book brought it all full circle," said veteran *Nightline* and ABC News correspondent Chris Bury. "Asked by Ted in that final interview about his dignity, Morrie said, 'My dignity comes from my inner self.' I found that striking because that's exactly where Ted's dignity comes from. He had this innate sense of dignity and fairness, which made him not only a world-class journalist, but a truly wonderful boss." Put simply, Ted found an unusual way to step away from *Nightline* with the kind of grace and nobility that Morrie would have appreciated.

That's to be expected from the "gold standard," which Ted has proved to be throughout his illustrious career.

"I spent 15 years working side by side with Ted Koppel," Bury told us. "He was the best boss I ever had in my life, bar none. Smart, tough, demanding, compassionate and fair. In terms of his intellect, we were all in awe because he's just sort of naturally very smart. But beyond that, he was just so curious about every story and wanted to get it exactly right. He prized accuracy and he drilled that into us. You had to be accurate with Ted because he despised factual errors.

"People wanted to work hard for Ted because Ted worked so hard and would never ask you to do anything that he wouldn't do himself. A lot of television anchors are in the business because they like to be on TV. Ted was not one of those. He loved reporting from the field and understood the two most important words in journalism: 'Go there.'" If Ted wasn't doing the reporting himself from somewhere in the field, his correspondents were. Bury said, "Ted would send you somewhere and his last words as you were going out the door would be, 'Surprise me.'"

Robin Sproul told us how Ted was a one-of-a-kind newsman and truth seeker; he was driven by the pursuit of truth, not a desire for the spotlight. Bury backed that up, saying, "Most television anchors want their show to have the camera on them. If you had a great story, Ted would turn over the entire 30 minutes to you. If you had been in Haiti busting your butt for a month and came back with really good stuff, Ted would say, 'Well, why don't you take over the show tonight?' I mean, that kind of generosity is just unheard of in broadcasting. But he knew that if you made the show really great it would make him look good (too). I've never seen anything like it before or since, at least in network news."

Ted received many honors throughout his distinguished career: 25 Emmy Awards (including a Lifetime Achievement Award in 2007), eight Alfred I. duPont-Columbia University Awards, three George Foster Peabody Awards and two George Polk Awards. It was my honor to personally witness his induction into the National Association of Broadcasters' Hall of Fame in 2001.

Television critic Tom Shales wrote the following: "In the 25-year history of *Nightline*, millions tuned in not because Koppel seemed like a man who thought he knew everything but because he gave the impression of wanting to know everything."

Ted Koppel is a WINNER who had an innate sense of world affairs and the role of journalists in holding governments to account. He surrounded himself with people who believed passionately in his mandate to report stories, really serious stories, and report them well. And he worked relentlessly to "bring people together who are worlds apart" during his long and remarkable run as anchor of *Nightline*.

DAVID MUIR

"For more than a decade, David has been front and center reporting on the biggest stories of our time, helping drive us forward with tireless dedication, hard work and good humor. ... David has made his reputation reporting from the ground on every big story of recent times, and we know that when the big stories happen, wherever they happen, David will be there for us and our audience."

James Goldston, former president of ABC News when naming David Muir to succeed Diane Sawyer as anchor of *World News Tonight* (June 25, 2014)

Scores of his classmates copied the moves of star Syracuse big man Derrick Coleman.

Or the batting stance of New York Yankees legend Don Mattingly.

Or maybe the pass rushing prowess exhibited by New York Giants linebacker Lawrence Taylor.

Sports idols and dreams of winning championships drive many youthful visions of glory, of prestige, of reaching the top.

David Muir approached the concept of "winning" in a completely different manner. The then-teenager aimed his lofty ambitions toward a decidedly different pursuit.

"(When) I was a kid growing up in upstate New York (in the 1980s), at 13 years old I began writing to the local news reporters in town," said David, who now anchors the nation's highest-rated network evening newscast, ABC's *World News Tonight*. "And as a kid, I could not put into words what it was that drew me to this discipline — to journalism. But I recognize now, certainly as an adult and as someone who learns every day in this fascinating job, that I wanted to see the world beyond my backyard and beyond my community."

David — who also co-anchors the ABC News magazine show *20/20* and leads the network's special events and breaking news coverage — timed his teenage return from after-school outdoor games to 6:30 p.m. Eastern Time, not the dinner bell.

Why?

That's when Peter Jennings would anchor *World News Tonight*, and that's who David would admire, emulate and ultimately honor as a successful journalist himself.

"I didn't realize that one day I would literally see the world," said David, who helped lead ABC's coverage of the 2012 Presidential campaign before ascending to the *World News Tonight* anchor role on Sept. 2, 2014. "I remember being the only kid playing outside excusing myself to go in and watch the evening news. I was always drawn to Peter Jennings. I'm sure as a 13-year-old, as a young man, I was very impressionable. Peter had this James Bond globetrotting style, if you will, but it was more than that. It was the conversation he was having with America every night. And I was drawn to that, along with his hunger, his curiosity and his globetrotting. When I look at what it is I'm drawn to now as a journalist — and I often take *World News Tonight* on the road all over the world — the kinds of stories I'm drawn to and the people I'm drawn to hopefully follow in that great tradition."

They do — and the public has been drawn to his demeanor, his unique brand of reporting, and truth-telling. When David first sidled into the *World News Tonight* anchor chair, ABC trailed NBC by more than 1 million viewers in average nightly viewership. By spring 2021, Muir's leadership had helped propel *World News Tonight* back to the top, by an average of more than 1.5 million nightly viewers.

That's a big leap forward — and it wasn't accomplished via smoke and mirrors.

"David Muir is an extraordinarily gifted broadcaster," Martha Raddatz, ABC News chief global affairs correspondent, told us. "During these times, I understand why the public is turning to him to watch (*World News Tonight*) more than any other (network news) show. David is really authentic. He cares about people. He reaches out to people. David is a really collaborative colleague. He wants all of us to be the best we can be and wants people to know that we are a team."

David's on-screen persona matches his true personality: caring, hard-working and devoted to fact, not fiction.

"I hope that (my approach) follows in that great Jennings tradition," David told us. "When I go out in the field, everywhere from Iraq to Afghanistan, from Fukushima (Japan) to Somalia ... for me, it's not about proximity to power, it's about proximity to people. When you look back at Peter Jennings and the body of his work, you remember the moments of Peter Jennings with the children. And you remember the moments with Peter Jennings out there with the people and absorbing his surroundings. I think that is what fuels me today. I'm grateful to have been influenced by him as a young man in journalism, and I'm certainly grateful, looking back, that I had the chance to work at ABC News while Peter was still the anchor of *World News Tonight*."

So often, the lofty dreams we nurture as teenagers never come to fruition. David's most fervent wish did: to become a worthy heir to Peter Jennings' anchor seat. No rim-rattling dunk, home run stroke or quarterback sack can match that level of winning in my book.

Or as David, with a hint of self-reflection, told us, "I hope that the conversation we're having with America, even in these heavy times, is a continuation of the conversation I gravitated to as a kid."

David is a WINNER because he embodies many of the same attributes that made Peter Jennings great. He succeeds because truth serves as his guiding light, and he's willing to go wherever it leads him so we, too, can make informed decisions vital to the maintenance of our democracy.

ROBIN ROBERTS

"Robin is one of those people who enrich your soul, who are authentically who they are, and who want to see you and who change you when you see them. It's (with) the quality of her listening, her attention and her compassion that she understands so much of the world ... how we're different and how we're essentially connected. And she has the best smile on TV!"

Diane Sawyer, former anchor of *World News Tonight* and co-anchor of *Good Morning America*

Longtime ABC news executive Robin Sproul fielded the phone call. It came from President Barack Obama's communications director, Dan Pfeiffer, in 2012. As the conversation unfolded, President Obama wanted to do a "big deal interview" but the overture came with a few strings attached.

"(He) wanted to give the exclusive to one person," Sproul told us. "And that person was to be Robin Roberts."

The award-winning anchor of ABC's *Good Morning America* was the perfect choice — even as the main topic for the interview remained nebulous by design.

"It was all with the understanding that they couldn't tell me the topic," Sproul added. "While you never turn down an exclusive interview with a sitting president, I kept thinking why do they want Robin? And then it slowly dawned on me that the topic would be gay marriage and it *would* be big. Robin did an extraordinary job on that interview and deservedly won awards for it. ... (She) is open and warm and friendly, and as smart as can be. The Obamas, as so many other newsmakers have learned, knew they could talk to her."

Robin's own sexuality was the focus of an email exchange between the two of us following a Facebook post of hers in late December 2013. I wrote to her, saying, "Well now, that little old year-end Facebook post of yours has caused a bit of a stir. I look forward to the day when such an item won't be considered 'news' by the mainstream media or otherwise. But in the meantime, after all you've been through the past few years, any blowback you get will be like a walk in the park. And you will always have the love and support of your family, colleagues and friends — that's what matters most!" In her reply, Robin said simply, "It certainly was not my intention to cause such a stir. Just grateful for my life and all it richly entails. My brother said the same thing you did: The people most important to me will always love and support me. And that is all that really matters. We should all be so lucky."

Robin is so much more than a deeply respected interviewer and journalist.

She's simply a "force," as ABC *World News Tonight* anchor David Muir put it. "Authenticity is her most powerful weapon, if you will," David said. "It's what makes her stand apart from so many others."

Robin stands tall as a force for good. An authentic and caring soul. An empathetic person who shares personal stories that have inspired millions.

"Robin Roberts came from a family of such great faith and strength and laughter," said her legendary ABC colleague, Diane Sawyer. "I think all of the Roberts — her parents, sisters and brother, who I love so much — as this rare event where shining, radiant, fun, guiding lights were born. Robin is one of those people who enrich your soul, who are authentically who they are, and who want to see you and who change you when you see them."

And the smile that Diane calls the best on TV? It's also completely genuine, even as Robin has faced more adversity in the past 15 years than many of us will encounter in a lifetime.

She was diagnosed with breast cancer in 2007 and another form of cancer, myelodysplastic syndrome (MDS), in 2012. These health challenges could have prompted a "Why me?" But not from Robin. *Never* from Robin. She instead embodied her mother's sage advice: "Make your mess your message."

"Robin's journey during my time leading ABC was different from all the others," said Anne Sweeney, the former co-chair of the Disney Media Networks. "She had to battle breast cancer in 2007 and just a few years later had to deal with MDS and a life-saving bone marrow transplant (from her sister, Sally-Ann Roberts). It changed me as an executive and made me understand the profound responsibility we have to one another.

"It was important for her to know that everyone at *GMA* was waiting for her. Every morning, (co-anchor) George Stephanopoulos would say her name. No one asked George to do that, but he did it and I think it really solidified a bond that so many people felt. He would talk about her as the captain of the ship. Robin's return to *GMA* in February 2013 was a joyous and memorable day for all of us at the network."

Robin has helped guide her colleagues as much as she helps to guide the audience through trying moments not only for the country, but some trying personal moments along the way for her. "Robin has left many of us in awe of her ability to step up and make the rest of us feel at ease in moments when she has been tested the most," David Muir told us. "And quite frankly, there were moments when we wanted to wrap our arms around her, but the truth is it was her taking care of everybody else ... (with) the power she has in connecting with her colleagues and the audience. It's not manufactured. And you couldn't if you tried."

It was a pleasure to turn the tables when interviewing Robin in March 2016 on the set of *Good Morning America*. We were recording a series of vignettes to help promote our mutual friend Dick Vitale's annual gala that raises funds on behalf of The V Foundation for the fight against pediatric cancer. Robin was scheduled to be one of Dick's honorees at that year's gala, and her inspiring spirit shined throughout the 30-minute interview.

I asked Robin for her reflected thoughts on having received the Arthur Ashe Award for Courage at the 2013 ESPYS, and she emotionally recalled having that high honor bestowed upon her.

"That was such a special night because when I was diagnosed with MDS it was (holding back tears) ... my mother had passed away shortly before that. There was a time when I thought, 'Oof, I don't know if I am going to make it.' Then, to be standing on that stage among your peers and people you have so much respect for and be a part of a program like the ESPYS, all the while thinking of Jimmy V (Jim Valvano) and the countless people who had won that award before me. And to be standing on that stage with my partner, Amber (Laign), and family there, and just to be able to look out at the crowd and say, 'I am a symbol of this too shall pass. I am a symbol of whatever it is that you're going through … just keep moving.' I was especially grateful because Arthur Ashe was a very dear friend and to be seen as worthy of an award with his name on it … as you can tell (again, with tears), it's still a moment that touches me."

And touches countless others.

Robin doesn't mince words, nor emotions. She epitomizes the term "authentic," which is an overused adjective, but one that perfectly — and almost singularly — describes her.

Robin is among the most talented, courageous and resilient people to have enriched my career and blessed my life. It was a joy to be backstage with her at the National Association of Broadcasters (NAB) Show in Las Vegas in April 2018 only moments before she was presented the NAB's highest honor, the Distinguished Service Award. Robin's name is now included among those on the list of individuals to be bestowed NAB's highest honor, including: Edward R. Murrow, Bob Hope, Lowell Thomas, Walter Cronkite, President Ronald Reagan, Dick Clark, Barbara Walters, Peter Jennings, Mary Tyler Moore, Oprah Winfrey and Michael J. Fox.

With an identity all her own and an unbreakable spirit, Robin is a WINNER in every sense of the word.

For more than 10 years now, George Stephanopoulos has worked alongside Robin as co-anchor of *Good Morning America*. George pointed to another word that encapsulates who Robin is: soul. "She leads with her soul. You can feel it in the morning. You can feel it in the way she carries herself," George said. "And you can feel it in the way she treats everyone. It's a soul that is determined to spread good in the world … and she does it in a way that feels grounded and whole and loving and nurturing."

DIANE SAWYER

"Diane Sawyer always thinks very deeply and creatively and tries to understand not just the story, but the underlying currents of the story; the parts that you wouldn't know about or have thought about. She sees the indirection, the subtlety, the nuance of a story better than anyone."

David Westin, former president of ABC News and current anchor at Bloomberg Television

"I'll have your back."

Those words perfectly framed then up-and-coming ABC News journalist David Muir's relationship with his esteemed and celebrated colleague, Diane Sawyer.

David is now the anchor of ABC News *World News Tonight*. Diane, who has been a star in the industry for more than 40 years, was the anchor from 2009 to 2014. And no matter what situation her correspondents faced, she could instantly put them at ease and help them craft their finest work.

"Diane always wanted us to know if it was uncomfortable (in the field), 'Don't you worry about a thing, because I'll have your back,'" David told us. "If you talk to any number of journalists who have come into her orbit, many would echo that sentiment. She'd send you out into the field to tell the stories of average people; to give people who don't have a voice a voice. There were multiple moments in the field where I was a correspondent filing for Diane's broadcast where we would be in a breaking news situation. I would look at her, she would look at me, and I knew exactly what it was I needed to do and what my job was in that moment. To have that experience with someone whom you admire, respect and revere is an extraordinary thing that I hold on to until this day."

Diane is a seeker. And she never quits.

"You haven't seen competitiveness until you've seen it in Diane Sawyer. And yet, she always did it in the most obliging way," David Westin, her former boss and president of ABC News, told us.

Diane also has an undeniable allure.

"Diane has true charisma," said former ABC executive Anne Sweeney. "Thinking of her interview style, she has the ability to get people into a very, very comfortable place without even realizing that they're answering questions they probably swore they'd never answer."

Diane joked to us that she'd once been "maybe the most disastrous weather girl in the history of television" early in her career, but her ability to tell stories and coax truth out of people — both famous and unknown — has made her one of America's great broadcasters for nearly half a century.

"Doing an interview with her was always something people wanted to do, simply because they wanted to be able to say they had done an interview with Diane Sawyer," said Robin Sproul, who served as a vice president of ABC News for 25 years.

Believe it or not, Diane was once adrift like many of us are from time to time. But sage wisdom from her father helped crystallize her commitment to make a difference in this world. "I came back from college and I had no idea what I was going to do," Diane told us. "And my father sort of asked me three questions: 1. 'What do you want to do?'; 2. 'Where could you do it and feel it was adventurous?'; 3. 'Does it help people?' He said, 'If you've got that intersection of your joy, and feeling it's meeting a need in the world, then you're home. That's your whole career.'"

So Diane embarked on a remarkable journey, eventually swam ashore and still seeks out every distant island. Uncertainty — and adventure —

is her guide. Diane's *Hidden America* special reports for ABC News have given voice to the voiceless and illuminated truths long obscured by the partisan squabbles that play out as theater in Washington, D.C.

"It's not always about the interviews with the famous and infamous," Diane said in a deeply reflective way. "I'm always amazed at the eloquence, the resilience, the enormous intelligence and brilliance of people who are not in the magazines. And that you can wander up that hill and any mountain in eastern Kentucky and find a universe of ideas and hope and talent, and the continued belief in the possibility of life. Every single time it strikes me with a new thunderbolt that this is who we are. And if everyone is given a chance to thrive and dream, a way to do it and a way to get there, then the world is changed. I love setting out not knowing what we're going to find. Don't you feel sometimes that a lot of what's around us (are people) who feel like they've been there before? That you see the patterns in it and as such need to break the pattern and be able to go on what they used to call 'blue highways' — the back roads — and wander into a story that is as rich as any great novelist's? A story that has breathtaking dimensions involving someone that might not tell it if you hadn't wandered in their door?"

Diane's body of work has been recognized with numerous awards, including the Walter Cronkite Award for Excellence in Journalism in 2010. Roughly one year after attaining that high honor, she and David Muir were once again in the field together, reporting for *World News Tonight* in the wake of a devastating tornado that tore through Joplin, Missouri. They were about to go on the air when remnants of the storm blew through the makeshift set with such force that a small tent hastily erected for the broadcast was nearly blown away. "The crew was holding on to the lights and camera, while Diane and I were literally sharing a microphone," David recalled. "But we just went on the air. The wind and noise were so deafening in the moment that we just looked into each other's eyes, if you will, and knew what we had to do."

David then summed up his feelings about his predecessor, saying, "To this day, I still feel lucky to have the privilege to sit in the anchor chair and have a conversation with America, and know that Diane is watching, too. I often think, 'I wonder what she would make of this or that moment?' It's as though she's still standing there like that moment in Joplin when we were sharing a microphone. And I recognize that my experience is shared by many others — Diane has been a champion for so many of us who learned and watched her along the way."

A champion who will always "have your back." That goes for colleagues, friends and fellow citizens of the world alike.

"When they say 99% of life is showing up, it really is," said former ABC correspondent and current CNN anchor, Jake Tapper. "I would constantly show up (for Diane) and say, 'What can I do? Here are some ideas.' Diane was just like open arms, open doors; warm and sweet, and always so flattering in terms of respecting ideas. I can never thank her enough."

Nor can I.

Diane Sawyer is a WINNER whose anchoring, original reporting, in-depth investigations and long-form interviews have defined a remarkable career. There are few experiences throughout one's broadcasting career that can match the sense of pride that rises up when calling her a colleague, or the feeling of joy that comes from being the beneficiary of her friendship.

GEORGE STEPHANOPOULOS

"George is so smart. We can watch a State of the Union together on set and have completely different takeaways with my thinking in terms of foreign policy while he hones in on the political angle, and it's dazzling. His political brain is really dazzling."

———————

Martha Raddatz, ABC News chief global affairs correspondent and co-anchor of *This Week with George Stephanopoulos*

ABC News anchor George Stephanopoulos is rightly renowned for his curiosity, work ethic and persistent efforts to ferret out the truth.

But even calm, cool George — whom I first met in 2007 to discuss coverage of the 2008 Iowa caucuses — needs soothing strategies to help stamp out stress. Enter meditation, which George started practicing in recent years to assuage frayed nerves and an overloaded schedule.

"It's been one of the biggest life enhancers I could ever imagine," George told us. "Especially with the schedule I have doing at least three jobs at ABC, plus trying to live a life and be there for my family and my friends. What I've found is that 20 minutes (of meditation) twice a day creates several more effective hours in my day. Taking that time to be quiet, to contemplate, to meditate and to let my mind rest, charges me for the whole day."

George's day is always beyond full. He joins Robin Roberts and Michael Strahan to co-anchor *Good Morning America* each weekday morning. He also serves as host of *This Week with George Stephanopoulos* on Sundays. And he has a production company that produces primetime specials for the broadcast network and other projects for Disney's various streaming platforms.

How does George find the hours? How does he keep up his energy? By deeply valuing his loved ones — and devoting himself to numerous charitable causes.

"He's just a well-rounded, really smart guy," former ABC news executive Robin Sproul said.

George is also a deeply committed family man. He is both ambitious and attentive to his loved ones. That can be a difficult balancing act. Not for George. Meditation may have helped him manage his professional life, but integrity and empathy are the values that have always helped guide him in his personal life.

"Winning is having a life that includes a lot of love," George said. "Valuable relationships. Worthy work. And some broader and deeper sense of purpose. It's not defined by where you end up, but how you go about trying to achieve all those goals in any given day, in any given moment."

It's all in the breath. And in the breadth of George's work. That day in 2007 when we first met over breakfast in a Washington, D.C. hotel was all about our collaboration on presidential debates that would be held on the Drake University campus in Des Moines at the start of the 2008 political cycle. But it spurred a special relationship and friendship that continues to this day.

George is known for his intense preparation and I've always respected him greatly for that. So it was a surprise to me when he took the time and risked embarrassment when agreeing to my suggestion that he throw out the first pitch at an Iowa Cubs game in August 2007, mere days before one of the two debates we had been working on together.

George's "throw" was, well, not great.

But when well-known rapper 50 Cent (Curtis James Jackson III) tossed out a far worse effort several years later, it prompted me to chide George a little bit. "I will never, EVER again give you a hard time about your first pitch before the Iowa Cubs game in 2007. Mercy," I typed in an email. George promptly responded. "Hah. I can give Fifty a hard time at our (*GMA*) concert on Friday!" he joked.

George's ability to laugh at himself remains central to his character. He's as smart and competitive as anyone I've ever met. He's driven. He's immensely talented. But he knows that the hamster wheel we all tend to trod upon cannot — and will not — break him. It won't slow him down. It won't diminish his driving but giving spirit while navigating the vicissitudes of Washington. Even in 2020 and 2021, when extremism went into hyper-drive and when fact and fiction became grounds for routine debate, no matter the evidence, no matter the truth.

"You have to know why you're doing it and what you want to achieve from it," George said of his life in politics and journalism. "And none of it is perfect. I have stumbled along the way, but what I've learned and taken away most of all from trying to navigate the world of politics and media is that it's such an unpredictable, chaotic and in some ways confrontational world. You're forming and reforming alliances, working with people over a long period of time, having tough conversations, but also (knowing) that in all those relationships you must try to be as direct and honest and candid as you can possibly be."

George is an incredibly kind and generous man. It was my privilege and pleasure to serve with him on the board of the Broadcasters Foundation of America where he continuously made vital contributions in terms of both time and treasure to benefit fellow broadcasters in need.

George has proved himself on every stage, at every stage, throughout his career. We returned to Drake University in December 2011 for another presidential debate. He teamed up this time with Diane Sawyer as co-moderator, and it was presented on ABC just weeks ahead of the Iowa caucuses. The duo was a tour de force.

"There was never a more fun preparation than watching those two co-moderators and brainiacs, George Stephanopoulos and Diane Sawyer, prepare for that debate," Robin Sproul told us. "It was a very heavy time, but nonetheless fun process to be involved with. I recall walking out of the prep sessions and saying, 'I don't know if it could be much better than that!'"

I couldn't have agreed more with Robin's assessment. George and Diane did a fantastic job with what ended up being one of the most-watched debates in the 2012 political cycle.

Today, George cycles through meditative states. For at least 20 minutes at a time. Up to twice a day.

Serenity meets solemnity for both our political system and one's life purpose. Deep breaths. Deeper thoughts — and words.

"Winning is the kind of fulfillment that comes with all the things I talked about," George said with some degree of reflection. "Your loving family. Good friends. Work that's important to you that you can do with integrity. To me, if you are pursuing all those things and doing so with a sense of balance, that is happiness."

George Stephanopoulos fully grasps what a meaningful career and balanced life are all about. Moreover, he is a WINNER who I'm proud to call a longtime network colleague and close friend.

BARBARA WALTERS

*"Barbara's fierce determination was unlike anything
I had ever seen or experienced. It was singular ... she
was larger than life. Barbara got up every morning,
looked at the world, and tried to figure out, 'How am I
going to conquer it today?' She never, ever stopped."*

Ben Sherwood, former president of ABC News and
former co-chair of the Disney Media Networks

Iowans have earned a reputation for being kindhearted and courteous.
It's what is often referred to as "Iowa nice" by some folks. So, while said
in an obviously good-natured manner, it nonetheless took me by surprise
when Barbara Walters said to me on more than one occasion, "I like you
even though you are from Iowa." It later dawned on me what — and to
whom — Barbara was not so subtly making reference.

Harry Reasoner, a native of tiny Dakota City, Iowa, was a highly
respected newsman for decades during a decorated career that took him
to the top spot at ABC News: the anchor chair. But Reasoner didn't
exactly welcome Barbara into the co-anchor's seat in the mid-1970s. The
three-time Emmy Award winner was skeptical of Barbara and felt she
hadn't necessarily earned her spot alongside him.

Put simply, there was nothing "Iowa nice" about the way he treated
Barbara. And he couldn't have been more wrong.

"The blood was so bad between us … that Harry's cronies on the crew took to using a stopwatch to note my airtime … (and) Harry's hostility soon began to show on the air," Barbara wrote in her 2008 autobiography, *Audition: A Memoir*. "I remember reaching toward him at the end of one broadcast, in a friendly manner, just to touch him on the arm. He recoiled, physically recoiled, in front of millions of people."

I lean into all of the above not to disparage or discredit Reasoner, who was an accomplished journalist in his own right. He became widely known after covering the assassination of President John F. Kennedy for CBS News. It was there that he teamed up with Mike Wallace to turn *60 Minutes* into the popular and incredibly influential newsmagazine program that it continues to be to this day. Reasoner had joined ABC News in 1970 where he first co-anchored the evening news with Howard K. Smith before taking over as the sole anchor in 1975.

I refer to all this solely to provide a framework from which to examine — and celebrate — Barbara's groundbreaking rise through the field of television journalism, where she is revered as a tough-as-nails trailblazer, world-class interviewer and competitor of the highest order.

Legend. Icon. The First Lady of Broadcast Journalism. There are simply not enough superlatives to describe the career of Barbara Walters. Highly regarded for her unique interviewing technique and solid journalistic work, Barbara was the first woman given the title of "co-host" for a network news program while working at NBC on the *Today* program. She made headlines in 1976 after signing a million-dollar contract with ABC that would make her the first woman to co-anchor an evening network news program and the highest paid journalist — male or female — at the time.

Reasoner's resistance to sharing the spotlight with a female co-anchor led to a rocky and frustrating start for Barbara at her new network. As Barbara put it ever so tactfully to Oprah Winfrey many years later, Reasoner was her "unwilling co-anchor." But while he may have been condescending, the old-guard media were blatantly rude at best — and downright sexist at worst. Barbara left the network's flagship evening news program in 1978 after two years of poor ratings; Reasoner left ABC altogether around the same time and headed back to CBS where he reassumed his old role on *60 Minutes*.

Undeterred, Barbara doubled down to carve out her niche as a crack interviewer and tack-sharp reporter. She went on to become an amazing contributor to the ABC Television Network over the course of the next 40 years.

"Barbara Walters was clearly a 'winner' for how she reshaped broadcast journalism and created her unique interview brand," former ABC News president David Westin said. "And Barbara had to do it from a position of weakness, not strength, as she was patronized throughout the early stages of her career. She reinvented herself with the help of (legendary television executive) Roone Arledge who was there with her at the time."

Barbara increased the focus on her primetime specials composed of conversations with heads of state, newsmakers, celebrities and sports figures. The first show of this nature aired in December 1976 and featured an interview with President-elect Jimmy Carter and his wife, Rosalyn. A tenacious pursuer of elusive people in the news, these specials quickly resonated with viewers while also earning begrudging respect from many of her critics.

In November 1977, Barbara went "mano a mano" with Walter Cronkite as they both snagged a joint, high-profile interview with Egypt's President Anwar el-Sadat and Israel's Prime Minister Menachem Begin. According to *The New York Times*, Cronkite was heard to say after the interview, "Did Barbara get anything I didn't get?" She later scored an exclusive interview with former President Richard Nixon in 1980 — the first live interview after his 1974 resignation.

"Barbara Walters is just an extraordinary person," former ABC executive Robin Sproul told us. "The list of people she's interviewed is just so long and impressive."

In June 1978, Roone Arledge unveiled his plans for *20/20*, a newsmagazine that has been a staple on ABC's primetime schedule ever since. Barbara was reunited with her former *Today* co-host Hugh Downs when she came on board in 1979 as a correspondent. In 1984, she became Downs' co-host and would remain in that role for the next 20 years.

Barbara had more than "arrived." She had become a crucial draw for ABC News' special programming — and helped the network's overall ratings spike.

"Barbara's fierce determination was unlike anything I had ever seen or experienced," said former president of ABC News and former co-chair of the Disney Media Networks, Ben Sherwood. "Barbara would be the first to tell you that she's not as glamorous or iconic as Diane Sawyer, or as incandescent and statuesque as Robin Roberts. And yet despite her diminutive size and Boston accent, she demonstrated an irrepressible drive and larger-than-life determination for five decades! If you think about the staying power of celebrity, there are only a handful of people who have been able to maintain that level of success, influence and stardom for five decades. Barbara spent more than 50 years at the very top of the television ecosystem as the queen of broadcast news. It's a singular achievement."

She did it without a hint of elitism. Barbara treated everyone with respect, as illustrated in a warm, personal anecdote Anne Sweeney, another former co-chair of the Disney Media Networks, shared with us.

"My career at ABC began as a page that was assigned to the news desk," Sweeney said. "A woman named Genevieve was in charge of all the pages and she had three rules: 1. Pick up the phone on the first ring; 2. Do not touch anything on my desk; and 3. Do not ever talk to Barbara Walters. So Barbara would come in and she must have thought I was studying mime in school. She would regularly walk by the desk and say, 'Well, hello.' Barbara was always gracious and beautiful and very purposeful as she did so. I would just nod and smile because I had been emphatically told, 'Don't talk to Barbara Walters.'

"Barbara never failed to say, 'Hello, how are you?' and I would just bow my head or make gestures. So years go by and I'm now in charge of the entire ABC television network, and I tell her this story. Barbara just laughed and said, 'Well, I'm so happy I was nice to you. Can you imagine how my life might have turned out differently had I not been?' She became a very dear and treasured friend."

And ever true. Barbara demonstrated a constant need to "win" and did she ever. It was a character trait deeply ingrained in her while growing up.

"Barbara was a fierce competitor. Fierce. Boy, she did not want to ever lose at anything," David Westin told us. "Barbara explained in her autobiography, *Audition: A Memoir*, why that was. Because of her childhood, she felt like every day was an audition. It didn't matter how successful she was, how wealthy she was or how much prestige she had. Every day, Barbara came in and felt like she had to prove herself from scratch."

And while she had an ego, her caring personality turned that into a positive. A large part of that ego hinged on how Barbara treated others, and that has always been with class, dignity and a preternatural sense of curiosity.

"Barbara Walters was a singular talent," said Anne Sweeney. "I admire so many things about her, but one that I deeply admire and appreciate is her intense focus. She listened so carefully when you watched her in interviews. It was remarkable what Barbara heard behind the word, seeing her get inside somebody's head in front of the next thought. So, it was that remarkable ability to listen. And then to ask questions that could only be answered with truth because, if you didn't, she'd go right back in."

Robin Sproul added, "When Barbara wanted a presidential interview, she usually got it because even if they didn't think they were going to win, they wanted their 'Barbara Walters interview' as a gift to their grandchildren."

She's been a gift to all of us. Iowans. Americans. And television viewers around the world.

Any opportunity to spend time with Barbara creates fond memories. In September 2005 we happened to arrive at Carnegie Hall at the same time for a memorial service celebrating the life of Peter Jennings, who had died from lung cancer a couple months earlier. It was an honor when she asked me to accompany and escort her to a seat inside.

In February 2008, the Broadcasters Foundation of America presented its annual Golden Mike Award to Anne Sweeney. This black-tie event at the Waldorf-Astoria in New York City was hosted by Tom Bergeron, longtime host of *Dancing with the Stars*. Actress and singer Vanessa Williams, who was starring in *Ugly Betty* at the time, was the guest performer. Barbara and I were among a handful of colleagues whom Anne asked to "present" her for the high honor during the program. There are few things in life more intimidating than having to follow Barbara Walters on stage and speak to a sold-out crowd in the Waldorf's main ballroom!

Barbara would occasionally reveal her sense of humor to me. Such was the case at the end of a letter she sent to me in December 1997 that ended with, "Please let me know if there is anything that I might do for you. And tell your wife she has terrific taste."

When it came time to lend a hand with community events, Barbara and her fellow *The View* co-hosts could always be counted on. They often supported "Bras for the Cause" and would typically have a little fun while doing so. In a public service announcement for the November 2009 dinner, Barbara said, "*The View* has contributed to this event in the past … and this entirely volunteer effort provides funds to screen and detect and treat and hopefully cure breast and cervical cancers all across Iowa." She then added with a wry smile, "I am just relieved that we weren't asked to sign a bra again this year!"

Barbara is a true original who seldom took no for an answer. When faced with obstacles, she saw challenges and worked to overcome them, sometimes against startlingly long odds.

On her final day as co-host of *The View* in May 2014, she asked David Muir, anchor of ABC's *World News Tonight*, to walk her out on stage. David recalled, "What she did not know was that many (other) legendary women journalists who had learned from Barbara — and who had followed in her footsteps — were waiting backstage to come out and surprise her on the set. It spoke volumes about her legacy that all of these accomplished women were willing to celebrate this one giant figure in journalism."

Near the end of the show, Barbara was joined on stage by female journalists from a variety of decades and networks: Jane Pauley, Deborah Norville, Katie Couric, Gayle King, Savannah Guthrie, Connie Chung and many more. Oprah Winfrey was there as well, and she told Barbara, "I'm here to celebrate what you've meant to me. … I want to thank you for being a pioneer … (for) paving the road we all walk on. You're really the reason we're all here."

So while this WINNER has undoubtedly left an indelible mark on broadcast journalism, her lasting legacy may well be her role as a pioneer for — and lasting imprint on — the countless female journalists who followed. Barbara spent more than five decades shattering glass ceilings in the world of network television news. There will *never* be another television news career quite like hers.

Bob Woodruff

"When I realized there was a job that existed in this world where I could be in the middle of huge world events and actually get paid for it, it was an epiphany for me."

———

Bob Woodruff, ABC News correspondent and
co-founder of the Bob Woodruff Foundation

Contentment.

It's an elusive state. It's hard to define and even more difficult to fully attain. It's also what eminent ABC News journalist Bob Woodruff pursues and most values in life.

Woodruff, whose life was forever changed — and nearly lost — when a roadside bomb tore through his vehicle as it rumbled through Iraq in 2006, had an experience that makes him understandably cautious when it comes to the concept of "winning" while pointing out that everybody has a different definition of what it is.

He'd been named co-anchor of *World News Tonight* only 27 days before an IED nearly killed him in the field. David Westin, the president of ABC News at the time, told us, "Bob is beloved by those who work under him. Every producer, every editor, every production assistant, they all adore him. He's got amazing energy and inner strength. It was those qualities that led me to name him co-anchor of *World News Tonight* with Elizabeth Vargas after Peter Jennings died."

Within the framework of a month, Bob had gone from the pinnacle of his craft to lying in a hospital bed fighting for his life. So perspective is strong with Bob. When he speaks, we all should listen.

"I feel pretty blessed that I was able to A), live and survive," Bob told us. "And B), recover to the point where my family is satisfied and that I'm able to work again. That has given me more happiness than probably others would have expected."

They say it's the little things that matter. Family. A child's laugh. A teachable moment. A second chance to do all the things one cherishes most in life.

Bob values all of the above. He's always been a seeker — a person driven by an unshakeable desire to elucidate truth.

He suffered a traumatic brain injury on that fateful day in Iraq and decided to devote the rest of his life to helping veterans who have lived through similar situations forge new beginnings in the wake of tumultuous times.

"Our foundation has been the most satisfying thing I've ever done," Bob said of the foundation he started with his wife, Lee. "Sometimes I ask myself if there was anything good that came out of the explosion that changed my life in an instant. I say, 'Yes, it has enabled us to have a direct impact on others.' There are real transitional problems within the government because in the wars in Iraq and Afghanistan, there were so many wounds. More wounds, percentage-wise, and fewer deaths, percentage-wise, compared to previous wars. So they had a lot of patients that needed to get back to their families and hometowns. Once they survived, there was a very difficult adjustment they still had to pursue.

"It was all very challenging, and the government was not quite ready for it. We later realized there was something our foundation could do to help with their transition back to life — something that would not compete with the VA — once they got out of Bethesda Naval (Hospital), Walter Reed (Hospital) or any of the other military hospitals where they were being treated."

Bob could have been bitter. He could have asked, "Why me?" Instead, he sought out ways to help, and then formed an organization devoted to doing exactly that.

"Bob Woodruff is a special human being," former Disney executive Ben Pyne said. "I remember attending his foundation's first 'Stand for Heroes' event at the old Town Hall Theatre in New York City. The network and its affiliate board were there to show their support. It was the year after Bob came back from Iraq and he was still recovering. The headliners that night included Robin Williams and Bruce Springsteen. Everybody on that stage and in the audience was so grateful that Bob was still with us because they just had so much respect for him."

Bob earned that respect — both before and after his tragic experience in the field. He isn't only a seeker. He's also a rebel, in the best sense of the word.

"I became a lawyer partly because my father said, 'Please don't be a lawyer,'" Bob said while describing his career's trajectory. "When I finally had the experience of working in journalism while still a lawyer, it changed my life. I was teaching young Chinese students about law when the Tiananmen Square massacre happened (in 1989). My wife was there with me and we witnessed horrific moments. Bob Simon from CBS News hired me to get his crew around town as a fixer. I watched how Bob reported on a huge piece of history. I decided to try to find those kinds of experiences in the world of journalism, so I made the change. I've never been one that loves to be trapped in a building. I always like to be out in the fields, you know, around the sand."

Bob knows he's lucky to still be with us. To continue reporting. To further his efforts to help us make sense of the world, one field, country, or continent at a time.

"There are just a lot of things in crises that are out of our control," Bob said. "Not in your hands. In some ways, it's a roll of the dice. There's no question that my recovery was impacted by the fact that I had friends and family. My wife said it was the four 'F's: family, friends, fun and faith.' Were they the reasons I was able to recover a little bit better than expected? It's very unscientific and unproven, but others have had similar experiences and confirmed that it has some meaning to it."

Bob Woodruff is a warrior who suffered unimaginable injuries in the pursuit of news, only to later make the most remarkable of recoveries.

Shortly before returning to work at ABC News in February 2007, he reflected on how so very close he came to dying. He spoke about the marble-sized rock once lodged against a carotid artery leading to his brain. "Had that rock traveled one more millimeter," he said, "I would have been dead. It is a miracle I'm alive."

Not just alive, but some would say better than ever. "Bob came back, and son of a gun, he came back in some ways better than he was before," David Westin, his former boss and dear friend told us. "He has a depth and a gravitas you only get by that kind of near-death experience. It's an extraordinary, extraordinary story. Having been close to him through that whole time and having remained reasonably close to him now, I never saw any resentment. I never saw any bitterness. I never saw any anger. Bob has moved on to a wonderful, new and uniquely different career."

Since returning to the job he loves, Bob has reported from around the world. He has traveled to North Korea eight times, reporting on the growing nuclear arsenal in the hands of Kim Jong-un. Since 2015, Bob has been the primary correspondent for ABC News throughout Asia. Miracle or not, it's great to see him back doing the kind of work that has been honored with numerous Emmy, Alfred I. duPont and George Foster Peabody awards.

The entire Woodruff family has shown how to make something positive come out of something so negative in their lives. Bob and Lee wrote a best-selling book, *In An Instant*. In the afterword they wrote, "Goodness and healing needed to emerge from such a devastating event." Their ongoing philanthropic efforts have more than cleared that bar.

Bob Woodruff is a WINNER and shining example of excellence, fortitude and resilience in all aspects of life: work, marriage, family and giving back.

WHITE HOUSE
CORRESPONDENTS

"Our role is to inform the public, seek the truth, ask tough questions and attempt to hold those in power accountable by shining a spotlight on what they are doing. ... What is at stake is the survival of our nation as a place where differing views are tolerated and debated, where election results are trusted and accepted, where people in power are held accountable and where the truth is accepted, even when it challenges our beliefs and our biases."

Jon Karl in his book, *Front Row at the Trump Show*

There is nothing new about a president of the United States criticizing, berating or even maligning the press. It goes along with the inherent nature of a relationship that is necessarily antagonistic at times. But in recent years the media have been the subject of increasing criticism and, at times, outright hostility.

In the first full month of his presidency, President Donald J. Trump added fuel to the fire when claiming that news outlets were "the enemy of the American people." According to a Pew Research Center survey conducted in March 2017, 94% of Americans said they had heard about the relationship between the Trump administration and the news media. And what they were seeing at the time concerned them: Large majorities felt the relationship was unhealthy and that the ongoing tensions were impeding Americans' access to important political news. Importantly, these concerns were widely shared across nearly all demographic groups and large majorities of both Democrats and Republicans.

No group of journalists has found themselves in the spotlight or the targets of criticism more than those who serve in the White House press corps. As Jon Karl wrote in the epilogue of *Front Row at the Trump Show*, the founding charter of the White House Correspondents Association serves as a reminder that a free press has played an integral role in the White House for well over a hundred years. Jon wrote, "… asking questions of the most powerful people in our government, reporting on their actions, attempting to hold them accountable. The charter will fade, presidents will come and go, and so will the individual journalists and news organizations who report on them … (but the role) has and will continue to survive challenging times and flawed reporters just as surely as it will survive flawed presidents."

My respect for the role and work of White House correspondents has been shaped by an admittedly distant view of a longtime network affiliate, and enhanced through a wide range of associations with several correspondents given the prestigious assignment of covering the White House for ABC News over the years. In keeping with the goal of this book, I wanted to provide some insights into the personal and professional lives — and "winning" qualities — of a few of them. There have been several with whom I've enjoyed spending time, including Sam Donaldson, Brit Hume and Ann Compton. In particular, I'll always recall fondly my visit to the White House in June 2014 at the invitation of Jon Karl, touring the James S. Brady Briefing Room and meeting with Ann Compton and up-and-comer Arlette Saenz. Now working for CNN, Saenz was promoted to White House correspondent in January 2021.

With the help of Rick Klein, political director for ABC News, I opted to profile three former White House correspondents who I know best: Jon Karl, Martha Raddatz and Jake Tapper. Rick validated my choices, saying, "I've had the pleasure of working with some of the greats of the game when it comes to the White House beat and so much more. And thinking about the three you've chosen to highlight, I'm struck by how differently they approached the job – all with the utmost professionalism, but all in their own ways."

While their personalities and approaches are different, each of the following profiles are intended to convey the depth of experience, commitment and sacrifice that are common to all of them. They are WINNERS for their tireless dedication to the pursuit of the truth and what *really* goes on at the White House, and for serving in a role that remains vital to our democratic process.

JON KARL

"Enemy of the American people? ... There's a reason the founders put freedom of the press in the very first amendment to the Constitution. As long as American democracy remains healthy, there will be reporters willing to pursue the truth — even if that means incurring the wrath of the most powerful person in the world."

Jon Karl on *This Week with George Stephanopoulos* (Feb. 19, 2017)

A Brooklyn cab driver turned the keys that opened Jon Karl's curious and lively mind.

That often-hailed working class New Yorker — Jon's stepfather — never graduated from college, but had clearly obtained a master's degree in how to lead a productive life.

"He served in the Korean War and (was in) the acknowledgements of my book," said Jon, who wrote the bestseller *Front Row at the Trump Show* while working as chief White House correspondent for ABC News, and is currently serving as the network's chief Washington correspondent. "My stepfather ended up writing a bunch of novels; a total self-made guy and a man of impeccable integrity."

Jon has followed in his stepfather's footsteps — not, of course, as a novelist, but as an incisive and widely respected reporter and nonfiction writer who deftly separates fact from fiction in the political realm.

Jon both "shows" and "tells." Truth is always his guiding light; the prism through which he cuts through spin and subterfuge.

"Jon Karl knows Washington," ABC News anchor George Stephanopoulos told us. "He loves Washington. But he is not of Washington. Jon knows how to maintain that critical distance that is necessary for any reporter, but especially reporters who cover the White House where it's so easy to become captive in that briefing room. He's never let that happen."

Jon has reported from our nation's political epicenter for many years now, but becoming an author, he said, revealed new ways to ferret out facts, and place them in the proper context. "The most important thing that I learned from the process of writing (*Front Row at the Trump Show*) is how important it was to take a step back and look at the events that I've experienced from a perspective (gained with) a little bit of time," Jon told us. "To go back and try to make sense of what happened. (To) talk to people who were in the center of these major world events and try to include all perspectives. It's an incredibly valuable experience. And one more thing about it is I learned people are so much more willing to talk about things in the past, than in the crush of breaking news. So I have learned so much more about the events I've experienced that I had no idea about at the time."

That's another reason why knowing history matters. News breaks briskly, but truth can be obscured in the present moment. That's harder to do with the passage of time and benefit of hindsight.

And Jon — like Martha, Jake and myriad other intrepid reporters who have covered the White House for ABC News and other news outlets — is adept at uncovering objective facts even as some try to twist and challenge them.

"There's always been misinformation out there," Jon said. "There have always been people who try to cast doubt on facts and (who) deny reality. But it's more prevalent today and that means a journalist has to get back to the basics of journalism, which is gathering facts and following the truth wherever it leads."

Jon found himself in a unique position while covering the Trump presidency owing to the fact that he had known Donald J. Trump longer than any other journalist on the White House beat.

"Jon leveraged a longstanding relationship with President Trump into some of the deepest and most informed reporting out there — during a time of unprecedented challenges for journalists," said Rick Klein, ABC News political director. "He juggled his roles as chief White House correspondent and president of the White House Correspondents Association in a way that made him the go-to voice for important advocacy on behalf of his colleagues — and for the First Amendment. He gained a reputation as one of the sharpest questioners of the Trump era, particularly during the COVID-19 crisis. But go back and look at some Obama-era press briefings and you'll realize Jon was doing what he has long done to administrations of all types — bringing critical accountability, accompanied by his generous good nature."

Jon learned all that from his stepfather, who plied the streets of Brooklyn in his yellow taxi. He learned it from Walter Fairservis, his anthropology professor at Vassar College who some believe was the real-life inspiration for the popular "Indiana Jones" character. Jon also learned it, of course, from his many colleagues and mentors — including Peter Jennings, Ted Koppel, Cokie Roberts, Diane Sawyer and George Stephanopoulos.

"And I got a chance to work with those people, which is pretty incredible," Jon said.

Amen. Jon and his fellow ABC News journalists who I've been fortunate enough to know are pretty incredible in their own right. They grasp what the word "winning" is all about when it comes to both their professional responsibility and personal growth.

"I think one of the most important attributes of a 'winner' is to learn the right lessons from loss; to rebound and improve after experiencing a disappointment," Jon said. "Other ('winning') characteristics are honesty and integrity and fairness. And yet another category of attributes includes energy, drive, and a dedication to self-improvement. You're always trying to push yourself to do a little better than you did before."

Jon Karl is a WINNER who, like his many colleagues, commands and deserves the utmost respect for seeking to serve the greater good by helping all of us sift through and better understand what truly matters.

MARTHA RADDATZ

*"I am soooo happy it is over and I survived. And
I thought Baghdad was tough? Bring it on!"*

Martha Raddatz, ABC News chief global affairs correspondent,
in regard to her work as co-moderator of the Donald Trump vs.
Hillary Clinton 2nd Presidential Debate (October 2016)

One of America's most incisive reporters, Martha Raddatz, gave college a try. She rejected it.

The well-traveled Idaho native and current chief global affairs correspondent for ABC News called herself an "idiot" for eschewing higher learning, but her impressive career arc indicates she may well have made the right call.

"I dropped out of college, which was really stupid," Martha told us. "But I felt like I wasn't motivated. I didn't like it. I wasn't learning that much. I just wanted adventure and (to learn) new things." And in her defense, she cited the fact that many people in TV are college dropouts. She added, "I think in some ways people who do that compensate for it in other ways. ... Peter Jennings was a high school dropout and you compensate for that by learning something new every day."

But as was the case with the intrepid Peter Jennings, Martha's instincts trumped academics. Her intelligence quashed indoctrination. Her quest for truth overshadowed any desire for bona fides.

Those instincts have been tested and put to good use while serving in the past as a White House correspondent for ABC News. "Martha knew not to be limited by the briefing room, that the stature of being in that room could be offset by how it could stifle your reporting and your view of the beat," said Rick Klein, ABC News political director. "She got out there in the country and the world to tell the stories that had White House components, with a remarkable ability to get somewhere just before everyone else would have a reason to want to be there. She also was an invaluable mentor to a next generation of reporters, many of them women, who learned from one of the best that nothing informs questioning better than direct knowledge."

Martha, who aptly described herself to us as "fiercely independent," has never stopped "getting out there" and being a seeker of knowledge. As a person. As a journalist. Or while covering national security, foreign policy or politics for decades now.

"Martha walks the walk. What she does is to get as close to the story as you possibly can. That's her great talent whether she's covering the military or global affairs," her colleague George Stephanopoulos told us. "She's on the ground or in the war zone — unafraid — so she can know in a visceral way what she's reporting on. And Martha brings that same intensity and 'need to be where the story is' when she's covering political campaigns. She goes out and meets voters where they live to better report what's on their minds. The key to her success has been living the story."

Speaking of being unafraid, I vividly recall an email exchange with Martha in 2016. Only days earlier she and CNN's Anderson Cooper had served as the co-moderators for a presidential debate between the candidates, Donald Trump and Hillary Clinton. Trump, as usual, brought bluster and bombast to the occasion. Martha kept her cool throughout — and kept the debate from completely careening off the rails.

"Hope you're doing well now that you're a couple days removed from the eye of Hurricane Donald," I joked with Martha in the email. "Nice job. You always do yourself — and us (ABC network affiliates) — very proud."

Martha responded with her typical sense of humor and flair. "Thank you, Ray!" she typed. "I am *soooo* happy it is over and I survived. And I thought Baghdad was tough? Bring it on!"

Martha's indefatigable spirit stands as a testament to ABC News' approach to news and politics. Truth is sacrosanct. Lies are refuted. Exploring and illuminating the issues that define our now-vast political divide serves as the guiding light for everyone within the organization.

We could joke about Trump's over-the-top showmanship. She could chart a path ahead, beyond the noise. Martha could get through anything — just as she had early in life.

"I was raised by a single mom and my dad died before my third birthday," Martha recalled. "I don't remember a lot about my early years. I think my mom had some depression issues — and I don't blame her. That wasn't an easy time for a single woman to raise a couple of kids, but I think I'm one of those people who knew what I didn't want to do. I didn't want to be sad and I didn't want to stay in one place. My mom was not the most optimistic person in the world and yet she encouraged me by saying, 'Don't be like me. You can do anything.' It makes me sad to think about her life and how she always said she was born 20 years too early as a woman. And yet, she was fiercely independent and early for her time in believing women could do anything."

Her daughter has no doubt proved that — as have countless other women, of course. "Fierce independence" obviously runs in the family, and we've all been enriched by Martha's hard-earned, real-life knowledge because of it.

"Somebody once told me it's disciplined curiosity," Martha said about being an esteemed reporter who has covered everything from war zones to tense and unpredictable presidential debates. "That's how I would describe our jobs."

My description is a much simpler one: WINNER.

JAKE TAPPER

"As a three-peat recipient of the White House Press Corps' most prestigious award, Jake Tapper sets the pace and standard for all journalists in Washington. ... A modern news machine, Jake keeps newsmakers honest and his audiences informed around the clock."

Ben Sherwood, ABC News president at the time, talking about Jake winning the White House Correspondents Association's Merriman Smith Award for an unprecedented third consecutive year (April 5, 2012)

Jake Tapper said his last words, stowed his microphone and signed off. His work was done.

That didn't necessarily please the then-fledgling, but nonetheless promising, reporter for ABC News. He knew the "big guns" were flying into Des Moines to report on the 2004 Iowa caucuses, so Jake — now the lead Washington anchor for CNN — went out with his producer, Max, to reflect and unwind.

Jake had done several live shots for *Good Morning America* throughout the Democratic campaign season and felt good about his work. So he, like everyone else, sat back with a cold drink to watch the caucus results roll in.

"I had been at ABC News for less than a year at that point and was having a tough time breaking through onto *World News Tonight* and *Nightline*," Jake told us. "It was clear that I was not going on air again that day with all the big guns like Peter Jennings, Diane Sawyer and Claire Shipman flying in. So Max and I were like, 'Okay, let's go out and celebrate.' So we went to Centro and the caucus results starting coming in. We heard John Kerry had won (the Democratic Party vote) and decided to head over to his event at the Hotel Fort Des Moines. After walking around and talking to some other reporters, we went to the hotel bar, Checkers. As I entered the bar, I saw her (Jennifer Brown). She was beautiful, and I walked right over and we started talking. It turned out she was from D.C. and was in Iowa to raise awareness and help get out the vote for Howard Dean. I don't know that I would say it was love at first sight, but basically it was like I met her and that was it. We got engaged the following year, we married in 2006, had our daughter, Alice, in 2007 and have been together ever since."

The Iowa caucuses can be described in many ways. Chaotic and messy. Unrepresentative. And yet deeply democratic. But for Jake, a dyed-in-the-wool Philadelphian, the event seemed quaint and earnest — until fate took a hand and led to him becoming a husband and father.

"Iowa is a part of the country that I was not at all familiar with being from a big (East Coast) city as opposed to an agricultural area," Jake said. "It's a great tradition, the Iowa caucuses. I don't know how much longer they're going to be in existence after the problems in 2020, but it's a great tradition. They measure enthusiasm. The people who vote really follow politics. They're not just run-of-the-mill voters. They are super informed and super involved."

Jake knows of what he speaks. His dogged approach to journalism sets him apart from almost all inside the Washington beltway. He's a "no bull" type of guy for whom truth remains ascendant above all else.

"Jake represents journalism at its best: providing the facts in proper context and holding those in power accountable for their actions and their words," said David Chalian, CNN's political director. "I've had the great pleasure of working with Jake both at ABC News — when he was the network's chief White House correspondent covering the (President Barack) Obama administration — and at CNN where his interviews as an anchor are the gold standard of accountability journalism. I've worked on producing several presidential town halls and debates with Jake as the moderator. These are events with incredibly high stakes — not just for the candidates, but for the journalists, too. And I always knew, with Jake at the helm, that we were in the best hands with someone whose intellect, preparation, determination and commitment to fairness are unparalleled in this industry. You do not want to be an elected official or a candidate for office being interviewed by Jake if you are not on your game and fully prepared to make the case based on facts."

Jake and I first met the morning after the Iowa caucuses in 2004, several hours after he serendipitously connected with his future bride. It had become a tradition that a guest from ABC News would speak to my Breakfast Club on the morning after the caucuses. The late Peter Jennings had made just such an appearance in 2000 after anchoring the network's caucus coverage from Des Moines the night before. But by 2004, the primary schedule in the early states was being compressed to the point that the ABC News political team needed to fly out on a charter flight directly to New Hampshire immediately after their Iowa coverage wrapped up. As a result, Peter Jennings was not able to make an encore appearance at the Breakfast Club gathering and relative newcomer Jake Tapper drew the short straw.

"I knew that I was a poor substitute for Peter Jennings but obviously did my best!" Jake told us. "It was a lot of fun, and Ray and I struck up a friendship and that was nice."

And long-lasting.

My service on the National Association of Broadcasters (NAB) board of directors from 2008 to 2015 involved attending regularly scheduled meetings in our nation's capital. It was a joy to skip out on an NAB event on one such trip and meet up instead for dinner with Jake and Jennifer. We talked about life's strange twists and turns involving the way they had met back in 2004 — and learned that their growing family now included a son named Jack!

News organizations like ABC will often change their White House correspondents when a new president is elected. That was the scenario when Jake was named senior White House correspondent the day after Barack Obama was elected president in November 2008. My wife and I had the pleasure of meeting up with Jake and Jennifer at the White House Correspondents Dinner in April 2012, where Jake was honored for an unprecedented third time in a row with the prestigious Merriman Smith Award which recognizes "presidential coverage under deadline pressure."

Jake's future success was shaped in part by his upbringing in Philadelphia, but colleagues and assignments like the one that once had him winding his way through Iowa helped define his personal and professional path as well.

"My mom and dad influenced me the most," Jake said. "Qualities they had like working hard and not having a defeatist attitude have gotten me where I am today. I learned similar lessons from Peter Jennings and Diane Sawyer: the idea of working hard, doing your best and showing up every day. Not every pitch you have is gonna get on air. In fact, most of them won't. Not every idea you have is gonna be embraced as a good one. But just constantly showing up and putting it all out there, and trying to figure out how to make it work instead of expecting people to just hand you things, will take you far."

Jake Tapper is a WINNER because he's cut from the same cloth as the great Edward R. Murrow. He doesn't suffer fools, nor liars. He cuts through nonsense and misinformation. And his commitment to excellence in journalism dovetails into an abiding devotion to the democratic ideals on which our country was founded.

3.
TELEVISION SPORTS

HOWARD COSELL

"He is not the one with the golden locks or the golden tan, but the old one, shaking, sallow and hunched, with a chin whose purpose is not to exist as a chin but only to fade so that his face may, as the bow of ship, break the waves and not get in the way of that voice."

Frank Deford in *Sports Illustrated* (Aug. 8, 1983)

Howard Cosell was arguably the most well-known — and controversial — sports broadcaster in my lifetime. His notoriety first arose during the early coverage of baseball's Jackie Robinson and boxing's Muhammad Ali (Howard's relationship with the latter dated back to when Ali's name was Cassius Clay), and skyrocketed after legendary television sports producer Roone Arledge assigned him to work in the *Monday Night Football* booth as a commentator.

But Howard was far more than just a "color guy" for ABC. He was as polarizing as an on-air personality could be, with audiences divided into one of two camps: they loved him or they loved to hate him. While often rooted in petty jealousy, he was also a lightning rod for criticism from broadcasting colleagues, sportswriters and media critics alike.

One can only imagine what our social media world, with Howard Cosell's presence in it, would look like today. Suffice to say, Howard would likely have millions of followers — and nearly as many detractors.

I point all this out in order to share a story involving Howard and me, one that requires a bit of background.

The Sertoma ("SERvice TO MAnkind") Club of Sioux City, Iowa, held an annual sports banquet and it often fell on me to book the keynote speaker. In 1977, the first year I participated in the event, Frank Gifford was the featured guest. I persuaded Bobby Knight to deliver the keynote speech in 1983. And in 1984, former Yankton College (South Dakota) stand-out and NFL All-Pro defensive end Lyle Alzado served as the after-dinner entertainment. Sadly, Lyle would die several years later at the young age of 43 from complications related to a brain tumor that he attributed to his use of anabolic steroids. He told *Sports Illustrated* before his death, "I started taking anabolic steroids in 1969 and never stopped. It was addicting, mentally addicting. Now I'm sick, and I'm scared. Ninety percent of the athletes I know are on the stuff. My last wish? That no one else ever dies this way."

Lyle was a gregarious character and amusing speaker. He died in 1992, just over eight years after his Sertoma appearance that inspired so many to reach for greatness.

Now, back to Howard Cosell …

It was a longstanding goal of mine for Howard to headline the Sertoma event, the proceeds of which benefitted youth organizations throughout the community. I was confident that Howard would attract a large crowd and generate record proceeds, and had reached out to him on several prior occasions. My best chance to make it happen occurred in early 1985 when a "private audience" with Howard was arranged for me by contacts in ABC's affiliate relations department. They had dutifully passed along my previous invitations but said, in so many words, that Howard finally had agreed to meet with me in person to discuss yet another invite. The catch? I would have to make the pitch myself.

The meeting was confirmed for Monday, Jan. 21, 1985, at 8 a.m. — the morning after Super Bowl XIX. There was no one around at that early hour in ABC's mid-Manhattan headquarters building at 1330 Avenue of the Americas and 54th Street. Not a soul. You could have shot off a cannon in the dark hallway leading down to Howard's office and not hurt anybody. At 7:55 a.m. sharp, I peeked my head around the corner of Howard's office and saw him sitting behind his desk puffing on a big stogie. "Mr. Cosell?" I said somewhat timidly. "I'm Ray Cole from Sioux City, Iowa. It's an honor."

Without getting up, Howard waved me in while saying in his distinctive voice with its familiar cadence, "Mr. Cole, please do come in and tell me why in the hell it is that you keep sending me these gracious but nonetheless bothersome invitations that would require me to make a damnable trip to some godforsaken place in Iowa." I recall thinking to myself, "Well, good morning to you, too, Mr. Cosell." What I said out loud was, "Please call me Ray." In the conversation to follow, he always called me Mr. Cole. I'm pretty sure Howard thought that calling me — a green 29 year-old station executive — by my last name and blowing cigar smoke across the desk at me was intimidating. For the record, it was! (Bob Iger, who was working at ABC Sports at the time, told me years later that he "could smell Cosell's cigars from five floors away!")

Instead of responding directly to Howard's opening salvo, I thought it might help break the ice by talking about the prior night's Super Bowl game. With that in mind, I started to regale him with my rehearsed observations of the game between the Miami Dolphins and the San Francisco 49ers. Just as I began to talk about Joe Montana's MVP-winning performance, Howard abruptly and bluntly shut me down. While exhaling another huge puff of smoke from his cigar, he gruffly said, "Mr. Cole, there are well over a billion people in China and not one of them gives a f**k about football." Once again, I recall thinking to myself, "Gosh, this is sure going well."

Howard quickly launched into a lengthy diatribe about everything that was wrong with sports. I listened to him go on uninterrupted for the next 45 minutes — though it seemed more like hours — without ever saying a single word. Howard talked about death threats he'd received from so-called sports fans and how his "bride" — that's how he referred to his wife, Emmy — was begging him to step away from television and all its craziness. He complained about the "jockocracy" that was increasingly responsible for placing former star athletes in broadcasting jobs after they retired even though many lacked, in his view, the proper journalistic or professional training. He made specific and unflattering references to several athletes who matched that description and had raised his ire. He also talked about the likes of Bowie Kuhn, George Steinbrenner, Alvin Ray "Pete" Rozelle and Allen "Al" Davis — all of whom he felt were largely "misunderstood and underappreciated."

Howard then pivoted to his special relationships with Muhammad Ali and Sugar Ray Leonard as a setup to the subject of his longest and most passionate tirade: boxing. It had been just over two years since Howard had called a WBC heavyweight fight between champion Larry Holmes and Randall "Tex" Cobb. Howard conveyed to me in loathing terms what he viewed as a "gross and disgusting mismatch" and disservice to the sport of boxing. He told me how his antipathy for the sport had been building up for more than 10 years prior to that fight, and of his inability to shake off the heartache of watching Muhammad Ali in the twilight of his career be "robbed of his health and stripped of his dignity."

However justified his earlier concerns, it was the Holmes-Cobb fight in 1982 that had clearly pushed Howard over the edge. He was incredulous that the referee had not stopped the fight after Cobb had taken "26 unanswered blows and his face looked like hamburger meat." Howard said the following on the air during the ninth round in regard to the fight's referee: "Doesn't he know that he is constructing an advertisement for the abolition of boxing?" Howard told me how he disregarded an order from director Chet Forte and ABC sports executive Jim Spence to interview the referee in the ring after the fight. Instead, he told the audience in so many words, "I will not dignify what you just saw with an interview. ... What you have just watched here tonight speaks for itself." The very next morning, Howard Cosell told his bosses that he would never call another professional boxing match.

What I had no way of knowing at the time of our January 1985 meeting was that Howard was quite literally walking me through an outline of his upcoming book that fully detailed his disillusionment with the state of sports in society. It was only after *I Never Played the Game* was published later in the year that I understood the true significance of the stream-of-consciousness denunciation of what much of his own career had been built on. Upon reflection, I found it to be far sadder than it was illuminating. The book was also highly critical of many of Howard's colleagues, and its publication led directly to the end of his television days on ABC. (Bob Iger confirmed that Howard "was pulled from the World Series that year after his book came out.")

At the conclusion of Howard's monologue, he finally returned to the purpose of our meeting saying, "Mr. Cole, at Emmy's behest, I am committed to reducing my obligations to ABC and eliminating any unnecessary travel. For those reasons and those reasons alone, I must graciously decline the kind invitation that you have persisted in extending for some years now. I do so with the knowledge that not experiencing all that Sioux City, Iowa, has to offer will always be a void in my life (yes, he actually said that with a straight face!). But I do respect your persistence and admire the good works of the organization sponsoring the event and have a good alternative for you."

Howard then picked up his phone, dialed an extension, and said to someone on the other end, "This is Howard. I have a gentleman from Sioux City, Iowa, who has a wonderful event that could benefit from the attendance of someone like you. Could you please come down to my office so that I might make an introduction?" I had no idea whatsoever who was on the other end of that brief call. But moments later, legendary tennis player Arthur Ashe walked into Howard's office. Arthur was working for ABC Sports at the time as a contributor to the award-winning *SportsBeat* magazine show that was hosted by Howard.

After a cordial introduction by Howard, I told Arthur all about Sertoma and their annual fundraising dinner. In doing so, I added that this event had never hosted a tennis player or, for that matter, an African American athlete or coach. I told him how great it would be if we could remedy both with his participation. Arthur said "yes" on the spot, and we quickly worked out a mutually agreeable speaking fee and date in April.

I was heartbroken to receive a certified letter from Arthur in early March advising that he was "dealing with a health problem and (my) doctors have informed me that I cannot travel at this time." It was more than seven years later in April 1992 when we learned that Arthur had HIV likely caused by a blood transfusion he'd received during heart bypass surgery in 1983.

Sertoma went on to hold a successful event in 1985 with former Chicago Bears player and coach, Mike Ditka, as the keynote speaker. But what I will always remember most about that year was my introduction to Arthur Ashe by Howard Cosell, and the lingering thoughts to this day of what might have been if only we could have hosted Arthur. I also live with the deep regret of not having saved the letter from Arthur that would no doubt be a special keepsake today.

There will likely never be another dominant sports personality like Howard Cosell given the emergence of cable sports networks and the passing of the monopolistic-like dominance of a three-broadcast-network universe. While pondering the years of isolation and bitterness that preceded his death in 1995, I recalled a sign that hung on the wall in Howard's office. It read, "The Rat Race Is Over. The Rats Won." Its seemingly deeper meaning was lost on me when noticing that sign at the time of our meeting 10 years earlier.

For many in my generation, we will not forget Howard's famous boxing call, "Down goes Frazier! Down goes Frazier! Down goes Frazier!" And we will always recall how, during a *Monday Night Football* broadcast, he broke the news of "An unspeakable tragedy, confirmed to us by ABC News, in New York City: John Lennon … shot twice in the back, rushed to Roosevelt Hospital, dead on arrival. Hard to go back to the game after that news flash."

Speaking about himself, Howard once said, "Arrogant, pompous, obnoxious, vain, cruel, verbose, a showoff. I have been called all of these. Of course, I am."

In spite of whatever flaws and shortcomings he may have had, Howard Cosell was nonetheless an estimable WINNER for being the seminal figure in sports of a generation, and for his trademark "tell it like it is" approach to sports journalism.

DICK VITALE

"An appetite for life, the energy level, a sort of unique way of being. Dick Vitale embodies all of that. ... The more time you spend with Dick, the more you understand him and the more you appreciate him. Doing so helps you understand why he is able to connect with people with such a genuine passion and compassion and authenticity. It's so powerful."

Chris Fowler, ESPN college football and tennis commentator

Pick a positive attribute.

ESPN icon Dick Vitale is its ever-loving — and very audible — personification. The sometimes bombastic and always genuine former college basketball and NBA coach churns through life on all cylinders and with no filter. Empathy frames his language. Cynicism is his enemy. Giving back is his guide.

"You wanna talk about a guy who epitomizes grit, passion and perseverance?" longtime ESPN analyst Fran Fraschilla asked. "Dick Vitale is the epitome of all that. What he's done to help build The V Foundation since its founding is incredible. When Dick gets to heaven, he's gonna be welcomed with open arms. He really will be. They're gonna be taking him right to a mansion because of what he's done for children and their families in this life. There are no words to describe it. There really aren't. It is mind-boggling what Dick has contributed to the cause of beating pediatric cancer."

Dick is known for his loud and colorful calls during games. It's what made him an icon. It's often dismissed as mere shtick. But it's not. If a person could embody sheer emotion, it would be Dick. The highs. The lows. He feels them all. And he then channels it in a positive way — along with the late, great Jim Valvano, whose optimistic and buoyant speech at the inaugural ESPYS in 1993 has become a clarion call for those who seek to become "winners" in the all-inclusive sense of the word.

"I think what Jimmy's speech did was touch on everything," Vitale told us. "It touched on (dealing with) tough times. The fight. The smile. To extend the hand. I mean, his great words about how things in your daily life should move you to tears, should move you to laughter and should move you to thought. I believe his speech will go on forever and ever. When we're all gone, that speech will still be right up there and really helping so many."

It has been a great privilege for our company to extend a hand in support of the Dick Vitale Gala. We have helped promote this annual event, and even produced a couple of telethons on our Sarasota station, WSNN-TV, to raise dollars for it. Since the first one held in 2006, the Dick Vitale Gala has raised over $44 million! Dick described me to Rob Gray in an interview for this book as "a man with a heart of gold." That was a touching thing for him to say. But if my heart is made of "gold," Dick's is constructed of a far more precious metal. His is a heart that beats to the rhythm of people suffering in his midst. A voice that exults in high-flying hoops exploits but resounds even more for people in need of medical help, of life-saving research, of hope.

ESPN's Mike Greenberg was one of the honorees at the 2018 Dick Vitale Gala. It was a pleasure for me to interview him in Bristol to help promote the event. Mike told me, "My memories (from working in Chicago) of Michael Jordan are of his just total determination. What I learned from him, and it applies to Dick Vitale, was a singularity of focus and total determination. Dick set about in his mind that his greatest priority was going to be The V Foundation. He was going to be leaving a lasting impact on the world (by) trying to do everything he could to eradicate pediatric cancer. His singular determination and focus in the pursuit of that has been inspirational. That's how Michael Jordan got to be Michael Jordan, and that's why Dick Vitale has been able to raise millions of dollars for cancer research."

Other ESPN colleagues see it much the same way. "Raising dollars for pediatric cancer research is what's most important to Dick Vitale," said play-by-play announcer Sean McDonough, who has called many games with Dick. "He's 'unbelievable!' as he would say. Even now in his 80s, his energy level and passion have not dropped off one bit. What he's done, particularly with his annual gala (to benefit pediatric cancer research), is incredible. There are times where I do want to say, 'Hey, Dick: I know this gala of yours is really important, but there's 10 seconds left to go in a tie game … could we not give out the website information right now?' But he's a hero to so many."

Dick is a hero for good reason, as McDonough properly noted. He is a giver, plain and simple. Touring children's hospitals alongside Dick has given me the chance to witness all of this. David Stark, who has headed up several such tours at Blank Children's in Des Moines, told us, "I mean, there was not a dry eye in any hallway he visited. It was clear that's who Dick Vitale is. He was only supposed to be at the hospital for a couple hours but he said, 'David, let's go to a different floor. Let's keep it going.' It's like he got energized by it — and we all did, too. He connected on a very personal level with patients and families he had never met before, but became best friends with, saying along the way, 'I'll take a picture with you. I'll sign this. I'm gonna build you up.' That was amazing to experience firsthand, and something I'll never forget."

And though he's a giver, Dick is also a feeler. He celebrates the highs while also fully absorbing the lows in life. A low like the one involving the passing of Austin "Flash" Schroeder in April 2015 following his struggle with T-cell lymphoma. We had honored Flash at a V Foundation event in Riverside, Iowa, just one summer before. It was sadly coincidental that Jim Valvano had passed away on the very same month and day — April 28 — in 1993. Or the low of seeing Nathan Njoroge pass away on the Fourth of July in 2020 following a courageous battle with the neuroblastoma he was diagnosed with at age 12. Nathan, who lived with his beautiful family in Clive, Iowa, directly across the street from us, was a patient at Blank Children's Hospital when Dick toured and spent time with kids there in June 2017. Both Flash and Nathan continued to "Win the Day" to the very end. Both were avid Iowa Hawkeye fans. Both were only 15 years old at the times of their death.

"Yeah, the lows are there. No question. It's just heartbreaking," Dick admitted to us. That's because his emotions are invested in each and every pediatric cancer patient like Flash and Nathan that he speaks to, connects with, or passes by with a smile and a wave. Dick wants to save them all. He strives to save them all. He knows, heartbreakingly, he can't.

"I love giving back because everybody's been good to me," Dick said. "I grew up in a great family with a mom and dad who were uneducated, (but) they had a doctorate in love. Their words always echo, 'Richie: Be good to people so people will be good to you.' I'm in 14 halls of fame now, and I can't run, jump or shoot. People have been so good to me and I feel like that makes me want to give back. I want the last chapter of my life (to be one) where people will say, 'Wow, he loved his basketball; he was energetic about his games, passionate.' But I hope they'll also be saying, 'You know what? He never forgot where he came from and was always willing to extend a hand with love in his heart to help other people.' To me, that's priceless."

And that's why, to me, Dick Vitale is peerless.

Michigan State Coach Tom Izzo might have put it best. He said, "Most people know Dick Vitale for his unmatched passion for basketball. And while that is certainly remarkable, what truly impresses me is his passion for life and for helping other people. It's a lesson that should serve as an inspiration to us all." I couldn't agree more.

The role Dick Vitale plays as college basketball's most recognizable and vocal ambassador, and his undying commitment to The V Foundation and many other philanthropic efforts, make him an indisputable WINNER with a capital "W".

RUSTY WALLACE

"It's our consistency that has gotten us this far, and there's really no need to be looking for some other game plan. ... This is my final season as a driver and I want to go out being remembered as a winner."

Rusty Wallace, when announcing the 2005 NASCAR Cup
season would be his last (Sept. 2, 2004)

Rusty Wallace ran his race team like a business. One of NASCAR's winningest drivers didn't want sycophants in the garage or the pits — nor in the broadcast booth. He sought out contrarians and innovators, anyone who could give him a few inches of edge under the hood or on the asphalt or behind a mic.

"I don't want 'yes' people around me," Wallace told us. "I just want somebody to be honest with me and give me really good feedback."

Now, Rusty *does* have an ego. How can a racer and broadcaster of his caliber not have one? I first met Rusty in 2005 around the time he broke ground on his signature Iowa Speedway in Newton, and we remained in touch throughout the track's construction. We jointly entertained sports directors from ABC stations around the country at the Texas Motor Speedway in 2006 after ESPN and ABC acquired the rights to once again broadcast NASCAR starting in 2007. A year or so later, we co-hosted a lunch with Iowa's governor, Chet Culver, and senior members of the state's economic development team, along with executives from Nationwide Insurance, as part of our efforts to lure a NASCAR Nationwide Series event (now known as the NASCAR Xfinity Series) to the Iowa Speedway.

I can be sure of this: Rusty was as collaborative as he was cocksure; he could be as demanding as he was impatient. And that's not necessarily a bad thing.

"Have you ever heard anyone talk about a patient race car driver?" asked longtime ESPN/ABC motorsports commentator Dr. Jerry "Doc" Punch. "If so, you will probably not recognize their name. That's because they likely didn't accomplish much in their career. Rusty was not patient. Neither was Dale Earnhardt. Neither was A.J. Foyt or Bobby Allison. That's not a quality that's associated with an ambitious driver like Rusty Wallace. Rusty was also very demanding, especially when it came to his race car. I don't think I've ever been around anybody who wanted more out of a car during a race. The car was never good enough, and that says a lot about who he was. He wanted the car to handle better and go faster. Rusty was sometimes very hard-headed about making adjustments to the car during a race. But that was just him — he was always relentless."

As for "winning?"

"Rusty was relentless to the point of being ruthless at times," Doc told us. "To compete at the level he competed at on the short tracks, you had to be that way. You had to be selfish and self-centered because everybody in those events wanted to win, and they wanted to take your place. Dale Earnhardt was the same way: He ran over people on the race track because his total focus was on winning. It didn't make any difference if you were a teammate, a friend or a relative! The most successful people in motorsports have always held a similar philosophy, and Rusty was exactly that way. Rusty and Dale had the same 'my way or the highway' mentality, which explains why they butted heads so often. But if you're a race car driver, it's a great way to not only survive but to advance."

Wallace, the 1989 NASCAR Cup Series champion and a guy who was voted one of the series' greatest 50 drivers, doesn't mince words when describing an approach to racing success that focused on the car as much as the car's driver.

"Well, this might sound very simple, but you can say all the hocus pocus you want, but if you don't know (crap) about your race car — about that thing that's making your living — you're gonna be in trouble. Understanding the car was everything to me. It was almost like my wife. I had to treat it well. I had to understand it. I had to take care of it. I had to do the whole thing if I was going to be successful. You can say stuff like, 'I exercise. I jump up and down. I hum at night. I do yoga' and (stuff) like that. And I'm like, 'No, no. That's not me.' I've never exercised a day in my damn life. I've never fell out of a race car a day in my damn life. I've been mentally focused every race I've ever been in, and so focused on the race car itself. Understanding that damn thing is unreal.'"

Tools of the trade. Wallace mastered such matters. He became both a great racer and an oval-based oracle by charting his own fast-paced path, not buying into fads or conventional wisdom.

All of that works for some. Not for Rusty.

"We can talk about 'winning' a long time," Wallace said. "You're not gonna win unless you surround yourself with smart people. Surround yourself with people that believe in you and are smart people that have been there, done that. My God, it sure does make life easier."

As adept as Wallace was on race tracks from Talladega to Richmond, he's remained equally successful in his broadcasting and designing careers. "Rusty was one of those rare drivers who grew up working on his car," said broadcasting colleague Punch. "He knew so much about cars that he had a lot to contribute as a commentator, and he was all energy and excitement. Rusty was always a pleasure to work with, and just a great guy to be around."

As for the Iowa Speedway, now a NASCAR-owned track that was hit hard by the pandemic in 2020, it is clear that it holds a special place in Wallace's heart. "There was no 'me' in that design team, I can tell you that," he told us while talking about the racy seven-eighths mile track. "Paxton Waters, the head-to-head architect is a super-bright guy. (Former track owner and the late) Stan Clement was there every single day saying, 'Hey, they're running the bulldozers here' or 'They're doing this there.' And I'm flying back and forth like every single Tuesday for over a year staying at the race track and getting to know just a ton of people in the community. It actually felt like my second home, and I really had a great time with a lot of people. And then to get that damn thing done and see the (first) race happen and have all the drivers say, 'Oh my God, this track is so much fun to drive on.'

"As a driver always wanting to design a race track that would race the way I wanted it to race, I hated coming off Turn 2 at some racetracks where the banking falls off and you can't pass anybody. It's follow the leader. Well, hell, that's not the deal at Iowa. I said, 'I'm going to bank up that damn Turn 2' (to) where you can drive into Turn 1 like a maniac and get on the throttle and have all that banking hold you to where you can just really rip around and try to pass people and then fly down Turn 3 and have almost the same feeling. Then, all of a sudden, you come off of Turn 4 and you go into that dogleg and the racetrack opens up and you're carrying speed that is similar to some of the intermediate tracks like Charlotte (Motor Speedway) — and it's only a seven-eighths of a mile speedway. And then to see the excitement of all the fans that supported the track ... seeing them show up at the track all jacked up and excited. Oh my God, what an amazing setting."

In June 2013, I was honored by the American Diabetes Association of Iowa — along with Dan Houston, Principal Financial Group and Gary Palmer, Prairie Meadows — with a Father of the Year Award. Rusty helped promote the award dinner by appearing in a public service announcement in which he said, "Three outstanding fathers who successfully balanced their professional lives while making an impact on the community." And if he hadn't already done enough, Rusty flew his private jet to Des Moines to join us and serve as the master of ceremonies. His presence made the honor all the more special.

"Rusty has experienced it all and built an amazing resume inside the sport of racing," former KCAU-TV sports director and current news anchor Tim Seaman said. "He's one of the top 10 NASCAR drivers of all time. All of that adds such an allure to his already magnetic personality. Who doesn't want to be around somebody who has had the kind of career that he's had with all the stories and different things he has to share? What makes being around Rusty so cool goes back to his 'winner's' personality. Being with him is always less about his being one of the best race car drivers ever, and more about who he is right now. That's what left such an impression on me and drew me in to whatever we were talking about."

Rusty has been inducted into four of stock car racing's major halls of fame, including the NASCAR Hall of Fame in 2013. He's a racing icon, whether driving, designing race tracks or analyzing each event with his keen eye and quick wit.

Russell William "Rusty" Wallace Jr. is a dynamic WINNER who transcends both acceleration and exhilaration.

Jay Williams

"It's amazing to watch Jay basically say no matter what the worst moment of your life is, you never want to be defined by it. No matter what it is. The fact that Jay will not allow one bad moment to alter the course of his life in any way, other than how he sees fit, is probably the quality about him that impresses me the most."

Zubin Mehenti, ESPN *Keyshawn, JWill & Zubin* co-host and radio host

His speed and skill were elite.

His instincts, peerless.

His basketball IQ? Off the charts.

Jay Williams possessed every trait a basketball coach at any level would treasure, but a life-threatening motorcycle accident abruptly ended his promising professional career.

So the iron-willed Duke All-American and national champion simply started a new one.

"Following my accident, I was at an intersection," said Williams, who has become an accomplished sports broadcaster at ESPN and *New York Times* best-selling author over the past several years. "I could have chosen to stop, put my head down and just stay there. Or I could choose to see the adversity as an opportunity to learn, grow and move forward — all the while understanding that playing professional basketball was no longer in my path and part of my journey. The latter mindset has been one that has propelled me in my life. My accident was an event where I could have made the choice to let it define me or could have made the choice to let it lead me to years and years of desperation.

"It is so instructive for so many people with the everyday decisions that they have a choice to make. It's relatable to everything that we feel maybe didn't go our way. When those inevitable setbacks occur, it's our choice to choose to learn from such experiences so we can find ways to navigate them differently the next time. But too often people get fixated and become so myopic on what they may have lost that they don't pay attention to what they could have gained."

Jay was a wizard off the dribble. He shined from the three-point line, too. He was a fiery captain and leader on the court. In an improbable comeback win at Maryland in 2001, he led his Duke team back from a 10-point deficit with only 54 seconds left to play. Jay scored eight points in the span of 15 frenetic seconds. "I thrived with pressure," Jay once said to me in an email. "Pressure makes diamonds."

There was nothing he couldn't do on a basketball court, until he drove a motorcycle into a light pole. The impact broke and mangled his left leg. It occurred just after his rookie NBA season with the Chicago Bulls. And it changed his life forever.

Jay resolved to help others rather than wallow in self-pity. His best-selling 2017 autobiography, *Life Is not an Accident: A Memoir of Reinvention*, serves as a testament to his ability to turn personal tragedy into universal inspiration; to transform grief and loss into growth and healing.

"Sports are just the door opener, man," Jay told us. "And that's why and how I use my platform."

Jay is wise. Thoughtful. Transfixed on the present and future, not the past.

"I remember thinking how Jay's been in the media for 15 years and if things had just gone another way that fateful day, I wouldn't be sitting here with him," said ESPN's Zubin Mehenti, who co-hosts the radio show, *Keyshawn, JWill & Zubin*, with Jay and former NFL star Keyshawn

Johnson. "He would be in the NBA and living a life that most of us could only imagine. Jay was very quick to point out when our show started that I had an NCAA basketball national champion and Super Bowl champion sitting next to me — a number two overall pick (in the NBA) and number one overall pick (in the NFL). And while Jay's NBA career was cut short, his high school and collegiate careers were amazing. Moving on from his disappointment has allowed him to do things that maybe he wouldn't have pursued if he was still playing in the NBA. The first day after the official announcement of our show, Jay called me and said, 'I want you to know one thing: I am so much more than a ballplayer.' His point to me was, please do not just ask me basketball-related questions or Keyshawn just football-related questions."

"So much more than a ballplayer ... "

Jay has proved that every day since his horrific accident. He could have asked, "Why me?" He could have been gutted by guilt since his hands were on the handlebars when tragedy eventually struck. But Jay shook his head, dusted himself off and moved forward — with purpose, with passion, with a focus on service to others.

"In sports, we are too often told that only the strong survive," Jay said. "No mercy. No weakness. All these things are what society tells us you need to be. But I've discovered that society can't really tell me how to be strong. I have to find that internally by indomitable will. It comes from where I find strength and not how other people interpret what (other) versions of how I should be strong are. I have found that other people can't change the energy I choose to give, regardless of whatever they say, or whatever they try to use against me. That is the energy that they have chosen to deal with and it doesn't have to be mine."

At the final game during his junior season at Duke, Jay's No. 22 jersey was retired at Cameron Indoor Stadium. But the degree to which Jay Williams is a WINNER extends far beyond his basketball accomplishments. While many athletes work their way back from an injury to compete in another game, Jay's recovery and fight was all about living life itself. The saying "Let your past make you better, not bitter" was one Jay learned to embrace. His story is told with remarkable honesty in his autobiography. I was deeply touched when Jay presented me with a copy of his book with the following personal note on the inside cover:

"Dear Ray, Thank you so much for allowing me to be a part of your team. You inspire me, my friend. And remember, 'Strength does not come from physical capacity; it comes from indomitable will.'" The latter is a Gandhi quote that Jay had tattooed on his body while playing at Duke.

Jay is someone who has truly inspired me and many others. Beyond his work for ESPN, Jay is the CEO and national director of special events for the Rising Stars Youth Foundation, which uses basketball as a vehicle to promote education and provide academic and financial assistance to students within the program. In January 2017, Jay accepted my invitation to keynote the Variety - the Children's Charity of Iowa annual black tie dinner. During my introduction of Jay that evening, I shared this quote from Martin Luther King Jr.: "We must accept finite disappointment, but never lose infinite hope." Those words are the embodiment of Jay's outlook on life.

In 2017, the National Collegiate Basketball Hall of Fame inducted Jay and other members of that year's class: Tim Duncan (Wake Forest), Rick Mount (Purdue), Paul Silas (Creighton) and John Stockton (Gonzaga). That's elite company. And Jay absolutely belongs. But it's his ability to find the deeper meaning behind superficial success that makes him a consummate winner, in every sense of the word.

Winning can be traced by statistics, highlights and championships. Jay's path is detailed via body art, which helps define him, but still only scratches the surface, hinting at the warm spirit and much deeper wisdom that lies within.

"I don't think a lot of people spend time thinking about what they want their purpose to be," Jay said. "They're too busy just living in the matrix and being distracted by all the things society tells them they should try to strive for. My tattoos like the one that says, 'What we do in life echoes in eternity,' are constant reminders of the positive mantra that I want to push into the world. 'To err is human, to forgive is divine,' is on my right forearm. I have a cross on my left pectoral (muscle), right over my heart, because I found my faith, too, when I went through my accident. I have, 'The Truth,' on my left ankle because I had this habit of telling little white lies when I was younger. And then there is the tattoo saying, 'Strength does not come from physical capacity, it comes from indomitable will.' I got that as a 20-year-old while thinking about strength.

"The aesthetic of strength does not come from physical capacity, it comes from indomitable will. I thought that — and felt that — at the time and I've lived that every single day since my accident. When I wake up in the morning all these reminders are in my face. I'm like, 'OK. That's my daily reminder. It's written there for a reason. Let's remember what your purpose is.' The tattoos serve as the road map of my journey."

It has been, and continues to be, the journey of a truly special person and WINNER.

4.
TELEVISION
ENTERTAINMENT

STEPHEN COLBERT

*"Ray! We gotta get to the bottom of this.
I propose an historic team-up between the
ABC5 team and 'The Colbert Report.' Y'all
can come here, or I can go there. The public
trust is at stake. The whole world is watching!"*

Stephen Colbert in an email to Ray Cole with a copy to Tom Purcell,
executive producer of *The Colbert Report* (Aug. 16, 2011)

Let's just say it was a chance meeting. I won't describe the specific place. It could have been anywhere, really, but it was a momentous occasion.

Suffice to say my first real encounter with television late night star Stephen Colbert ended with both of us washing our hands.

Now, let Stephen take it away ...

"It turns out that I have met Ray Cole and he has touched my Emmy (Award)," Stephen said during his opening monologue for an episode of *The Colbert Report* ten years — and many Emmys — ago. "See what happened was, in 2008, we had just won our first Emmy and naturally I went to the bathroom to celebrate. The only other gentleman in there who I didn't know was Ray Cole. He offered to hold my little trophy while I peed; I said I'd rather you hold my Emmy. In return — true story, true story — in return, when he peed I held his package by which I mean these little parcels he's holding down there (points to picture). So my apologies, (Ray) did touch my Emmy and when you have touched my Emmy, you have touched the best of me."

I laughed riotously at Stephen's joke, even though it was partly at my expense, and found it obviously good-natured.

The situation that framed it: an Iowa Straw Poll/Colbert Super PAC/ *The Colbert Report* episode that was about as crazy as any situation that I can recall in my 40-plus year broadcasting career.

Here's what happened: In 2011, Stephen established the Colbert PAC (a so-called "Super PAC") and it produced ads asking voters in the Iowa Republican Straw Poll to write in Texas Governor Rick Perry's name. The problem? The Colbert PAC ads encouraged voters to intentionally misspell the name as "Parry" with the "'A' for America." While my instincts have always been to err on the side of caution in such matters and grant access to qualified parties, we nevertheless declined to accept the ads in this case on grounds that their purpose was to cause confusion. As funny as the ads were, I did not want our station to aid and abet its clearly intended mischief. Interestingly enough, the other television stations in Des Moines did accept the ads — and take the Colbert PAC's money — as was their prerogative.

David Oxenford, a respected communications lawyer, would later write the following in a blog posting: "The station was not only within its rights to reject the ads, but had an even greater responsibility to vet the third-party ads since stations are theoretically responsible for the content in those ads."

Well, it became quite obvious that Stephen did not buy our reasons for the rejection when he absolutely lampooned us at the top of his show on Aug. 11, 2011. He personally dared me to "touch his Emmy" after pulling it out as a prop near the end of his rant. So the next day I called Stephen to remind him that I had, in point of fact, touched his Emmy! It made for a light conversation and we shared a good laugh.

But my decision did lead to a bit of legal wrangling — and some relatively thorny issues for our station, WOI-TV in Des Moines, Iowa.

"Stephen Colbert has twice mocked Des Moines ABC-TV affiliate WOI-TV on his Comedy Central show for rejecting the campaign spots produced by his political action committee," Jim Romenesko wrote for the Poynter Institute in August 2011. "Ray Cole, president of WOI parent Citadel Communications, says he's a Colbert fan but believes the station made the right decision. 'This was a close call for us. Our instincts are to grant access to our airwaves to qualified parties. We just felt this was too confusing. The straw poll isn't a real election, but ... it has real impact.' Rachel Paine Caufield, who teaches a political satire class at Drake University, thinks WOI has a point. 'This whole thing is like the cool kids playing a prank and the stand-up kid says: 'OK, this has gone too far.' They (WOI) might be doing the right thing, but they're not going to be cool.'"

We may, in fact, have been cooler kids than some thought at the time. Stephen kept the joke going for months right up through the 2012 Iowa caucuses. He started off *The Colbert Report* on Jan. 4, 2012, by once again turning to our news team: "Now, just because the Iowa caucus results are in doesn't mean I'm turning my laser focus away from the Hawkeye State. Other news organizations hit it and quit it. Wham, bam, thank you ma'am. I don't see how they can do that. ... Well, maybe I'm old-fashioned but I believe that hyping a news story is a sacred trust. And this caucus has left me with an unquenchable thirst for Iowa news. Well thankfully, ever since the Ames straw poll back in August, I have had a close personal relationship with WOI, ABC5, Des Moines' news leader. When IO-Want Iowa News, IO-Watch WOI! I'm an admirer of their Emmy-watching news team. So let's check in live to get the latest Iowa news. WOI news team, thank you for joining us."

It was a wild and crazy few months.

And no matter what anyone thought at the time, I did indeed — as noted earlier — hold Stephen's first Emmy. Much more importantly, he has always impressed me with his wit, compassion and ability to deliver political insights tinged with both humor and irreverence. Stephen is a one-of-kind WINNER who has established himself as one of the great political satirists of our time.

Stephen is a quality human being," fellow late-night veteran Conan O'Brien told *Variety* magazine's Cynthia Littleton. "You take away the suits and the noise on these shows, and you're left with just the person. That's something that shows Stephen in a really good light." Colbert had been honored with a George Foster Peabody Award just one month prior to Littleton's cover story for the magazine in July 2021. Presented in the wake of the pandemic and stressful times in our country, the Peabody jurors recognized *The Late Show* for "combining comedy with genuine goodness at one of our darkest hours."

Stephen now owns nine Emmys and counting — more than I could hold in almost any situation. And definitely more than I could ever hold at one time in a men's room.

MICHAEL J. FOX

"Life is a ride. Strap in, hang on and keep your eyes open."

Michael J. Fox in his book, *A Funny Thing Happened on the Way to the Future ...*

There are so many words to aptly describe Michael J. Fox: Actor. Husband. Father. Humanitarian. Author. Friend.

But golfer?

As noted in the prologue, Michael has described his golf game as a bit on the "horrible" side. But in fairness, he took up the sport to challenge himself only *after* being diagnosed with Parkinson's Disease.

Michael was my special guest and playing partner in the Principal Charity Classic Pro-Am in May 2009. He said at the time that learning to play golf after being diagnosed with Parkinson's was the "most optimistic" thing he had ever done. After attending the draw party the night before, we had a large gallery of his fans follow us around the Glen Oaks Country Club layout during the Pro-Am. Many of those followers were people who had Parkinson's or were supportive members of families dealing with Parkinson's. The respect and admiration shown to Michael was palpable, and something to behold.

We have since played together in numerous charity golf events, and our team even finished first at the Broadcasters Foundation of

America Celebrity Golf Tournament at Sleepy Hollow Country Club in Scarborough, New York in September 2011! "I am committed to showing that people with challenges can lead an active life," Michael wrote to me in an email around one of our outings together.

Michael does, indeed, live an "active life." He's also led a distinguished one marked by courage in the face of adversity. Michael turns challenge into platforms for growth — and does so in a way that inspires others.

"Michael might be about the best person I know," ABC News anchor George Stephanopoulos, a good friend of Michael's, told us. "He is so smart, so funny, and the whole world knows how talented he is. But even more than that, he is an incredibly loyal friend. You could not ask for a more loving husband. To watch his devotion to Tracy (Pollan, his wife) up close over all these years has been an education and a blessing. Michael is just an awful lot of fun to be around, and you'd never know the burdens he's carrying because he addresses the challenges with his famous optimism. And he maintains that not in a saccharine way, but in a way that's rooted in reality. It does not deny what's happening or deny what he's dealing with, but puts it in perspective. Michael shows everyone the importance of perseverance and hope while addressing what life throws at you."

It was my great privilege to nominate Michael for one of the television industry's highest honors: the National Association of Broadcasters' Distinguished Service Award. It is presented annually to broadcasters "who have made a significant and lasting contribution to the American system of broadcasting." Previous recipients are a Who's Who of television legends, and include William Paley, Edward R. Murrow, Bob Hope, Lowell Thomas, Walter Cronkite, Ronald Reagan, Dick Clark, Barbara Walters, Mary Tyler Moore and Oprah Winfrey. In my nomination of Michael, I specifically referenced his "tremendous contributions to both the entertainment and medical research communities." The award was presented to him in Las Vegas during the annual NAB Show on April 12, 2010. Playing golf together in the Philip J. Lombardo Charity Golf Tournament sponsored by the Broadcasters Foundation of America, followed by dinner at the Prime Steakhouse in the Bellagio, rounded out what will always be one of the most memorable weekends of my professional career.

So as it turns out, "horrible" golfing can lead to lasting connections. And giving one's time can reap rewards impossible to quantify. Michael — star of *Family Ties*, *Spin City* and the *Back to the Future* franchise along with many other celebrated films and TV programs — is determined to live his best life, and provide meaningful guidance on how to live yours.

"I look at life with humor and say, 'What's the good in this? What's the best I can take from this?'" Michael told *Good Housekeeping* magazine in 2013. "And usually the best I can take out of a situation is what makes me laugh. (That) applies as much to anyone who deals with any hardship or challenge as it does to a guy with Parkinson's. I really believe, let it be what it is. Accept it; know what it is you're dealing with. And if you do that honestly, and you really look at it and you're not afraid, then you'll see how much space there is around it and how much room there is for other things, other attitudes and other experiences."

Michael was diagnosed with Parkinson's in 1991. He established the Michael J. Fox Foundation in 2000 and offered one of the most heartfelt public eulogies to the iconic Muhammad Ali (who also battled Parkinson's) upon his death in 2016.

"Before I was diagnosed with Parkinson's, I admired him and I admired his athleticism, his poise, his class, his style, his stoicism, his belief in what he thought was right," Michael told *US Weekly* magazine. "(But) to have actually met him and joined with him in a common cause, in a common fight was … I mean, who else would you want in your corner?"

The same could be said for Michael, who has long been a tireless advocate and fundraiser for Parkinson's research among other important causes. He's selfless and self-aware. He knows his voice can help others, so he raises it to great effect.

Michael has addressed the "famous optimism" that George Stephanopoulos made reference to earlier. In a conversation with Michael J. Fox Foundation CEO and co-founder Debi Brooks, Michael said, "I'm absolutely an optimist. But I've learned you can be an optimist and a realist. The key to optimism is to accept the problem. … In life, it's about accepting and embracing. To be grateful for what you define to be grateful about. You can find something to be grateful about in anything. And that'll sustain your optimism."

While he has always insisted that, "I never set out to be heroic," it is nonetheless obvious that Michael is the public face of Parkinson's. He is very much a hero — and every bit a WINNER in the most profound sense of the word.

Jimmy Kimmel

"Watching Jimmy over the last 20-plus years has shown me how nothing comes easy no matter how much God-given talent you have. The reasons for the enduring success of 'Jimmy Kimmel Live!' have everything to do with Jimmy's 'winning' attributes: hard work, curiosity, determination, pride in your work and wanting to be the best you can be."

Rob Mills, ABC Senior VP of Alternative Series,
Specials and Late Night Programming

Jimmy Kimmel is an iconoclast. He challenges the status quo. He does it with humor — both sophomoric and sophisticated — and yet that belly laugh-based foundation is always rooted in a deep commitment to what can only be described as "The Golden Rule," even though Jimmy isn't an overtly religious man.

Kimmel entered the network television late night battles in 2003, when Jay Leno and David Letterman were vying for supremacy. Jimmy joined the fray almost as an also-ran "bro" type of comic except for his ability to set himself apart with rapier wit and an uncommon amount of understanding. He simply blazed a new path and now — some 18 years later — is a late night network TV mainstay.

"When you looked at what Jimmy was doing, it was undeniably brilliant and he made it look so easy," said Rob Mills, veteran ABC programming executive. Rob has witnessed firsthand the extent to which Jimmy understands that success has more to do with maximum effort than it does innate talent, adding, "If you don't give 100% week in and week out, you're not going to maximize your talent."

Jimmy *always* maxes out.

"He has a very strong work ethic and passion for what he does, which is to communicate and entertain," said ABC's longtime affiliate relations executive, John Rouse. "And Jimmy's not afraid to show a high level of empathy. (He's) just a good person overall who has a special way of connecting with his audience."

Jimmy and I met in 2002 when he was first introduced to ABC affiliates at a luncheon in New York City. He spoke enthusiastically about his new late night talk show that was set to launch the following year. However, he had to share top billing that day with, of all things, the Stanley Cup. Most affiliates opted to have their picture taken with the Cup even though it required putting on white gloves to hold it. Not me, as no gloves were required to touch or have your picture taken with Jimmy. Goodbye, Lord Stanley … hello, Jimmy Kimmel! And, sure enough, *Jimmy Kimmel Live!* made its debut on Jan. 26, 2003, immediately following the presentation of Super Bowl XXXVII on ABC. He became a valued network colleague, and remained a friend ever since.

Jimmy has long made a point to surround himself with family and close friends. Molly McNearney has been a co-head writer for *Jimmy Kimmel Live!* since 2008, and (more importantly!) Jimmy's wife since 2013. In July 2014 they welcomed a beautiful baby girl, Jane, to their family and in April 2017 had a second child, William "Billy" Kimmel. At just three days old, Billy had an emergency — but successful — open heart surgery at Children's Hospital in Los Angeles. There is little doubt that having a newborn child with a health condition changed Jimmy's approach to comedy — and outlook on life itself.

Jill Leiderman, a 25-year veteran of late-night television, served as the show's executive producer for 14 years prior to stepping down in May 2020. Erin Irwin, a co-executive producer has been with the show since 2004. Don Barris is a comedian who has "warmed up" the studio audience from day one. Jimmy and Don's relationship dates back to 2003 when they worked together on the made-for-TV reality film, *Windy City Heat*. The show's house band, Cleto and the Cletones, is led by childhood friend and saxophonist Cleto Escobedo III. They perform the show's opening and closing themes, play music in and out of commercial breaks and entertain the studio audience through the break. An interesting bit of trivia is that the show's opening theme is sung by the late Robert Goulet. Dicky Barrett, formerly a singer with the Mighty Mighty Bosstones, took over as the show's announcer in 2004.

Jimmy's cousin, Sal Iacono, is a writer and frequent sketch performer on the show. Guillermo Rodriguez is the parking lot security guard for the show and has been Jimmy's go-to sidekick for many years now. "Uncle Frank" Potenza, Jimmy's real-life uncle, also served as a security guard for the show and appeared on-camera regularly until he died from cancer in 2011. Frank was a warm, fun-loving guy and it was my pleasure to spend time with him on several occasions. Uncle Frank's former wife, Concetta "Aunt Chippy" Potenza, is also a show regular who Jimmy loves to play pranks and elaborate hoaxes on for the audience's — and his own — amusement.

In what might arguably be one of the biggest developments in the show's history, *Jimmy Kimmel Live!* flipped time periods with ABC News *Nightline* in 2013. This was not an easy decision for the network to make. I was part of a memorable conference call on June 8, 2012, with network executives, senior officials from ABC News who were understandably opposed to such a move, and their counterparts from ABC Entertainment who were in favor of it. The handful of ABC affiliate board members joining me on the call were brought in to the network's internal *Nightline* and *Jimmy Kimmel Live!* deliberations for the first time. In fact, the real purpose of the conference call was not divulged to any of us representing the affiliate body ahead of time.

All those on the call from News and Entertainment made strong, poignant arguments. News pointed out that *Nightline* was an important, award-winning program that had served the network well since 1979; it was still winning its time period in total viewers. Entertainment countered that *Jimmy Kimmel Live!* was on a roll and had earned the opportunity to compete more directly with *The Tonight Show with Jay Leno* on NBC and *The Late Show with David Letterman* on CBS. The respective arguments were made against the backdrop of widely anticipated changes involving the hosts of the competing late-night shows, perhaps giving ABC an opening to drive higher late-night ratings among younger demographic viewers. It then became clear that the network's top brass were looking for affiliates to weigh in.

After some awkward silence, I was the first to speak up and began by saying that the difficult question in front of us was the equivalent of being asked which one of our children we loved the most. I then shared my point of view that we should strike while the iron was hot and move *Jimmy Kimmel Live!* up to 11:35 p.m. ET. Though he was not on the conference call, Jimmy called me a short time afterward and thanked me for the support even though neither one of us knew at the time what the final resolution would be. It was not until Aug. 21, 2012, that the network officially announced the time slot switch to take effect on Jan. 8, 2013.

Looking back, I remain convinced it was the correct call. With the end of *The Tonight Show with Jay Leno* in February 2014 and David Letterman's retirement from the *Late Show with David Letterman* in May 2015, Jimmy is now host of the longest-running, late-night talk show on network television.

Other memorable experiences with Jimmy involve the Primetime Emmy Awards. The first such occasion occurred at the Emmys in 2008 where my wife and I had the pleasure of spending time with him. The following morning I participated as outgoing chairman of the ABC board of governors in a closed-circuit feed to affiliates that originated from the *Jimmy Kimmel Live!* set in the El Capitan Theatre. Jimmy came in early, still dressed in his tux from the night before, to kick off the affiliate presentation; it was obvious that he had enjoyed a long night of celebrating at Emmys afterparties.

Jimmy served as host of the 64th Annual Emmy Awards in 2012 and was later invited back for an encore performance as host of the 68th Annual Emmy Awards in 2016. Jimmy rocked it from the outset with an opening video bit featuring Jeb Bush as an Uber driver for *Veep*, and Jimmy hitching a ride on the *Game of Thrones* dragon. Hosting an awards show is no small task, but Jimmy has a knack for keeping the program moving. His mother, Joan Kimmel, even contributed to the lively atmosphere by passing out 7,000 peanut butter and jelly sandwiches in the middle of the telecast! Jimmy poked some fun at himself as well: Moments after his "Best Variety Series" nomination lost out, old nemesis Matt Damon strolled on stage. "I missed the last category," he deadpanned to Jimmy. "Did you win?"

As enjoyable as attending the Emmys as Jimmy's guest was, it was the intimate, private afterparty that he and Molly hosted that was even more memorable. Every bit a foodie, Jimmy recruited five of his celeb chef pals and several mixologists to pair each dish with specialty cocktails for the star-studded affair at The Lot in West Hollywood. Members of the Kimmel family (including PB&J sandwich maker, Joan), cast members from *Jimmy Kimmel Live!*, Emmy award winners and nominees alike, and other friends of Jimmy's were there. And yes, even Matt Damon showed up with his wife, Luciana Barroso.

With his experience hosting awards shows — the Primetime Emmy Awards (twice), the American Music Awards and the ESPYS — Jimmy was more than prepared to serve as host for the 89th Academy Awards in February 2017. He told *Deadline Hollywood* that the most important lesson learned from previous hosting jobs was to prioritize the audience response over all else. "People get overly focused sometimes on the audience at home," he said, "and the audience at home is used to responding to other people laughing. So if you get dead silence in the room, even if there are people at home who might think it's funny, it's not going to be seen as a success."

Jimmy's Oscars hosting gig earned him rave reviews. *Variety's* Sonia Saraiya said Jimmy nailed the "perfect, quintessential host move" when he joked that he knew he'd screw up the telecast somehow after *La La Land* was incorrectly named best picture instead of *Moonlight*. The Academy of Motion Picture Arts and Sciences wisely announced in May 2017 that Jimmy would return to host the Academy Awards in 2018. He told *E! News*, "If you think we screwed up the ending this year, wait until you see what we have planned for the 90th anniversary show!" For the record, his second turn hosting the Academy Awards produced more positive acclaim — and none of the controversy associated with the first one.

Attending the White House Correspondents Association dinner in 2012 was made all the more special by the fact that Jimmy was the host. Jimmy and President Barack Obama exchanged some pretty good zingers that night, including this one from Jimmy to Obama: "Remember when the country rallied around you in hope for a better tomorrow? That was a good one." It was arguably one of the best WHCA dinners in history, and President Obama would later accept an invitation from Jimmy to be a *Jimmy Kimmel Live!* guest on March 12, 2015, for what was one of the highest-rated shows of the year.

Despite having the word "live" in the show's title, *Jimmy Kimmel Live!* has not aired regularly on a live basis since 2004. There were just too many guests who liked to challenge the network's lawyers and censors! Attending a taping of the show for broadcast later that same evening is still every bit as much fun. While it's been my pleasure to attend well over a dozen such tapings, a couple of more memorable occasions stand out.

ABC-TV held an affiliates meeting in May 2010 at the Hollywood Roosevelt Hotel just down the street from the El Capitan Theatre. One of the meeting's highlights was the day affiliates and network executives showed up for a taping, though I'm not sure having a bunch of "suits" make up nearly the entire studio audience was Jimmy's idea of a good time.

Another enjoyable show experience occurred around the ESPYS in July 2012. Following their win over the No. 2-ranked Oklahoma State Cowboys on the gridiron the prior November, the Iowa State Cyclones were nominated for an ESPY in the "Best Upset" category. It was truly enjoyable to host Coach Paul Rhoads and four of his players at a *Jimmy Kimmel Live!* taping where that year's ESPYS host, Rob Riggle, was one of Jimmy's guests.

And finally, it was especially memorable to attend a taping in July 2019 with the entire Cole family for the first time, and have Jimmy and then-executive producer Jill Leiderman greet us afterward.

Jimmy was born in Brooklyn, New York, and grew up in the Mill Basin neighborhood before the family moved to Las Vegas when he was nine years old. He has made a habit of returning to his roots on a regular basis for *Jimmy Kimmel Live!: Back to Brooklyn*. Guests for these special shows in years past have included David Letterman, Michael J. Fox, Howard Stern, Bill Murray, Chris Rock, Alicia Keys and Jay-Z. It was fun to join Jimmy in October 2018 when the show originated for the fourth time from the Brooklyn Academy of Music's Howard Gilman Opera

House. Julia Louis-Dreyfus and Bebe Rexha were among the guests that night. It was even more fun to join Jimmy and the entire cast and crew at their wrap party held later at the infamous Hometown Bar-B-Que.

Jimmy hosted an entire week of shows from the Zappos Theater on the Las Vegas Strip in April 2019. Susan and I had the pleasure of attending the final taping that week during which Jimmy hilariously crashed a wedding ceremony with the assistance of Celine Dion and David Spade. As is always the case with the Brooklyn shows, Jimmy's love for Las Vegas shone through the entire week. Just a few months later, he opened "Jimmy Kimmel's Comedy Club" in Las Vegas at The LINQ Promenade. In a genuine show of love for his hometown, Jimmy announced that all of the profits from the comedy club would be donated to deserving Las Vegas charities.

Jimmy is the kind of guy who can help keep you very humble. For example, Diane Sawyer sent me a note in June 2014 just after the announcement that she'd be stepping down as anchor of *World News Tonight*. She wrote, in part, "Ray, your wonderful mind and heart have been like a GPS for me in the 15 years I have anchored a daily broadcast at ABC." A humbling sentiment, to be sure. Upon learning of Diane's note, Jimmy was not to be outdone and sent me a note of his own. It read, "Ray's wonderful mind and heart have been like UPS for me. I especially love when he wears those little brown shorts." Everybody deserves a friend — and ego check — like James Christian Kimmel.

Like the legendary Johnny Carson and David Letterman before him, Jimmy is a WINNER who can always be trusted to put a smile on the face of his audience at the end of a long day. We can only hope he soldiers on for many more years to come, and that his longstanding feud with Matt Damon lives on as well in what has become one of the most celebrated bits in late night television.

With The Walt Disney Company's **Bob Iger** and the Cole family at Blank Children's Hospital in April 2018. Bob made a special trip to Des Moines to participate in a dedication ceremony during which a Disney-themed silhouette mural was unveiled. (Photo credit: Carolyn Vaughn, Blank Children's Hospital)

Our daughter Brittney with **Peter Jennings** in Los Angeles, CA in June 1988 during an ABC affiliate reception. The next morning Peter led the questioning of Vice President George H.W. Bush as part of a panel discussion that also included David Brinkley, Sam Donaldson and George Will.

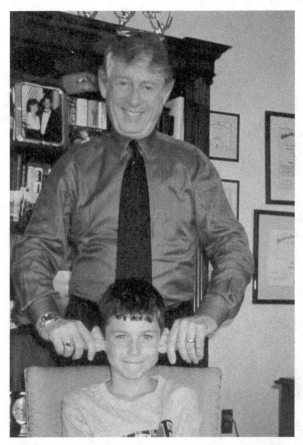

Our son Brandon with **Ted Koppel** in June 2000 sitting in the renowned *Nightline* anchor's office. Our family was vacationing in Washington, D.C. and stopped by the ABC News bureau to watch a taping of that night's show.

With **Barbara Walters** at *The View* in November 2006. Also pictured (l-r) are former co-hosts Rosie O'Donnell and Elisabeth Hasselbeck, longtime ABC affiliate relations executive John Rouse, and opera star/guest co-host Beverly Sills. (Photo credit: ABC-TV)

With **Rob Lowe** and members of the Cole family in June 2007 following the Principal Charity Classic Pro-Am draw party. We enjoyed a special dinner on the eve of the famous "birdie" Rob scored in the Pro-Am event the following day.

With **Robin Roberts** at the "Bras for the Cause" gala in Altoona, Iowa in November 2008. Robin was the keynote speaker at this event which raised funds for breast and cervical cancer programs across the state. (Photo credit: PhotoJeania Inspired Photography)

With **Stephen Colbert** immediately after the 60th Annual Emmy Awards in September 2008 where The Colbert Report had been honored with its first-ever Emmy award.

With (l-r) **Todd and Aaron Thomas, Kenny Mayne** and **Ben Jacobson** in July 2010 at the ESPYS Golf Classic. On stage at the ESPYS the following night, the Thomas brothers were honored with the Arthur Ashe Award for Courage and Coach Ben Jacobson accepted the Best Upset award for Northern Iowa's win against top-seeded Kansas in the NCAA Men's Basketball Tournament.

With cable television pioneer and iconic ESPN executive **George Bodenheimer** at the ESPYS in July 2010.

With **Dr. Mehmet Oz** and his wife Lisa at the Broadcasters Foundation of America's Golden Mike dinner in New York City in February 2012.

With **Jon Karl** at the White House in June 2014. The visit included a personal tour of the West Wing and a stop at the podium in the James S. Brady Briefing Room.

With ESPN's **Stuart Scott** at the ESPYS in Los Angeles in July 2014. Stuart is holding the Jimmy V Award for Perseverance that had been presented to him just a few hours earlier.

With **Michael J. Fox** at the Sleepy Hollow Country Club in September 2014 where our team finished second in the Broadcasters Foundation of America's celebrity golf tournament.

With **Bernie Saggau** at the Iowa Hall of Pride in March 2016. His vision led to the building of this unique attraction that showcases the achievements of the many WINNERS that Iowa's communities and schools produce.

With **Lesley Visser** and **Dick Vitale** in April 2016 during the *Dick Vitale Telethon* on WSNN-TV in Sarasota, Florida. This broadcast was presented only weeks ahead of Dick's annual gala to raise funds for The V Foundation and pediatric cancer research.

With **Jay Williams** at the Variety - the Children's Charity of Iowa's black tie dinner in January 2017. Jay was the keynote speaker and shared his inspirational personal story.

With **Gary Thompson** and his wife Jan at the Iowa Hall of Pride in June 2017 following a reception honoring the hall's director, Jack Lashier. We are pictured alongside a sculpture of the "Roland Rocket" that is part of the high school basketball exhibit.

With **Diane Sawyer** in her office in the ABC News world headquarters building in New York City.

With **David Muir** and **Martha Raddatz** in May 2018 at an ABC affiliate meeting in New York City. Also pictured is Cecilia Vega who now serves as chief White House correspondent for ABC News.

With **Robin Roberts** and **George Stephanopoulos** at *Good Morning America* in October 2018. The show has garnered high ratings and won multiple awards since the two of them teamed up as anchors more than ten years ago.

With **Jimmy Kimmel** and the Cole family in July 2019 shortly after the taping of that night's *Jimmy Kimmel Live!*.

With **Phil Lombardo** at the Broadcasting & Cable Hall of Fame induction dinner in October 2015. My boss, mentor, partner and friend for the past 35 years was inducted later that evening for his enormous contributions to the broadcasting industry, most especially his leadership of the Broadcasters Foundation of America.

DR. MEHMET OZ

"Whatever you choose, do it fully — with passion and childlike enthusiasm."

Dr. Mehmet Oz, cardiothoracic surgeon, professor
and *The Dr. Oz Show* television host

Perfection can be the enemy of progress. It can lead to self-paralysis. It can dim creativity and crush curiosity — and since nothing in life or nature is, in fact, "perfect," the single-minded pursuit of it becomes a fool's errand.

Few people I've met understand this dynamic better than Dr. Mehmet Oz, the son of Turkish immigrants, who has learned that discomfort leads to growth; that momentary failure fuels ultimate success.

"I restarted all the time," Mehmet, a world-renowned heart surgeon, told us when describing the development of his popular, long-running TV program, *The Dr. Oz Show*. "I don't think I was a particularly good interviewer when I started. I was too quick to rush to solutions and not patient enough to hear what the real issues were. That's a big problem if you get into emotional problems, because you can't fix an emotion until you hear it.

"There are many examples of things that I failed at. My goals were about changing the way Americans thought about their health. It was to get them to realize they could become the real experts on their own body.

If they would do that, then they could do the things they needed to do to get healthier. So as long as what I was trying to do was along those lines, I succeeded in the moment that I was failing."

Mehmet addressed the subject of "winning" further, telling us, "People say it isn't about whether you win or lose, it's about how you play the game. And when I was a kid, I didn't subscribe to that. I cared about winning or losing. It mattered to me a lot. I did not want to lose. Why would you ever want to lose? I didn't realize what the true meaning was. The meaning is not that it doesn't matter that you lost. Of course it matters that you lost. You shouldn't want to lose.

"But there's something more important than winning and losing. If you don't play the game right, if you cheat or break the rules, if you are disrespectful when you win, if you do the things that make you a lesser person, then people aren't going to want to play with you. Win or lose, you're going to end up doing it by yourself. That's just life. But if you do the honorable thing, win or lose, you get to play again and again. That's the long game, right? Not the three-hour afternoon match, but the long game and you get to keep playing. So long as you keep playing, you'll be fine. That's part of the vision."

Dr. Oz's vision has helped millions live better, more health-conscious lives. He's an authority on health matters but has never stopped learning. That's another critical component to "winning" — a ceaseless drive to discover more about the world as well as more about one's self.

"Constant learning is definitely critical," Mehmet said. "There are a couple aspects to being a constant learner. First, there has to be a humbleness — and a willingness — to understand your approach to understanding complex issues. One of the reasons I went into medicine (stemmed from knowing) that I'd never master it. I knew I could be better than anyone else, but not perfect. So that's one issue, a humbleness about what you're dealing with. Then you have to get people working with and under you that you trust. People you trust who are going to challenge you and not tell you what you want to hear. That's the key to becoming a leader."

Dr. Oz's parents overcame myriad challenges when they emigrated to the U.S. from Turkey in the 1960s. In the wonderful book, *Journeys: An American Story*, compiled by Andrew Tisch and

Mary Skafidas, Dr. Oz notes that his parents often reminded him how early on they would collect cans to help make ends meet. Their example of finding success in the moment — and being willing to embrace risk and the possibility of failure in pursuit of a better life — guides him to this day.

"I've gained a lot of appreciation for what it took for my parents to come to this country from Turkey and leave everything they had there behind," Mehmet told us. "They wanted to seismically change the world they were living in. America was the pinnacle of that world, and they wanted to be a part of it so they made the big move. What this emphasized to me is that disruption can be a very healthy process. Not destructive, but disruptive. And to look at what's out there and think, 'This could be better. I am going to just do it and not complain or whine or moan about it.'"

As we have stayed in touch over the years, Dr. Oz has acknowledged the extent to which his voice is a powerful one. But he also knows he must raise it in order to make a difference; he believes strongly that it's everyone's responsibility to passionately do the same.

"Use your voice to be the biggest, best person you can be," Mehmet told us. "You have to ask yourself, 'If I don't do it, then who else will?' If we all do that, good things will happen as we talk more and more about doing the right thing. Evil is not when bad people do bad things; it's when good people let bad people do bad things and don't call them out. All of us must use our voices."

Dr. Mehmet Oz is a WINNER, and I was both eager and proud to acquire *The Dr. Oz Show* at some of our company's television stations when it launched in 2009. It has since won numerous Daytime Emmy Awards for both Outstanding Talk Show Informative and Outstanding Talk Show Host. Dr. Oz has always shown me his authentic self, and my faith and trust in him as both a colleague and friend has always proved out.

5.
EXTRAORDINARY IOWANS

GOVERNOR
TERRY E. BRANSTAD

"I watched Terry Branstad up close and very personal. ... This small-town guy from Leland, Iowa, had the strongest work ethic of anyone that I've ever known. He absolutely just churns all the time. It was interesting to see how he took that to a level of political and governmental success where he never lost an election. By most measures, he is the most successful political figure in Iowa history."

Chuck Offenburger, former "Iowa Boy" columnist
for *The Des Moines Register*

On December 14, 2015, Terry Branstad served his 7,640th day in office, making him the longest-serving governor in the history of the United States.

By the time he stepped away from the Iowa governorship for the second and final time in May 2017, Branstad had served as the state's chief executive for a total of more than 22 years.

That's staggering longevity. And it's a testament to Branstad's ability to foster goodwill and broker agreements that united both sides of the aisle for much of his gubernatorial career.

"Winning" often entails bringing people together who might otherwise remain worlds apart.

"You can't imagine the heat I took from the state's Democrats in 2014 when I endorsed Branstad — not to mention, my wife, Susan!" Bill Knapp, the iconic Des Moines businessman and Democratic Party supporter, told us. "But I'm not just a Democrat. I'll vote for a Republican or an independent if I like him or her. I'm going to go for the person and not the party. I just thought that Branstad had done a good job and gave him credit for that."

Longtime Des Moines business leader Suku Radia also recalled, with some astonishment, how Branstad was able to garner Knapp's support.

"Terry Branstad is a pretty remarkable guy in terms of just how much service he has given to Iowa," Suku told us. "I'll always remember having lunch with Bill Knapp in 2012 when he said to me, 'You know what? I've made peace with Terry Branstad. He's running again and I gave him $50,000.' That says a lot about Governor Branstad, how he managed to go from being in Bill Knapp's doghouse to becoming a friend of Bill's. After that, whenever Bill had a party of some sort or the other, it was always interesting to see Governor Branstad where we'd never, ever seen a Republican before!"

How did Branstad do it? In part, it was because he governed at a time when politics were less tribal. Representatives of the government, with some exceptions, tended to serve in the interest of the "greater good" — and there was at least some common agreement as to what that truly meant.

Branstad, much like his predecessor and mentor Robert D. Ray, personified the shared notion that whatever one's political bent — left or right — common ground could always be found.

"I don't know that anybody ever traveled the state as much as he did," recalled Chuck Offenburger, former columnist for *The Des Moines Register*. "When he started off and based on the first few times I was around him, I thought this guy was going nowhere. He was about as bad a public speaker as you could hear with no discipline as he'd go off on tangents and ramble on … He totally changed over his career, of course, and by giving so many speeches he got darn good at it! What I did notice about him from the start — in the (Iowa state) legislature first and then as lieutenant governor (to Robert D. Ray) — was how under-regarded he was by his opponents. They always thought it was going to be easy to beat him. Except he never lost!"

Truly, never.

Branstad, who went on to be President Donald Trump's ambassador to China, stressed that to us with a more than a hint of pride.

"Well, I never lost an election," Branstad said. "I ran for state representative, lieutenant governor and governor. Several of my campaigns for both lieutenant governor and governor involved primary challenges as well. A lot of the success was all about hard work. It was about focusing on your constituents and working hard to represent them. I feel really honored that my biggest victory was the sixth and last race for governor in 2014 where I carried 98 (of 99) counties and beat Jack Hatch by about 22 points."

Branstad's first stint as Iowa's governor helped strengthen a robust relationship the state held with China. His predecessor, Governor Ray, had established that bond. Branstad simply deepened it.

"Governor Ray went to China and approached the Chinese government about having a sister state relationship," Branstad told us. "I signed the sister state agreement with the governor of Hebei (China) during my first year as governor in 1983. He then invited me to bring a delegation to China in 1984, and we were there for the 35th anniversary of the founding of the People's Republic on October 1, 1984. The next year in the spring of 1985, Xi Jinping came to Iowa with an agriculture delegation. He was only a county-level party secretary at the time.

"Iowa is known for its friendliness and hospitality, and we really did a great job of hosting him and the entire delegation. They visited farms and factories and to this day Xi Jinping has fond memories of that visit. It was his first trip to America and he calls everyone involved old friends. We've all stayed in touch with him over time. Our sister state relationship has remained active and that, I'm sure, is a major reason why Donald Trump chose me to be the ambassador to China. In their culture, longtime personal relationships are really important."

That's universally true, as well.

"Governor Terry Branstad is the epitome of a public servant," said Scott Raecker who worked for and alongside Branstad and Governor Ray. "Governor Branstad's career is legendary as the longest-serving governor in the history of our country in addition to serving as the U.S. ambassador to China at a critical time in our two countries' relationship. His achievements are rooted in a tremendous work ethic, his love for Iowa and his ability to build relationships with people — especially people that are new and different.

"I witnessed his evolving relationship with Governor Ray over the years, and observed a true and deep friendship that eclipsed any political connections," Raecker added. "When Governor Ray passed away, Ambassador Branstad was on his way back to China from the U.S. He turned around and immediately came back to Iowa in order that he and Chris (Mrs. Branstad) could pay their private respects. They arrived back late at night and went directly to the Capitol where Governor Ray was lying in state. The ambassador and Mrs. Branstad placed a wreath of white and blue roses with a banner that read simply, 'Mentor.' It was a moment that will forever capture the connection between these two great public servants."

Iowa Senator Chuck Grassley said it well when talking about Branstad's ambassadorship appointment in a speech on the floor of the U.S. Senate: "The fact is, he (Branstad) has been an ambassador for Iowa to the nation and to the world for his entire career. He will bring Midwestern humility and level-headed leadership to the job. He is a workhorse who is unafraid to get in the trenches to get the job done."

Governor Branstad is a WINNER who served his native state with purpose and passion, and whose influence will be felt for generations to come.

WILLIAM C. KNAPP

"For some years now, Bill Knapp's favorite line has been, 'I worked really hard to make a lot of money, and now I'm having so much more fun giving it all away.' I once told Bill that at the rate he's giving it away, he may die broke! Bill laughed and said, 'That's not very funny, because it may be true!' True or not, I will tell you this: Bill Knapp is as generous as they come."

Suku Radia, retired president of Bankers Trust

Bill Knapp drew his first breath three years before the onset of the Great Depression.

Growing up on a family farm in Southern Iowa, he learned the value of hard work at the crack of dawn and well into the milky-skied night.

"My upbringing taught me a work ethic more than anything else, but it also proved to me that it was probably not the way I wanted to live," Bill, an Iowa business icon, told us. "You had to milk cows twice a day, 365 days a year. I learned how you couldn't control the prices and you couldn't control the weather. I knew good and well I was not (meant) for the farm, because I wanted to be somewhere I had more control."

So Bill, a World War II veteran now in his 90s, shunned the pastoral life, and embraced a hectic and exhilarating existence in the world of real estate and commercial development among buildings wrought from brick, mortar and steel.

Always forward-looking. Always the aggressor. Always proactive.

"You know, if you wait for someone to call you, they'll never call you," Bill told us. "You've got to call and reach out to people. That way, you can forge new and mutually beneficial relationships."

Bill, like most of the "winners" we talked with, is all about the "win-win" situation. He built his multimillion dollar business empire with a keen business acumen and sense of fairness. Bill convinced people his gains would be shared with them.

It's a giving quality that has transformed civic life in Des Moines — and greatly endowed institutions like Blank Children's Hospital.

"Bill Knapp is obviously a pillar of our community," said David Stark, the chief executive officer at UnityPoint Health-Des Moines, who oversees operations at Blank. "UnityPoint and Blank have been blessed to enjoy a four-decade relationship with him. Bill's handshake is his word and that has proved to be true on many deals I've been a part of with Knapp Properties. He has left what I would say is an indelible imprint on the community through his tremendous generosity."

Don't expect Bill to revel in the fanfare that frames his philanthropy. He does the right thing because *it's the right thing*. Period.

Bill is also a staunch Democrat. Viewed and respected as a "kingmaker" by many in the party, he has been a key figure at both the local and national levels. But that didn't stop him from bucking his party in the 2014 Iowa gubernatorial election. Bill chose to support Republican Terry Branstad, who sought — and attained — an unprecedented sixth term.

Why?

Because as noted in the Terry Branstad profile earlier in this chapter, Knapp has shown a willingness to put the person above the party. That was especially true in the case of Branstad who, in Knapp's mind, had done a good job as governor and deserved credit for that.

It's doubtful that Bill agreed with Governor Branstad on many policy points. But he had seen Branstad, especially as a protégé of Iowa Governor Robert Ray, act in Iowa's best interest in the past, regardless of their respective party lines. Branstad, who later served as former President Donald J. Trump's ambassador to China, told us that receiving

Bill's endorsement was one of his biggest accomplishments. "Just because somebody wasn't for you the last time, doesn't mean you can't win them over," Branstad said of earning Knapp's endorsement.

Bill — a lifelong humanitarian who has given countless millions of dollars away to help those left behind — made that subjective call based on what he'd seen from Branstad in the past. Memories help frame current reality and doing the right thing at the time doesn't guarantee it turns into the right thing for the future.

"I always value the present," Bill said. "You've got to value the present. And I've always said this: If your mind can conceive it, and if you can believe it, you can achieve it. That's not original. That's just something that I've long believed in."

Even when he milked cows twice a day. Even when the world beyond his visible horizons seemed far away. Even during the brutal 98-day Battle of Okinawa in 1945, which helped seal the Allied Forces' triumph in World War II.

Only 17 years old at the time, Bill sought and received the necessary permission from his parents to fight "in a war we had to win" and enlisted in the U.S. Navy. He was assigned to the USS Catron and eventually saw intense action piloting a landing craft that repeatedly hit the beach. He would return to Okinawa in 2015, nearly 70 years to the day, and shared these reflections with Mike Kilen of *The Des Moines Register*: "It was pretty traumatic to see. It's hard to explain how bad it is in war. You can't imagine it. When you've been there, you can't understand how anyone could settle anything with war. We ought to do everything on Earth before that."

The boy who had left rural Iowa out of a patriotic sense of duty returned to his native state as a man with a new outlook on life. One wherein he understood firsthand "how tenuous it could be, and we better live every day."

Five years before the aforementioned *Register* article was published, Bill wrote a $250,000 check to cover the entire cost of an Iowa Honor Flight trip for World War II veterans. He hoped it would be a "trip of a lifetime" for some of his fellow Iowa veterans. It was — and has been for veterans on several other Honor Flights since.

Bill would often tell me during our occasional lunch conversations to always "treat your word as bond" and to never "give another person a reason to question their trust" in you. That sage advice, and his "doer not a dreamer" mentality, have made lasting impressions on me.

"I do things and move on," Bill told biographer William Friedricks. "I don't dwell on the past; if you do, you lose focus on the present."

What makes Bill Knapp such a unique brand of WINNER is the breadth and depth of the impact he's had on those less fortunate. Evelyn Davis, founder of the Tiny Tots Childcare Center for low-income families, wrote the following in a note to Bill in December 1986: "I can never thank you enough for being my friend. I don't know how or why you do all you do for us and others, but I am more than glad the Lord sent you my way."

I, too, am fortunate to call him a friend — and all of Iowa can be glad the Lord sent this special person and WINNER our way.

GOVERNOR
ROBERT D. RAY

"When confronted by scenes of human suffering, Robert Ray responded, not as a political candidate doing an electoral calculation, but as a Christian following a moral imperative from the parable of the Good Samaritan. ... Through his actions, Governor Robert Ray answered the eternal question: 'Am I my brother's keeper?'"

Ambassador Kenneth M. Quinn, in his eulogy for Governor Ray
(July 13, 2018)

The late, great governor of Iowa, Robert D. Ray, embodied the word "character."

So it's only fitting that his legacy as a beloved and broadly supported governor was the establishment of an enduring initiative called "Character Counts!"

Its six pillars?

Trustworthiness, respect, responsibility, fairness, caring and citizenship.

Ray, who served as Iowa's governor from 1968 to 1982, was the state's first five-term governor (in his early years, Iowa's governors were elected to two-year terms). He was respected by everyone in the state, even as some pushed for more progressive policies. Bob, as his friends called him, truly was a man in the middle — and a man of high principles.

At the request of his successor, Governor Terry E. Branstad, Governor Ray chaired the Iowa Sesquicentennial Commission, a colorful multi-year 150th anniversary celebration of Iowa becoming a state in 1846. That work led to a Ray-inspired vision of enhanced civility through character and ethical leadership, and the founding of the "Character Counts!" program in 1997. It eventually migrated to The Robert D. and Billie Ray Center at Drake University where it continues to make an impact in Iowa and around the world.

"Governor Ray was a wise leader who was known as a good listener and contemplative decision-maker. He was an exemplar of civility with a conviction that your adversaries in life should never be enemies — and could always become friends," said Scott Raecker, who was at Governor Ray's side as the lead executive at both the Sesquicentennial Commission and The Ray Center. "To those who had the privilege and honor to know Governor Ray, he was a friend to everyone."

"Bob Ray was liked by everybody, whether you were a Democrat or a Republican," Des Moines business icon and Democratic Party activist Bill Knapp told us. "He was really someone who just knew how to get things done and how to get people to work together. When it comes to Republicans, as far as I'm concerned, he was one of the best that there ever was."

Governor Ray was fair. Principled to a fault. He thrived as a politician in an era where there were "liberal" and "conservative" public servants on both sides of the aisle. Ray's ability to bring consensus to bear in the past is one of his enduring legacies.

"Governor Ray was a classic," said celebrated Des Moines business leader, Suku Radia. "He was not a person who would ever say, 'This is the Republican way,' or, 'This is the Democratic way.' He always stood for doing the right thing, as opposed to worrying about whether any one person or party was going to be upset. Governor Ray didn't think or take action along party lines. Never. He was one of the greatest governors we've ever had in Iowa."

My first memorable interaction with Governor Ray occurred in 1982 at the annual summer convention held by the Iowa Broadcasters

Association (IBA). He and local radio legend Forrest "Frosty" Mitchell were co-owners of several Iowa radio stations, including powerhouse WMT in Cedar Rapids. While the Drake Bulldogs were his favorite team, Ray was an enthusiastic Iowa Hawkeye fan as a result of being a color commentator for Iowa Hawkeye football games in the 1950s and 1960s alongside Frosty. Governor Ray was inducted into the IBA Hall of Fame at that 1982 convention, an honor that would coincidently be bestowed upon me more than 30 years later.

The breadth and depth of our relationship grew after our company acquired WOI-TV in 1994, and our family moved from Sioux City to Des Moines. We later became fellow members of The Breakfast Club, Ltd., resulting in our regular attendance at weekly breakfast meetings, along with occasional social gatherings involving our wives, Billie Ray and Susan Cole. He became a role model that I would frequently turn to for advice. At the time of Ray's passing, his grandchildren shared that one of the qualities they admired most about him was that he was "always more interested in your opinion than telling you his opinion." That was overwhelmingly my personal experience and remains a good lesson for us all.

Governor and Billie Ray were active supporters of Variety - the Children's Charity of Iowa and were the honorary co-chairs of the 2002 telethon. In large part due to Governor Ray's encouragement, Susan and I agreed to serve in the same capacity for the 2012 telethon. He spurred me on in a similar way to serve as the admiral of Easter Seals of Iowa's 2013 Raft Regatta at Camp Sunnyside. Governor Ray was a highly visible supporter of Easter Seals and Camp Sunnyside, where for decades he was an active participant in their annual Pony Express Ride and honorary admiral of the annual Raft Regatta.

"Let your light shine. Everyone can do something to make a difference in this world," Governor Ray often said. "We might not be able to do it all but we can do something, and isn't there great satisfaction in that?"

Indeed, there is. Or was. Or maybe can be, once again. Governor Ray's array of character-building initiatives reflect both a bygone era and hope for the future. We are all in this together — whether there's a global pandemic or not. And character truly counts the most when fear reigns, and hope wanes.

"My dad (Coach Ed Thomas) was big on character and considered it one of the most important traits to develop in others," said Aaron Thomas, the principal and head boys basketball coach at Aplington-Parkersburg High School (Iowa). "It was all about your name, your word and your character. Governor Robert Ray embodied all of that, so to see my dad recognized by the 'Character Counts!' organization was an honor that meant an awful lot to my family. It was an unbelievable testament to my dad because he strived to be a man of great character. That really mattered to him. To be recognized for what he did, how he lived his life, and the impact he had on others would've been a huge deal to my dad." Coach Ed Thomas was a "winner" on a truly epic scale who is profiled later in this chapter.

Governor Ray rose above party politics. He unified a state — and, yes, a very homogeneous one — by listening to every voice, regardless of party or ideology. He set the standard for how to treat people and lived the Golden Rule.

In the late 1970s Iowa became a worldwide leader in the humanitarian re-settlement of refugees from Laos, Cambodia, Thailand and Vietnam. It was Governor Ray who welcomed these so-called "boat people" to his state. He knew the move would be unpopular in some circles and that there would be xenophobic pushback, but he did the right thing anyway. "I decided we couldn't sit here in the middle of Iowa, in the land of plenty, and let them die," Governor Ray told *The Iowa City Press-Citizen* in 2003. "They had to risk everything, their homes and members of their family." As was so often the case, a "Do unto others as you'd have them do unto you" philosophy guided him to a compassionate if not necessarily popular course of action.

Governor Ray simply chose to do the right thing at every turn. And if that's not a "winning" quality, I don't know what is. Around the time he stepped down from office in 1982, Governor Ray offered this advice to his successor. "There's only one way to run this office, and that is to listen to the people," he said, and then choose a position and "stay with it and take the flak. And if they don't like you, let them get another governor." That successor? Terry E. Branstad.

"I learned a lot just by observing and watching the way he handled things and from his ability to connect with people," now-former Governor

Branstad told us. "Even in meetings when he had to give people a 'no' answer, he did it in such a diplomatic way that they came away feeling good about it. And when people would write him a nasty letter (which was rare), he would oftentimes come back to work at the Capitol in the evening just to call and visit with them. It was such a disarming practice. Here your governor is, still working at 9 o'clock at night, after you've written him a nasty letter and he extends the courtesy of calling you? Yes, I think that was very disarming and one of the many successful techniques that he used."

Scott Raecker served as the executive to Governor Ray's role as chair for almost 25 years. They presided over more than 100 board meetings together. What developed over those years was a working relationship that evolved into a beloved friendship.

"Governor Robert D. Ray was one of those uniquely larger-than-life individuals. His favorite titles in life were husband, father and grandfather," said Raecker. "And yet, he was a man who had a profound commitment to serve others along with a guiding moral compass that was deeply rooted in his strong, yet quiet, Christian faith. Governor Ray rose from his modest roots to become a beloved governor and international humanitarian who inspired Iowa, and the world, to open their doors to unknown refugees — saving hundreds of thousands of lives along the way. He was a man who had a humble spirit and viewed his life purpose as the opportunity to serve others."

Governor Robert D. Ray was a quiet, plain-spoken man known for his civility — a WINNER with the highest integrity, moral clarity and character.

BERNIE SAGGAU

"Bernie Saggau is the most visionary person
I have ever met. He had this idea that Iowa
was a special place and we ought to recognize
Iowans and their unique and noteworthy
accomplishments. That is how his dream for the
Iowa Hall of Pride came about. Through sheer
force of will, his vision became a reality."

Jack Lashier, director of the Iowa Hall of Pride (retired)

When Bernie Saggau spoke, no one's mind dared wander.

Not because the revered former executive director of the Iowa High School Athletic Association (IHSAA) was bombastic behind a podium. Nor because he was overly slick. No, Bernie effortlessly earned rapt attention from his audiences because he exuded both earnestness and authority — and people consequently hung on his every word.

"When I would do speaking engagements, everybody expected a talk about athletics, given my unique background," Bernie told us. "But I just used the athletics theme to get my message across to kids (of) how important they are, and what they could be and couldn't be. I was never afraid to talk about patriotism and I'd talk about how you'd better get up and go to church because faith is important in your life. I would talk about how you've got to have goals in your life. (And) in the latter years, I would talk about hate, given my belief that hatred is one of the major problems in our country today. And, you know, the kids would listen. I didn't use notes and always talked from my heart, and that seemed to help get the message across."

Integrity. Sportsmanship. Citizenship. Patriotism. Overcoming obstacles.

Bernie's deeply held values endure because they matter. He has embodied them throughout his life dating back to his days as a three-sport student-athlete at what was then Buena Vista College (now University) in the late 1940s. His voice carried then, too, despite — or maybe because of — his diminutive stature.

"When I was in college, I was kind of a freak," Saggau recalled. "In my freshman year I weighed 120 pounds and played football. I had some lucky things happen to me, and had some success. Well, all of a sudden, in Northwest Iowa, the (elementary and high) school people would hear about me, and they'd read about me, and they would think, 'You know, maybe he would do a good job talking at our athletic banquet — and I'd be cheap! That was one thing they were looking for, I'm sure."

Maybe, but they also got tremendous value for whatever modest speaking fee Bernie collected in those days.

It's impossible to overstate the impact Bernie's more than 38 years leading the IHSAA — and his countless motivational speeches delivered across the state and the country — have had on the well-being of young and old alike.

"Bernie has always been an amazing public speaker," said Jack Lashier, who served as the longtime director of Saggau's legacy project, the Iowa Hall of Pride. "He could communicate and connect with little kids, with high school kids, and with adults. Bernie just has the ability to communicate on all kinds of levels. He could have done anything he wanted to in the sales world or as a motivational speaker. He could have done anything. Iowans were just lucky to have him in the role he played at the IHSAA for all those years."

Saggau first served under the IHSAA's then-executive director Lyle Quinn before ascending to that role himself. Even then, he turned heads with his integrity, commitment and bold ideas.

Quinn asked his new employee, "What's the first thing you're going to do?" Bernie shared with us how his answer to that question was as candid as it was direct. He told Quinn, "I'm going to go out and call on every high school in the state." It got real quiet in the room before Quinn followed up with, "Every school?" To which Bernie replied, "Yep, I'll make it to every school to tell them my name and that I'm working for the association. If you ever have a problem, call me. And if I cannot answer your question, I'll go find the answer for you."

In Bernie's first year at the IHSAA, he made it to about 85 percent of the schools and the following year he visited the rest of them. As Bernie summed it up, "It makes a difference when people know that you care about them and that you're not so smart as to have all the answers."

Bernie began a well-deserved retirement on January 1, 2005. Just a few months earlier, a "Tribute to Bernie" dinner was held at the Sioux City Convention Center. It was an honor for me to be asked to serve as the master of ceremonies as Bernie was toasted — and occasionally roasted — with great joy and fanfare. Bernie wrote to me afterward to say, "It was a night I will long remember, and you made it twice as memorable by doing such a great job as master of ceremonies." To receive such a warm compliment from one of the most prolific public speakers our state has even seen was incredibly gratifying.

Bernie's success clearly wasn't just built on well-crafted talks. His actions have made indelible impressions on high school activities programs across the country. He remains the longest-tenured director in the history of the 50 state high school associations, and he is a member of the National Federation of High School Athletic Association's Hall of Fame.

"I mean, you talk about a guy who had a 'winning' attitude," said Tim Seaman, longtime sports director and current news anchor at KCAU-TV in Sioux City. "Bernie's drive and personality propelled him to the top of high school sports in America. He was really respected by anyone and everyone who was involved with high school sports, and yet he was just always so welcoming."

Bernie's always welcomed — and celebrated — too.

Two decades after his Buena Vista football career came to an end, he became one of the first members of the school's athletics hall of fame.

"Buena Vista announced the names of three former players for their inaugural hall of fame class," Bernie said. "They picked two really great players ... and me. I believe they selected me for the same reason I was recruited way back when. It was about my leadership, faith in teamwork and belief that if you give 110 percent you'll have success in whatever you do in life."

Bernie's message never changed much. Timeless wisdom rarely does. I'll never forget the first time our paths crossed. It was 1974. Bernie delivered the commencement speech at Kingsley-Pierson High School (Iowa), my alma mater. My future bride, Susan Henry, was a year younger than me and a member of the graduating class. My mind didn't wander as Bernie gave a remarkable speech that night.

I've long since learned what a dynamic and nationally renowned public speaker he is. In fact, Susan and I had dinner with Bernie and his late wife, Lois, in 2004. We laughed about the coincidence of Bernie having spoken at Susan's graduation. He told us that he had spoken to well over 1,000 student bodies across the country during his time at the IHSAA. While I was serving as president of the Siouxland Officials Association in the early 1980s, Bernie accepted my invitation to be the keynote speaker at our annual dinner. He truly valued the bond and special fraternity that coaches, referees and high school administrators enjoy, and "blew the roof off the house" as was so often the case whenever and wherever he spoke.

Bernie also graciously accepted many other invitations to speak at events for me over the years, such as "Best of the Class" programs our television stations conducted to honor the top academically ranked high school seniors at graduation time. I can personally attest to how his speeches always had themes and messages that touched on the values he held most dear: integrity, sportsmanship, citizenship and patriotism.

When it came to imparting a lasting message on values, ideals and character, you could not find a better person or WINNER than Bernie Saggau to be the messenger.

COACH ED THOMAS

"Whatever you do in life echoes through eternity."

Coach Ed Thomas

Aaron Thomas cherishes his childhood memories of being a coaching icon's son.

He remembers playing near the Aplington-Parkersburg High School (A-P) practice field as his dad, Ed, worked to extract every measure of effort, accountability and talent from his football players. He recalls hanging out in the weight room as Dad encouraged his players and students to pile on weight plates, perform one last rep and dig deep to develop both physical and mental strength. He can reminisce about the bus rides to and from games, the state football titles and the eager, gritty commitment of the players.

"My dad would always say that nothing great is ever done without enthusiasm," Aaron told us. "My mom (Jan) said the same thing, too. Both of them were tireless workers, willing to help others."

Ed Thomas guided four Falcons players to productive NFL careers: Casey Wiegmann, Brad Meester, Jared DeVries and Aaron Kampman. That's a stunning number given the community's relatively small size. ESPN went so far as to dispatch Kenny Mayne, the witty *SportsCenter* anchor, to Parkersburg in 2003 to interview Coach Thomas for a segment on the *Sunday NFL Countdown* show that explored his uncanny ability to turn out NFL-worthy players. But however often Thomas found himself in such a spotlight, it truly never was about him. Not ever. Even on June, 24, 2009, when a former player suffering from mental health issues entered the A-P weight room and tragically shot Thomas to death.

Ed Thomas was 58 years old. He was doing what he loved: helping young people grow and develop into the best version of themselves they could be. He was beloved and respected on a truly massive scale, which made his killing all the more senseless, all the more soul-shattering.

"Some things are inexplicable," Kenny Mayne told us while drawing on his own deeply personal experience with loss. "While we may never know the reason for some things, we can honor whoever has left us in the very best way possible. When we lost our twin boys, I remember coming out of that wondering if I would ever be ready to be back on TV and say anything that's funny, or for that matter, would anything ever be funny in life again? But I remember it kind of hit me one day that the best way to honor someone is to continue living life to your fullest. Their memory wouldn't be blessed by you giving up or becoming bitter or changing who you are. It doesn't mean you don't still suffer the pain of the loss, but it means that you continue to be the best you. You have to find the joy in life again, no matter what things you suffer."

Aaron Thomas, and the entire Thomas family — his mother, Jan and brother, Todd — found serenity and perspective by offering up forgiveness. They forgave Mark Becker, the former player who had shot their husband and father that day. They forgave the Becker family. All of them needed to heal. The tight-knit community needed a path forward fueled by faith and compassion, not hatred and vengeance.

Just 13 months earlier, Ed Thomas had helped the Parkersburg community heal following a devastating EF5 tornado that claimed nine lives and destroyed scores of homes and buildings, including the high school. They would rebuild — but that effort first necessitated the healing of hearts and minds. Only then would the brick and mortar-based work prove to be durable. Ed and Jan Thomas helped lead the charge on both fronts. They chose to elevate others in the wake of such a catastrophic event. They chose to "find the joy in life again."

"I would point to the example of how both my mom and dad lived their lives," said Aaron Thomas, who is now the principal and head boys basketball coach at A-P as well as a powerful public speaker. "They taught us that it can't be about you, that you have to be selfless and that you must be able to see the hurt and pain others are going through."

And do something about it. In the aftermath of Ed's death, his family immediately responded to the tragedy with understanding and empathy. That's what Ed taught. It's also how Jan, her sons and their families would strive to model their lives going forward.

"The thing that struck me was the forgiveness and kindness from the Thomas family," said ESPN's Rece Davis who, along with colleagues Herm Edwards and Chris Spielman, journeyed to Parkersburg in 2009 to broadcast A-P's season-opening football game against their neighboring rival, Dike-New Hartford. The game marked the Falcons' emotional return to the field for the first time following the tragic shooting at the school two months earlier, and ESPN presented it to a national audience.

"You know, it would have been very easy for someone in their situation to show a lot of bitterness, especially toward the family of the young man who was mentally ill and committed the crime," Rece continued. "That would have been easy. Instead, they took the harder road. They took the road of forgiveness and understanding that there were others suffering, as well. The dignity and class and character that the Thomas' showed will forever be imprinted on me. I just have so much respect for the way their family handled such a tragic situation. When I think of all the things that Chris, Herm and I saw during our visit, what stuck with me more than anything else was how they took a horrific tragedy and helped greatly promote the healing."

The special broadcast was less about the high school football game played that August night, and more about revealing the story of the community's resilience and who Coach Ed Thomas was. Davis delivered a moving soliloquy prior to signing off the broadcast and making the toss to the late-night *SportsCenter*:

"There is no satisfying answer as to why this town has suffered so much devastation. In a span of 15 months, life in this heartland hamlet was altered permanently but their faith remains steadfast.

The man who inspired and left them is no longer here to enjoy the fruits of his labor. But Ed Thomas' work — his lessons, his life — are still fully evident. When you get knocked down, you get up and go. You don't quit. Tonight offered closure to some, another chance to get up and go. Just as Ed Thomas would have wanted it."

It was watching this game and hearing Rece Davis' words that later inspired me to nominate the Ed Thomas Family for the Arthur Ashe Courage Award. Presented annually at the ESPYS, this honor is bestowed upon individuals who "reflect the spirit of Arthur Ashe, possessing strength in the face of adversity, courage in the face of peril and the willingness to stand up for their beliefs no matter what the cost." The strength, courage and faith shown by the family in the face of their tragic loss were extraordinary.

My nomination included the requisite biographical information on Coach Thomas' career: the extraordinary win-loss record, the state titles, the numerous players who went on to find success in the college and professional ranks and his being named the NFL's High School Coach of the Year in 2005. It, of course, also included the details of his inspirational efforts to help rebuild the community in the aftermath of the destructive tornado.

While it no doubt helped to have ESPN executives familiar with the story in light of the 2009 broadcast, it was still no easy task to convince the ESPYS selection committee that the Thomas family deserved to have their name immortalized alongside the many outstanding individuals whose names appeared on the list of previous recipients. That list includes Jim Valvano, Muhammad Ali, Dean Smith, Billie Jean King and Pat Tillman. The prior year's honoree was the former president of South Africa and anti-apartheid leader Nelson Mandela. Steadfast in my admiration for the Thomas family, the nomination concluded with the following statement: "Courage can manifest itself in many different ways, but the courage to forgive may well be among the most powerful."

It was truly gratifying to learn in March 2010 that the ESPYS selection committee agreed that the Thomas family story was one of immense courage, one that transcended sports. In making the announcement, then-ESPN senior executive John Skipper said, "The Thomas family showed us how people can come together under extraordinary circumstances that would normally drive them apart."

"Our family is humbled and honored to be selected as the Arthur Ashe Courage Award winner," said Aaron Thomas at the time of the announcement. "To be mentioned in the same sentence as past winners is more than anything our family could have imagined. This award is a great testament to the type of man my father was. We are merely following his example and what he would expect. Even through the toughest of times, we know how my dad would have handled the situation."

One of the enduring images of Ed Thomas shown during the award presentation at the ESPYS in July 2010 was the sight of him standing stoically on the sidelines with his arms folded, and the superimposed words he lived by: "Faith, Family and Football." It meant a great deal to the family and his many former players for his story to be shared — and his legacy elevated — with such a wide audience. "To have my dad's story told on a national level and then get the feedback we received from people about how it touched them, or changed their mindset about losing a loved one, or being wronged by somebody else was more than probably any of us — or my dad — could have ever grasped," Aaron said. "It was gratifying to see the impact he made even after he passed away."

"Coach Thomas' story was such a powerful story that needed to be told and it still needs to be told (perpetually)," said former A-P, University of Iowa and Green Bay Packers player Aaron Kampman. "You'd give up all of it (ESPYS, Ashe Award, etc.) to have Coach Thomas back. But the concept that something beautiful can still come out of something so ugly and terrible, that's the reality. I think that's the great hope. It's what resilience is really all about in the end and ties into so many different areas of life. It was an opportunity modeled first and foremost by the Thomas family.

"It was not without pain, not without grief and not without suffering. But they still made a choice to move forward and to get up the next day, and do the things that you are asked to do as a leader and hold that responsibility with honor. Coach Thomas used to say (that among) the greatest gifts that God has given us is the opportunity to choose, and you can demonstrate that in different ways."

The values Coach Thomas epitomized truly took what it means to be a WINNER to its most rarefied level. Among them was the fact that each of us can choose our response to any situation, and how the harder path is often the right one to follow. Hopefully, those hard, but inspiring, choices will endure.

GARY THOMPSON

"I had the pleasure of working with Gary Thompson on the old Cyclone Television Network. He was as genuine, caring and respectful a person as you will ever find. It was during this period of time that I was able to gain a greater appreciation of just how accomplished Gary was as an athlete, as a coach, as a broadcaster, as a businessman ... and as a person."

John Walters, the "Voice of the Cyclones" and
former sports director at WOI-TV

The old Iowa State Armory erupted. Fans flooded the floor. Cyclones star guard Gary Thompson — aka "The Roland Rocket" — exulted, reveling in the upset as future NBA Hall of Famer Wilt "The Stilt" Chamberlain shuffled off the court along with his talented Kansas Jayhawks teammates.

The date: January 14, 1957.

The score: Iowa State 39, Kansas 37.

While Gary didn't score the winning basket (Don Medsker did), he played a key role in the triumph over the player who would become one of the NBA's all-time greatest big men. And Gary would go on to be named the Big Seven Conference (later to become the Big Eight Conference, and currently known as the Big 12 Conference) Player of the Year at the end of that same season.

"Everybody remembers 'the Wilt game' in large part because Iowa State won it," Gary told us. In keeping with the kind of person he is, Gary remembers it most for what eventually sprang from the victory. Years later, he sent letters of support to Chamberlain when he was battling heart problems. He had also sent him notes when Kansas retired his uniform number. Time passed. Gary became a successful broadcaster and businessman. Chamberlain became a celebrity and a legend before passing away in 1999 at the age of 63.

About eight years later, memories of "the Wilt game" morphed into a permanent bond between Gary and Chamberlain's sister, Barbara. All because of those unanswered letters — which Chamberlain had saved and Barbara discovered while presiding over his estate.

"(Wilts' sister) called me out of the blue," Gary said. "She thought it was pretty nice that we had competed against each other and wanted me to know that he had kept the letters I'd written to him. And from that conversation, we became good friends. Wilt had left some money (to the University of Kansas) so she invited us to have lunch with the chancellor and share some special activities. The United States Postal Service later came out with a national postage stamp (featuring Wilt) and Barbara invited us to join her when the stamp was unveiled in Philadelphia. It's a relationship we have kept up. Our philosophies of faith and life are much alike and it's been a very good association."

Winning in basketball, business and life has always driven Gary, who excelled as a broadcaster for 34 years. He offered illuminating color commentary for basketball games at the local and national levels, and worked with such luminaries as Jay Randolph, Bob Costas, Dick Enberg and Jack Buck.

Gary also remains active and influential with Iowa State's athletics department. In fact, it was his guidance that helped lead to the hiring of the current director of athletics, Jamie Pollard, who has since become one of the most respected ADs in the country.

"If he hadn't supported me, there's a good chance I'm not the athletics director," Pollard said. "And No. 2, during the interview process, Gary was so passionate about Cyclone alums and former student-athletes. Wisconsin (where Pollard had been an assistant AD) had what was considered one of the strongest letterwinners organizations in the country. Gary was intrigued by that because at the time Iowa State wasn't doing a ton on that front, and he was convinced that the school needed to do a better job of staying connected to its former athletes.

"I'm really proud of how in the last 15 years we have grown our letterwinners organization immensely," Pollard continued. "We have multiple full-time staff members and we do so much to reach out with a 'Once a Cyclone, always a Cyclone' message. None of that would have been possible if it weren't for the passion Gary Thompson had for his alma mater and for all the student-athletes that wore Cardinal and Gold before and after him. I think it speaks volumes for how Gary has always been about so much more than himself. That's one of the reasons we named the Iowa State Male Student-Athlete of the Year award after Gary Thompson (in 2019)."

Gary's No. 20 basketball jersey was the first Iowa State jersey ever retired. He was a rare two-sport All-American who also starred as a shortstop on the Cyclones' baseball team. He never stopped honoring his rural roots, which helped him fine tune the rare art of balancing humility with high achievement; he had an unwavering commitment to "winning" without compromising one's principles in the process.

"Gary was hardly a physical specimen," said Chuck Offenburger, longtime columnist for *The Des Moines Register*, who also penned the excellent biography, *Gary Thompson: All-American*. "I mean, gosh, he was a little guy. Even he said, 'You know, when I was a freshman at Roland, I came into a game and hit a couple of big shots. But I was so little and underdeveloped at that time.' Gary said that was his story that freshman year. And it continued in his sophomore year when he led the Rockets to the state tournament. As he kept knocking down these long-range shots — not a jump shot, but a set shot — the media just went crazy over them. Gary said that opened doors for him, with that exposure early on leading to every other bit of success to come later in life. Much the same thing happened at Iowa State."

And behind the mic.

Gary's ability to describe the game during broadcasts was both prodigious and down to earth. Details mattered. Insights gleaned from his playing days peppered his commentary. A true passion for the game

— and those who played it — permeated every sentence. It didn't matter if he was broadcasting a high school state tournament game or a national college game of the week. "I loved doing it because it allowed me to still be associated with the game," Gary told us. "Many people came up to me over the years to say, 'I bet you love being on television.' I would always say in response, 'No, that's really not what's important. What's fun about broadcasting is being able to see a lot of great games and to come in contact with a lot of great coaches and players.' Being around and associated with people who loved the game as much as I did was the most important thing."

Perhaps that's why the larger-than-life Chamberlain kept Gary's letters. Perhaps that's why Gary — the ultimate competitor and gentleman — is universally respected. Perhaps the "Roland Rocket" always knew the game, not one game, defined one's relationship with "winning."

Big or small. Outside or inside. Dreams take flight either way — and can spiral to heights few would dare dream of even attempting to reach.

"We went to the state tournament one year and there was nobody back home in Roland except the guys in the fire department!" Gary said. "In that state tournament, we played three schools: Davenport, Waterloo West and Des Moines East. They were all big schools, among the largest in the state. Our coach taught us to believe that those kids were just like us and if we did, 'A, B and C,' in the game, we had a chance to win. That small-town, small-school experience has served me well throughout my life."

Gary's interest in athletics and the timeless lessons they provide has never waned. And he continues to be as loyal and steadfast supporter of Iowa State athletics as you will find anywhere. Susan and I were guests of Gary and his wife, Jan, in their private suite when the Iowa State Cyclone football team upset No. 4-ranked TCU in October 2017. No Cyclone fan in sold-out Jack Trice Stadium cheered louder — or smiled more — after the victory that day than he did.

Gary has been inducted into both the Iowa and National High School Halls of Fame. He is a member of the Iowa State University Letterwinners' Hall of Fame. In June 2005, it was my distinct honor to nominate him for induction into the Iowa Broadcasters Hall of Fame.

Gary Thompson is a WINNER who has long been a champion in basketball, in baseball, in golf, in business and — most importantly — in life.

6.
MAKING A DIFFERENCE

BROADCASTERS FOUNDATION OF AMERICA

"Simply put, the person sitting down the hall, in the studio, or in the cubicle next to yours could be tomorrow's (grant) recipient. Because as long as they have worked in the industry and have a qualifying need, the Broadcasters Foundation is there for them, and for everyone in radio and television."

———————————

Deborah Parenti, publisher of *Radio Ink* (Aug. 28, 2017)

Anonymous grant recipients trace the Broadcasters Foundation of America's legacy of giving:

There's the email from a mother of four school-age children who had recently lost her husband, a former broadcaster: "Without your help, I would have lost what little bit we have — our apartment, our car, everything."

In another email, a television broadcaster from South Carolina wrote this in the wake of Hurricane Florence: "I was brought to tears when I received the (emergency) grant check in the mail. To know there is support from the broadcasting community during these hard times makes them a bit more bearable."

And then there's this heartfelt note from a 40-year broadcast engineer who developed Stage 4 chronic kidney disease as he neared retirement: "As you know by now, I could not make it ... or still be alive ... without your help. God bless you all."

The ever-charitable Hall of Fame sports broadcaster Dick Vitale often talks about the simple, yet courageous, act of "extending your hand."

It's easier to do so when our loved ones are hurting; it can be more difficult to do when the person in need of help is a complete stranger.

But Dick plays no favorites, nor should we.

It's been my great privilege to serve on the board of the Broadcasters Foundation of America (BFoA) — a vitally important organization that provides desperately needed aid to people in the broadcast industry we know and people we don't know. It plays no favorites.

The BFoA's stated mission: "To improve the quality of life and maintain the personal dignity of men and women in the radio and television broadcast profession who find themselves in acute financial need due to a critical illness, accident, advanced age or other serious misfortune."

Some recipients of this needed assistance are news anchors, reporters, meteorologists, sports anchors or radio program hosts you recognize. Others work quietly behind the scenes. I'm talking about talented photojournalists, producers, directors, production assistants, promotion and marketing directors; digital specialists, music and program directors; account executives, traffic and sales managers; broadcast engineers and IT techs, business and administrative staff, and more.

So many more.

So what happens when one of our own needs a helping hand? When a fellow broadcaster has an accident or medical emergency with a long road to recovery ahead? Or when a hurricane, wildfire or severe storm leaves behind unexpected damage?

What happens when they have nowhere to turn?

The BFoA extends that helping hand.

This giving philosophy can be traced back 70-plus years. It was back then that a simple "lend a helping hand" approach led to the formation of the Broadcast Pioneers. Years later, the charitable concept first conceived by the Broadcast Pioneers was built upon in a manner that expanded its outreach to the entire country. We know it today as the Broadcasters

Foundation of America. But the overarching goal remains the same: to provide an anonymous safety net to broadcasters who find themselves in need. This is accomplished via monthly grants to those who are unable to work due to an illness, accident, advanced age or other serious misfortune. Medical bills or long-term care expenses can leave a family in desperate need of help; these grants can help fill the gap between income and expense.

"Our only goal is to provide aid to those in our industry who need it most," said Scott Herman, current chairman of the BFoA. "Our grant recipients are hard-working broadcasters from across the country, who have been hit by challenging — often life-altering — circumstances. Together, we can help them get through the toughest times."

When natural disasters hit a community, broadcasters are some of the first on the scene, reporting live. These events all too often affect the lives of broadcasters as well, and leave some in dire financial need. In such situations, the BFoA provides one-time grants to broadcasters who need financial help to rebound and recover from disaster. For example, the U.S. was hit hard in 2017 by hurricanes Harvey, Irma and Maria. They devastated parts of Texas, Florida and Puerto Rico. In California, record-breaking wildfires ravaged parts of the state. The BFoA distributed over $300,000 in one-time, emergency grants. Our response to natural disasters, when the lives of fellow broadcasters are turned upside down by nature's fury, is immediate.

The resources needed to meet this goal are raised through a combination of special events and two annual fundraising drives.

The Guardian Fund was established to ensure that financial assistance is available in perpetuity to fellow broadcasters who find themselves with an acute need. Contributions to this fund are used exclusively to support the benevolent outreach of the BFoA.

A second corporate-focused initiative, the Angel Fund, further enhances the BFoA's ability to reach out to broadcasters in need by working in tandem with the Guardian Fund. It is important to point out that when the process of issuing monthly grant checks to a qualified broadcaster begins, particularly involving the elderly, the BFoA stays with that individual throughout his or her lifetime so long as a need exists.

A number of special events such as the Golden Mike Gala, the Celebrity Golf Tournament, the Philip J. Lombardo Charity Golf

Tournament and the Leadership Breakfast are held throughout the year to raise both awareness and additional funds. These fun, mission-driven get-togethers remind us how grateful we are to call ourselves broadcasters, and for the blessings in our individual lives. We are also compelled to reflect on those in need — and what we, collectively, can and must do to help.

No one individual has done more to help than Phil Lombardo. In the acknowledgments as the beginning of this book, I referred to Phil as "an experienced broadcaster with a burning entrepreneurial spirit in his soul." He has been an industry leader for over 50 years including serving as joint board chairman of the television and radio boards for the National Association of Broadcasters. But Phil's lasting legacy will be the manner in which he redefined the BFoA's mission and set it on its current course.

Phil served as chairman of the BFoA from 2000 to 2015, and continues today in an active role as chairman emeritus. He has played a seminal role in the growth and impact of the BFoA. Just over $60,000 in assistance was given out to broadcasters in need back in 2000; in 2020, the BFoA awarded more than $1.7 million in monthly and one-time emergency grants.

No board member is more familiar with Phil's leadership and contributions to the BFoA than Bill O'Shaughnessy, president of Whitney Global Media. "Few quarterbacks of our altogether unique foundation have had the lasting and significant impact on our calling as chairman emeritus Lombardo," Bill told us. "All the while he kept us true to our mission and firmly focused on our noble work among hurting and almost forgotten colleagues, past and present. I know of no more generous guy than Phil Lombardo."

While the names don't matter, the connections do. Supporters of the BFoA mission understand that delivering assistance to the suffering among us enriches us all.

"While in the hospital, my daughter read me your lovely, life-saving, generous letter assuring me of the Broadcasters Foundation of America's continued support," a broadcaster wrote upon learning of our anonymous assistance. "It brought true tears of joy to my eyes, and this compassion was some very, very warm news, indeed."

Such support has a massive impact. In the words of another anonymous grant recipient, "All of you are my angels on Earth. I don't know what I would have done without you."

The Broadcasters Foundation of America is a WINNER because of its unwavering commitment to serving fellow broadcasters in times of need. We're all "winners" when we extend a helping hand — to people both familiar to us and those whom we've never met.

ESPYS

"When you die, it does not mean you lose to cancer. You beat cancer by how you live, why you live and in the manner in which you live."

Stuart Scott, while accepting the Jimmy V Award
for Perseverance at the ESPYS (July 16, 2014)

Robin Roberts is the ultimate personification of Jimmy Valvano's legacy. And in quoting him, her grace and power shine through his inspiring words.

"'Don't give up. Don't ever give up,'" Robin told me in a 2016 interview while sharing her reflected thoughts on Jimmy V, The V Foundation and the ESPYS. "I close my eyes (and) think about the (1983 North Carolina State) national championship and how Jim Valvano went running around looking for someone to hug.

"I remember the first ESPYS, and how Jimmy courageously stepped out there and delivered that memorable speech," Robin continued. "It's a little-known fact, but I was the very next person on that stage after he accepted his award and made his powerful remarks. I remember being in the wings and watching it, never knowing that I would be one of those people that he made reference to when announcing the foundation that night. He said, 'It may save somebody's life, it may save someone you love.' I had no idea that the foundation would potentially save my life. So the ESPYS are very special to me for that reason."

As they are to me.

As a native Iowan, I take special pride when teams or people from my home state are honored in meaningful ways. That was especially true at the ESPYS in July 2010.

Just one year earlier, the Arthur Ashe Courage Award was presented to Nelson Mandela, the former president of South Africa and anti-apartheid leader. So to be in attendance when the ESPYS awarded that same high honor to the family of an Iowan — an individual who had been one of the state's most prolific high school football coaches — was beyond gratifying. An executive vice president of ESPN at the time, John Skipper, felt the same way, saying, "To tell the story of a regular person like Ed Thomas, and to honor a high school coach and feel the soul of sports at the local level, was quite special."

Ed Thomas was the longtime football coach at Aplington-Parkersburg High School (A-P). While working with student athletes in the Falcons' weight room on June 24, 2009, Coach Thomas was shot and killed by a former player suffering from mental illness. Beyond the school's renowned success on the gridiron, Thomas had also played a pivotal role in helping the community come together and heal after a devastating tornado the previous year. His life story, and the manner his family responded in the face of such tragedy, was beautifully told in a video tribute shown just prior to the presentation of the Arthur Ashe Courage Award to his wife, Jan and sons, Aaron and Todd Thomas.

It was both a painful and heartwarming occasion. One of his former A-P players, Aaron Kampman, had gone on to play at the University of Iowa and in the NFL for the Green Bay Packers. Kampman, along with three other former A-P players who also were playing in the NFL at the time, made the effort to be present at the ESPYS that night. Coach Thomas was a WINNER on a truly epic scale and was the subject of an earlier profile in Chapter Five of this book.

There were other Iowans in attendance at the ESPYS that year as well. University of Northern Iowa head basketball coach Ben Jacobson and two of his players, Ali Farokhmanesh and Adam Koch, basked in the celebratory atmosphere. After all, it's not every day that the

Panthers are featured on a national stage let alone win an ESPY in the Best Upset category.

"It was not one of those deals where we went out there, hung out in the hotel until the awards show, accepted it, and then got out the next day to go home," said Jacobson, the Panthers' longtime and highly respected coach whose team had knocked off No. 1-overall seed Kansas in the second round of the 2010 NCAA Basketball Tournament. "We had the opportunity to get involved in everything that was going on for the entire three days, which included playing in the ESPYS Golf Classic and attending all the parties. That's what made it so much fun for us. You talk about a way to top off or kind of put an exclamation point on an incredible two-year run, we go to the ESPYS and win one! It was a once-in-a-lifetime experience."

As it turned out, another group of Iowans would enjoy a similar experience just two years later and it also came about as the result of an ESPYS nomination in the Best Upset category.

With a monumental, double-overtime 37-31 football victory over No. 2 Oklahoma State, the Iowa State University (ISU) Cyclones garnered national attention in November 2011. It came as no surprise when they were invited to the 2012 ESPYS, and it was my pleasure to host the ISU contingent consisting of head coach Paul Rhoads, linebacker Jake Knott, running back Jeff Woody, quarterback Jared Barnett, and cornerback Leonard Johnson. Woody and Knott, rivals in their high school days, had become close friends. "Who would have thought back in 2009 — the year we graduated from high school — that we would ever do anything that would come close to being on ESPN, let alone be going to the awards show with all those sports celebrities?" Woody said at the time.

While the ESPY was awarded to the Los Angeles Kings for their Stanley Cup upset championship, the ISU players nonetheless took home fond memories of walking the ESPYS red carpet, attending the ESPYS show and parties, and even being special guests at a taping of the *Jimmy Kimmel Live!* show. "We were welcomed and felt such a part of it," Rhoads, now an analyst for perennial Big Ten and national power Ohio State, told us. "I mean, we were hobnobbing and rubbing elbows with an array of top athletes and celebrities, but never felt like we didn't belong."

There are countless other ESPYS memories having nothing to do with teams or people with Iowa ties.

It's almost become a ritual to cross paths at the ESPYS with former network colleague and friend Robin Roberts. The first such time was in July 2008 when she joined ESPN's Stuart Scott as co-presenter of the Jimmy V Award for Perseverance. The presentation was made all the more poignant knowing that the two of them had recently shown remarkable perseverance of their own: Robin while beating back breast cancer, and Stuart during a fight involving a cancerous appendix that was discovered during a routine appendectomy. As life would have it, perseverance was a virtue that both Robin and Stuart would need in abundance as new health crises later emerged for both of them.

In 2012, Robin was diagnosed with myelodysplastic syndrome (MDS) that was believed to be a complication of her breast cancer treatments years earlier. It required her to take an extended leave of absence from *Good Morning America* to receive a bone marrow transplant, a procedure in which the donor cells from her sister, Sally-Ann, were injected into Robin's system. Robin returned to the air on Feb. 20, 2013, and proclaimed, "I have been waiting 174 days to say this: Good Morning America!" off the top of that day's show.

Robin was honored with the Arthur Ashe Courage Award at the ESPYS in 2013 where basketball star LeBron James served as the presenter. In her moving acceptance speech, she reminisced about being backstage in 1993 when Jim Valvano gave his monumental speech after being presented the first-ever Arthur Ashe Courage Award. Robin said, "I never imagined that I'd be able to be standing here 20 years after Jimmy V's speech and say that because of everyone who has responded to his challenge, because of all the donations, research and support, mine is one of the lives that's been saved." She concluded her acceptance remarks with a heartfelt message for the audience in the theater and viewers watching at home: "I draw strength from you. You give me the courage to face down any challenge … to know when fear knocks, to let faith open the door."

As for Stuart, his cancer returned in 2011 and then again in 2013. He was presented the Jimmy V Perseverance Award at the 2014 ESPYS. I sat down and spoke with Stuart in a courtyard outside the JW Marriott on the morning of the awards show, and he clearly understood that he was a man facing his own mortality. Robin later told me that ESPN had put her on "stand-by" to accept the award on Stuart's behalf in the event his lack of strength prevented him from doing so himself. But step on stage he did, with a message every bit as inspiring as Robin's had been the year before:

"When you die, it does not mean that you lose to cancer. You beat cancer by how you live, why you live and in the manner in which you live. So live. Live. Fight like hell and when you get too tired to fight then lay down and rest and let somebody else fight for you."

Following his brave fight involving more than 50 infusions of chemotherapy, radiation and multiple surgeries related to his cancer treatments, Stuart Scott passed away on Jan. 4, 2015.

"I will continue to keep fighting — sucking the marrow out of life, as the marrow sucks the life out of me." Those were only a few of the passionate words spoken by renowned *NBA on TNT* sideline reporter Craig Sager while accepting the Jimmy V Perseverance Award at the EPSYS in 2016. Having been diagnosed with leukemia in 2014, Craig continued to work during his battle with the disease and throughout the course of his many treatments. One of the few things he hadn't accomplished during the course of his storied 44-year career was working an NBA Finals game. So in an "across the aisle" expression of support and admiration, Craig was invited by ESPN to work Game 6 of the 2016 NBA Finals on ABC. It was a "win or go home" game for the Cleveland Cavaliers who beat the Golden State Warriors, 115-101, to even the series.

In an email sent just moments after the game to my friend and then-ESPN executive John Wildhack, I said, "Game 7! Sager's postgame interview with LBJ (LeBron James) was perfect. Any chance he's healthy enough for an encore? Again, congrats to you and TNT on the classiest of moves." In a prompt reply, Wildhack wrote back to say, "Ray, this was the only game he could do due to his medical schedule. Was great to have him be a big part of tonight. ... Hope he makes it to the ESPYS. He's in rough shape." It was only then that I fully grasped the dire nature of Craig's condition.

Much like Stuart Scott had done in 2014, Craig summoned the energy needed to appear on stage wearing one of his patented brightly colored jackets. Following an introduction by then-Vice President Joe Biden, he said, "Time is something that cannot be bought, it cannot be wagered with God, and it is not in endless supply. Time is simply how you live your life." Craig ended his speech with inspiring words about hope: "I see the beauty in others, and I see the hope for tomorrow. If we don't have hope and faith, we have nothing. I will never give up, and I will never give in. I will live my life full of love and full of fun. It is the only way I know how." There were but a few dry eyes in the house.

Craig passed away on Dec. 15, 2016.

John Quincy Adams, our nation's sixth president, once said, "Courage and perseverance have a magical talisman, before which difficulties disappear and obstacles vanish into air."

The ESPYS relate perfectly to this quote in the form of presentations like those noted above around its two pillar awards: the Arthur Ashe Courage Award and the Jimmy V Award for Perseverance.

On the surface, the ESPYS celebrate achievements in sports, but does so with depth, heart, soul and a firm recognition that the human spirit — both the good and bad elements — undergirds all of the "wins" that are deservedly celebrated.

No one better exemplified the "soul" of the ESPYS than its longtime executive producer, Maura Mandt. We had lined up an interview with Maura for this book but, tragically, she passed away on Feb. 28, 2020, before we could talk to her.

Maura had been the driving force behind producing the aforementioned heartfelt, tear-inducing, but ultimately soaring tribute to Coach Ed Thomas. "Maura came to Parkersburg — so very different from New York City — and just absolutely loved being in small town Iowa," said Aaron Thomas. "She attended a track meet, and then really dug into my dad's story with her vision of how to best tell it in the 10-minute video that was later shown at the ESPYS."

Maura's hands — and compassionate touch — helped shape the path of the ESPYS; her handprints were on each and every element of the production.

"Maura Mandt was a 'winner' through her determination," former ESPN president John Skipper told us. "She had a goal and would do whatever it took to make the ESPYS special every year."

She always succeeded, too.

"There is one word that best describes Maura Mandt: relentless," said Connor Schell, the former ESPN executive and producer of the acclaimed *30 for 30* documentary series. "She was someone who didn't stop and it was always in pursuit of making whatever it was she was working on better. ... Her interests were never compromised. They were always, 'How do we make this one story inspirational? How do we make this one moment more powerful? How do we deliver something that no one's ever seen before? How do we raise more money for The V Foundation?' ... Maura was really one of a kind."

So are the ESPYS.

That's because great storytelling drives every facet of the production. That's what Maura wanted and demanded. That's how they will hopefully continue as both a tribute to her and everyone who's been honored — in both triumph and tragedy — over the years.

The ESPYS also play a vital role in supporting ESPN's partnership with The V Foundation. John Skipper said, "Through the lasting words of Jim Valvano, Robin Roberts, Stuart Scott and so many others, the ESPYS have always provided a wonderfully inspirational forum. In turn, they have a lasting impact by strongly supporting The V Foundation and the critical fight against cancer."

So while the ESPYS recognizes winners, it is itself a WINNER for the special way it celebrates the emotional connection fans have to their favorite sports, players and teams — all the while raising funds for The V Foundation to help support the best and latest cancer research.

Jim Valvano would no doubt be proud of how this connection between the ESPYS, ESPN and The V Foundation has grown since 1993, and the manner in which the related efforts have led to breakthroughs and discoveries. But Jimmy would be the first to point out that the game is far from over. There's still a lot of time remaining on the clock, and much work remains to be done before a final victory over cancer can be declared.

PRINCIPAL
CHARITY CLASSIC

"He's the incurable optimist. She ruins your morning. He lights up a room. She burns a hole in your wallet. He makes you want to seize the day. She makes you want to seize a 7-iron and toss it straight into the nearest lake. It's an odd marriage, this union between Michael J. Fox and the game of golf. He's a walking inspiration; she's a succubus with sand traps. And yet, somehow, it works."

Sean Keeler, writing about Michael J. Fox and his golf
game following play at the Principal Charity Classic in
The Des Moines Register (May 28, 2009)

Rob Lowe has often been cast by Hollywood as a heartthrob. Occasionally, he's a villain. His enduring acting career has garnered many accolades and earned him numerous awards.

But when inviting Rob to be my first "special guest celebrity" golfer at the Principal Charity Classic (PCC), I had no idea he would stroke, er stoke, a bit of controversy during his round at Glen Oaks Country Club in West Des Moines.

"Rob Lowe got himself a birdie," sports columnist Sean Keeler wrote in *The Des Moines Register* in 2007. "Unfortunately, it was a goldfinch, and it wasn't moving. On the par-4 fourth hole at Glen Oaks Country Club, Lowe's approach accidentally struck what appeared to be a young goldfinch in mid-flight. The murder weapon? A sand wedge."

Now, the goldfinch is a beautiful bird. It's Iowa's state bird. And while the demise of one of these glorious creatures is indeed very sad, the good news is the population is nonetheless thriving — and despite Rob's accidental strike against one of the species, this PGA Tour Champions event is thriving as well and has become a key driver for charitable causes in Iowa and beyond.

"The Principal Charity Classic is truly a global event," said Dan Houston, chairman, president and CEO of Principal Financial Group. "We have golfers from all over the world that compete. We have clients and guests that come from all over the world, and so for Des Moines and central Iowa, it's a great calling card to say, 'Doing more business in Des Moines should be top of mind.' So that's certainly one benefit, but this is the most important one: $30 million raised for children's charities since 2007, impacting 130,000 young people every year. You'd be hard pressed to find another PGA Tour Champions event that is more impactful in the community. There are other tournaments with a bigger purse, but in terms of driving meaningful results for children's charities, ours is one of the best."

It's *the* best, in my humble opinion.

Many of the PGA Tour's biggest names went on to play on the Champions Tour: Jack Nicklaus, Arnold Palmer, Lee Trevino, Gary Player, Fred Couples, Tom Watson, Jay Haas, Tom Kite, Craig Stadler, Davis Love III, Tom Lehman, Hale Irwin, Frank "Fuzzy" Zoeller, Bernhard Langer and many other legends.

Since 2007, the tour stop in Des Moines has been fortunate to have the Principal Financial Group as its title sponsor, and Wells Fargo as the presenting sponsor. It was my great privilege to serve on the PCC executive board from 2008 to 2014, and work alongside Principal executives and community leaders like Barry Griswell, Larry Zimpleman and Mary O'Keefe. My primary assignment was to arrange for the participation of celebrities in the PCC Pro-Am event that always precedes the 54-hole professional tournament.

Here's a list of a few of these celebrities along with a little background on their appearances:

2007 – Rob Lowe. Rob had a recurring role on the ABC hit drama *Brothers & Sisters* during the 2006-07 television season. Steve McPherson, the then-president of ABC Entertainment, happened to mention to me on a call that he was about to sign Rob to a deal making him a primary *Brothers & Sisters* cast member. I only half-jokingly suggested to Steve that he make any deal contingent on Rob agreeing to play golf in the PCC Pro-Am. Believe it or not, that actually worked!

The amazing Rob Lowe/goldfinch story deserves one final footnote. Principal Financial Group is a company that employs many capable actuaries. So it was not a surprise when someone asked what the odds were of Lowe actually hitting a goldfinch with a golf ball. Remarkably, it was determined that the odds were substantially greater than him getting hit by lightning, becoming a saint or even being elected president. "It turns out there's roughly a 1 in 240 million chance of this happening with all factors taken into consideration," said Ellen Lamale, chief actuary at Principal. "Even with the odds in his favor, it looks like our feathered friend was really just a sitting duck."

2008 – Jason Taylor. While playing defensive end for the Miami Dolphins, Jason Taylor was a six-time Pro Bowl selection and NFL Defensive Player of the Year in 2006. More impressively, Jason was honored with the Walter Payton Man of the Year Award in 2007, an honor recognizing both on-field achievements and off-the-field contributions.

Upon learning that Jason would join the season six cast of *Dancing With the Stars (DWTS)* in March 2008, I immediately extended an invitation for him to play in that year's PCC Pro-Am. What neither of us anticipated is that he and his partner, Edyta Sliwinska, would advance to the competition's finals! Further complicating matters was the fact that the Dolphins had a new man in charge: Bill Parcells.

According to published reports at the time, Coach Parcells was upset that his star defensive player was missing OTA's (organized team activities) because of the *DWTS* commitment. The notion that Jason would be stopping in Des Moines to play golf en route to his home in Miami only added to Parcells' anger. While feeling enormous pressure to cancel his PCC appearance, Jason honored the commitment he had made several months earlier. It meant arranging for Jason and his family, a nanny, and the family dog to fly via a private jet from Los Angeles to Des Moines and then on to Miami following his round, but it all worked out! The guy who helped make it happen was Gary Wichard, a well-known sports agent who served as the inspiration for the movie *Jerry Maguire*. Sadly, Gary died less than three years later after a year-long battle with pancreatic cancer.

Jason Taylor was inducted into the Pro Football Hall of Fame in August 2017.

2009 – Michael J. Fox. Several big names had committed to playing in that year's Pro-Am, only to back out for a variety of reasons. It's worth noting that no celebrity has ever been paid an appearance fee of any kind by the PCC, but such an arrangement "qualifies" their participation in a way that can often result in a late scratch. That was the case in 2009 as we found ourselves scrambling to find a last-minute celebrity participant.

Michael J. Fox was about to release his new book, *Always Looking Up: The Adventures of an Incurable Optimist*, and it was being published by Hyperion Books. ABC and Hyperion, both divisions of The Walt Disney Company at the time, worked in tandem to produce a May "sweeps" primetime special with the same title. It was a wonderful program and included a feature segment with Michael and actor/comedian Bill Murray playing golf together. Bingo! I had met Michael on a couple of occasions during the time his hit show *Spin City* was on ABC. Less than 24 hours after the special had aired, Michael agreed to be our special guest celebrity at the PCC draw party and Pro-Am.

Michael has talked about how his friend, Clark Gregg (from the *Avengers* television and movie franchise), describes him while teeing off: "He says 'You look like you're between two subway cars with a foot on each platform.' He then says, 'And you hit the ball 220 yards, and I don't know how you do it.'" However he looks playing it, Michael loves the game of golf.

Amazingly, Michael never took up the sport until after being diagnosed with Parkinson's disease. When announcing his appearance, the PCC said in a release, "Actor Michael J. Fox will be in West Des Moines to golf in the Principal Charity Classic Pro-Am. (He) is an inspiration to millions of people around the world. His optimism, generosity and dedication to helping others demonstrate the spirit of The Principal Charity Classic."

2010 – Teri Hatcher. Michael J. Fox is a tough act to follow, but Teri was more than up to the challenge. I had met the *Desperate Housewives* star in 2006 at an ABC Upfront in New York City, then again the following year at the Television Critics Association's Summer Press Tour in Los Angeles.

It was at a poolside reception at the Hollywood Roosevelt Hotel in 2010 where I was able to coax her into making a PCC appearance. At the Pro-Am Draw Party the night before she played, Teri graciously offered to contribute an item to the benefit auction. It consisted of her hosting a private dinner for up to eight guests at Napa Rose, her favorite restaurant, which is located at the Grand Californian Hotel in Disneyland. The winning bid was nearly $20,000 with all the proceeds going to support the PCC's charities. Teri was a truly great sport.

2011 – John Buccigross. As noted earlier, buttoning up celebrity commitments at the 11th hour was the norm but this year topped them all. Michael J. Fox had such a great time in 2009 that he looked forward to making a return visit. It was just too easy, or so we thought. I received an unexpected phone call on Memorial Day, just one night before the draw party, and learned that Michael was experiencing serious back problems. A plane trip in light of his condition was problematic enough, but any thought of a golf game was now entirely out of the question.

I immediately reached out to my good friend at ESPN, George Bodenheimer. In the span of an hour, we had worked out the details for John Buccigross, an ESPN *SportsCenter* anchor and avid golfer with a single-digit handicap, to pinch hit for Michael.

Buccigross is a world-class guy who made a great impression during his stay. He has gone on to become somewhat of a legend among professional and college hockey fans for his hosting of the Buccigross #overtimechallenge on Twitter.

It was fun to welcome Bucci back to Iowa in June 2019 when he played as my partner in the Des Moines Golf and Country Club's annual member/guest tournament.

2012 – Chris Harrison. As the longtime host of *The Bachelor* franchise on ABC, Chris was someone that I'd crossed paths with regularly at affiliate meetings, the ESPYS Golf Classic and other events over the years. We had extended invitations to him on several occasions to play in the PCC Pro-Am. This was the year we made it happen! Chris had an enjoyable time playing even though his round was frequently interrupted by young ladies holding flowers and asking, "Chris, will you accept this rose?"

An important lesson addressed in the next chapter of this book — one that's illustrated by the generosity of celebrities like those named above — is about the importance of giving back to others. "One of the themes you notice with 'winners' is they associate with other 'winners' who are doing good things," said David Stark, the CEO at UnityPoint Health-Des Moines and PCC board member. "They also recognize how they can do even bigger and better things by working together."

The PCC has now awarded more than $30 million to deserving tournament charity partners since 2007. They include these four outstanding organizations — WINNERS all — which are dedicated to serving children in the community:

- Blank Children's Hospital
- MercyOne Des Moines
- United Way of Central Iowa
- Variety - the Children's Charity of Iowa

The Principal Charity Classic is a WINNER for the way it succeeds in its mission to raise dollars for local children's charities. That has never been more evident than it was in 2020 when, despite the event being canceled due to COVID-19, a record $6.7 million was raised in support of Iowa kids.

"The dollar amount is impressive and reflects the generosity of our community during a difficult time," said Nick Cecere, senior vice president of Principal Financial Group and chairman of the PCC board of directors. "More than 95% of our sponsors, ticket holders and volunteers chose to donate to this year's event or allocate their donation to next year's tournament. That is an incredible testament to our collective resilience, and it makes a huge difference in the lives of Iowa children."

"We pivoted several times, but never lost focus on the tournament's purpose," added tournament director Douglas K. Habgood. "To give back to Iowa kids at this level during a time like this is remarkable."

The 2020 tournament trophy — which would typically be engraved with the name of the year's golf champion — appropriately bears the name "Iowa Children" as the winner in what was an unprecedented year.

VARIETY - THE CHILDREN'S CHARITY OF IOWA

*"I see Variety associates and friends from all around
the world and they ask, 'How in the world do you
generate $4 million or more a year?' Well, it goes
back to the people of Iowa ... they just care about
our state, they care about our communities and,
most of all, they really care about our kids. And they
are very philanthropic by nature."*

Sheri McMichael, executive director of
Variety - the Children's Charity of Iowa

Sheri McMichael calls herself "a hugger."

It's an admirable trait for anyone to have, but especially for the
executive director of Variety - the Children's Charity of Iowa.

"We encounter difficult situations that absolutely break your
heart," McMichael told us as the charitable organization was revamping
fundraising plans because of the COVID-19 pandemic. "(With) those
kids, there are two things that are our first priority: love and structure.
When you see these kids and know they don't have the structure and
don't get love, you immediately notice it. They'll often ask before they

leave if they can have a hug. So we know that we've given them a bright spot in their day."

Hugs, of course, were mostly put on hold while COVID-19 infections spiked across the U.S. and across the world. That compassionate touch — so vital, particularly for children — had to be conveyed in less conventional ways, and Variety maintained its laser-like focus on its mission to improve the lives of young people with physical or mental disabilities, or difficult family situations.

"There are a number of reasons why the Variety organization here in Iowa has been as successful as we've been," Sheri told us. "It starts with the foundation of the four guys who said, 'We're going to do a telethon … We're just going to do it and see if it works.' With their tenacity, they raised $150,000 the first year. The second thing is the ability for Variety to keep the money raised here in our communities.

"The dollars benefit children in our communities, and help make Iowa the best possible place it can be for our kids. The citizens of our state know that we are putting the money where our mouths are. We put resources back in the community and operate with very low administrative costs. And finally, I'd say it is about who Iowans are. They just really care about our state, care about our communities and are very philanthropic by nature."

Originally called The Variety Club, this organization founded an Iowa chapter in 1937. It yielded less than impressive results until the quartet of Stanley Reynolds, Ray Johnson, Mike Reilly and Steven Blank (those "four guys" Sheri mentioned earlier) founded the annual telethon in 1975. Since then, Variety - the Children's Charity of Iowa has raised more than $113 million, positively impacting organizations serving children in each of Iowa's 99 counties.

WOI-TV (ABC5) has always served as the home of the telethon production and broadcast. Our company acquired WOI-TV in March, 1994 just one week prior to that year's telethon. My very first meeting following the closing with the station's prior owner, Iowa State University, was held over lunch with Stanley Reynolds and Ray Johnson. Their dedication to the telethon and Iowa's children was undeniable, and we quickly reaffirmed our commitment to remain the telethon's home. In fact, we expanded the carriage of the telethon to include our stations in the Quad Cities (WHBF-TV) and Sioux City (KCAU-TV) the very next year. My wife, Susan, and I were especially proud to serve as honorary telethon chairs in 2012.

While the telethon is the organization's largest and most visible fundraiser, Variety hosts a number of other events throughout the year: Black Tie Gala, Sweetheart Charity Date Auction, Mommy & Me: Sweetheart Dance, Spirits of Spring, Savor Des Moines, the Miller Lite and Leinenkugel Golf Invitationals, Polo on the Green and the Two Days of Compassion Radiothon to name a few. The funds raised are used to support Variety's mission: improving the lives of children who are at-risk, underprivileged, critically ill or living with special needs. The challenge of this mission is met head-on through many different and valuable programs.

The statewide grant program funds nonprofit children's organizations that provide essential medical equipment for infants and children of all ages, and programming that helps children make positive choices. Another core program is the Compassion Fund, which provides much-needed financial assistance to families when a child is hospitalized.

"We've had a relationship with Variety at Blank Children's Hospital for 40 years," said David Stark, UnityPoint Health's chief executive officer. "Very few organizations can say they've had, from a charitable standpoint, such a deep connection with an organization for that period of time. Blank Children's was the recipient of the very first telethon dollars, which is unbelievable. There is literally not an area or department at Blank that hasn't been impacted by Variety during that period. It could be the emergency department, intensive care unit, nursery, therapy or developmental clinic. We're treating patients from all over Iowa — from every county — so Variety has truly had a statewide impact."

The organization is also well known for its Variety vans that transport children to activities, playgrounds and recreational opportunities. The very popular Kids on the Go program is all about mobility in the form of bicycles, helmets and locks given to children who might not otherwise own a bike. Variety even gives specialized bikes to children with special needs and recently expanded this program to include gait trainers, standers, strollers and specialized car seats to enable more children to experience the freedom to explore, engage and play.

One of Variety's more recent initiatives involves the building of Star Playgrounds in communities throughout the state so that children with special needs will have a greater opportunity to climb, roll, swing and laugh!

Variety Iowa is a recognized leader within the Variety International network compromising 44 offices in 13 countries. Three past presidents of Variety Iowa have gone on to serve with distinction as international presidents: Stanley J. Reynolds (1989–1991), Mike Reilly (1995–1997) and Jody Reynolds (2001–2003).

Stanley and Jody Reynolds, in particular, were the heart and soul of Variety Iowa. It was many years ago when their third child, Brigid, died at an early age from complications developed at birth. Jody told Stanley on the drive back from the funeral, "We are going to make her life count." The two of them devoted themselves from that day forward to serving children across Iowa and around the world.

Variety held a "Roast & Toast" in November 2013 to honor Stanley's 40 years of dedicated service to Iowa's children. In keeping with the spirit of the evening, it was a real pleasure for me to join other presenters in poking a little fun at Stanley. I started off with an old Winston Churchill line about the "modest little man with much to be modest about!" I later made reference to the fact that "many within the Variety family consider Stanley to be an institution; the rest of us think he belongs in one." But I concluded my remarks on a more serious and sincere note, borrowing heavily from a poem by Ralph Waldo Emerson: "To laugh often and much; to win the respect of intelligent people and affection of children; to appreciate beauty; to find the best in others; to leave the world a better place — and to know even one life has breathed easier because you have lived. This is to have succeeded." Every word of that verse was applicable to Stanley and Jody Reynolds.

Jody was immensely successful in her own right, and she contributed mightily to the Variety mission until her passing in June 2019. Notably, Jody was the first female president of both Variety - the Children's Charity of Iowa and Variety International. It was my privilege to give the opening address at Variety's North American Region Conference in October 2018 where Jody was deeply engaged, as always, and in the audience flashing the patented smile she was known for.

Variety is a WINNER for the countless ways in which it serves thousands of children across Iowa, helping them to fully share in the experiences of life — no matter the challenges — and encouraging them to reach their full potential.

THE V
FOUNDATION

"I was in the third row for Jimmy V's famous ESPYS speech on March 4, 1993. Everyone there that night saw his bravery and his courage. It was massive as Dick Vitale and Coach K had to help him to just get up out of his seat and on to that stage. Everybody, from the second he started walking up there, was sobbing knowing what he was giving to us in that moment."

Lesley Visser, 2020 Sports Emmy Lifetime Achievement
Award honoree and board member for The V Foundation

If he trembled, no one noticed.

If his voice cracked, no one cared.

If his strength seemed to be flagging, no one would have guessed it.

The late, great Jim Valvano's signature "Don't give up, don't ever give up" speech that helped usher The V Foundation into existence during the ESPYS on March 4, 1993, was a triumph in every sense of the word.

Jimmy was dying of cancer. He was both accepting of and driven by that immutable fact. He was fully determined to make a lasting difference in this world and fully delivered — both onstage that night and in perpetuity.

"I've seen the speech so many times that I have a lot of it memorized," said award-winning broadcaster Sean McDonough, who covered Valvano as a college coach and worked alongside him calling games for ESPN. "If I were listing the greatest speeches I've seen or heard, that would be No. 1 for me … particularly (given) how sick he was. If you just watched the tape and didn't see him being helped on and off the stage, or just saw him standing there at the podium, you wouldn't have any idea how sick he truly was. There was a lot of question by the people who were around him that night if he would even be able to make it down to the ballroom. So to me, that part of it was almost unbelievable, too. I watch it every year when the events for The V Foundation take place during 'V Week' on ESPN. They always play the speech and I'm glued to it every time."

Moved, too. Who could possibly remain stoic when listening to Jimmy's well-crafted and poignant words aimed to uplift everyone within earshot — or anyone who could listen and watch later — even as his own battle with cancer neared the end? His speech eclipses the term "iconic" and perfectly describes the ongoing work of The V Foundation, which has expanded into an organization that has awarded more than $260 million in cancer research grants since 1994.

They never, ever give up, just as Jimmy declared plaintively, while exhorting others to join the fight.

"The thread that pulls it all together is hope," said Susan Braun, who served as The V Foundation's chief executive officer from 2012 until her retirement in January 2021. "We see hope express itself in different ways in the work we do. Sometimes the hope is for a cure. Sometimes the hope is in the form of a new research finding that is stunning and we're seeing more and more of those. So hope can mean different things to different people, but what ties together the most beautiful and triumphant with the darkest and most tragic is hope. We strive to grow hope as much as we possibly can."

Action springs from that kind of hope. Struggling people draw strength from it.

Dick Vitale, ESPN's Hall of Fame basketball analyst, confirmed what Sean McDonough had told us earlier: that his close friend, Jimmy, could barely muster the strength to make it to the stage to accept the Arthur Ashe Courage Award that night at the inaugural ESPYS. But make it he did, and the powerful speech that followed began with him saying, "I'm going to speak longer than anyone else has spoken tonight. That's the way it goes. Time is very precious to me. I don't know how much I have left and I have some things that I would like to say." The words spoken in the next 11 minutes contained powerful lessons on how to live a full life: "If you laugh, you think and you cry, that's a full day. That's a heck of a day. You do that seven days a week, you're going to have something special."

It was during that same speech that Jimmy V — with the full support and backing of ESPN's then-president and CEO Steve Bornstein and the entire ESPN family — announced the creation of The V Foundation for Cancer Research. He dreamed of finding a cure for cancer and wanted to ensure that his fight, and the fight of so many others, would lead to victory. Although Jimmy lost his battle with metastatic adenocarcinoma less than two months after delivering his now-famous ESPYS speech, his dream to find a cure for an "incurable" disease lives on through cancer research grants made possible by The V Foundation.

"As someone who lost both his parents to cancer, I certainly understand the importance of, and have a great respect for, the research," said Rece Davis, ESPN *College GameDay* host. "I've seen it touch so many people, and so many of my colleagues during my 25 years at ESPN, and to see how dedicated people are is pretty amazing."

Jimmy V's message remains as strong as ever. His mission has only gathered steam since his death. His speech may be one of the greatest ever delivered, but its impact continues to grow as time marches on.

Lesley Visser, one of the most respected and accomplished sports journalists of our time, will never forget the words she heard from her seat in the third row. "At our (V Foundation) board meetings, we still play that speech decades later … and four times a year you sit there and you cry. I think it is Churchillian. I think it's one of the greatest speeches in the history of America."

Indeed it is. Jimmy's eloquence and earnestness merged so beautifully on that celebratory stage.

"Jimmy V's famous ESPYS speech touched all the bases," said Vitale, who has made it his life's work to raise money for pediatric cancer research. "It touched on dealing with tough times. The fight. The smile. To extend a helping hand. I mean, his great words about how things in life should move you to tears, move you to laughter and move you to thought were precious. If you do those things every day, as Jimmy said, you're going to have a full, full life. I believe in that timeless message, and I believe his speech will go on forever and ever."

And so it does. The V Foundation's mission remains the same: Make cancer a curable disease, at whatever cost, no matter how much sweat equity and fundraising it takes. As an organization, it is unwavering in that pursuit — just as Jimmy was, whether crying, laughing or sitting quietly in thought. Power resides in all of those places. He tapped into it — and we can, too.

"One of the things I've learned along the way is that whenever you go to one of their events or you're watching on TV and donate, all of those dollars go to cancer research and programs," Sean McDonough said. "I didn't always know this, but all the administrative expenses are covered by an endowment. That's an awesome thing, because sometimes with charities you wonder … (and you) ask yourself, 'How many cents on the dollar are going to pay the people running this and how many actually get to the reason why I'm giving the money?' I don't know if that's unique to The V Foundation, but I think it's something that certainly makes it special among many other things."

These "things" are too numerous to fully convey with mere words on a page. But what Jimmy did on March 4, 1993, ignited a movement. It's part of ESPN's culture and an achievement that if he were alive today, would likely have exceeded his expectations.

That's because of him. And us. And everyone who's chosen to support The V Foundation, including other prominent ESPN figures who were also lost far too soon.

Twenty-one years after Jimmy's venerable speech touched so many hearts and minds, ESPN *SportsCenter* anchor Stuart Scott spoke at the ESPYS on July 16, 2014. Stuart — who had been dealing with cancer for several years — rose to receive the Jimmy V Award for Perseverance. Stuart, like Jimmy roughly two decades earlier, would inspire many with his rousing and heartfelt speech on the same stage. He died the following January, but lifted Jimmy V's legacy to another level, along with his own.

"He walked up to that podium like nothing was wrong, gave a great speech, and then went backstage and collapsed," former ESPN president John Skipper told us. "Stuart was a fellow North Carolinian and Tar Heel, so we were quite close. I remember going to see him one night on the late *SportsCenter*. During the commercial break, he put his head down in his hands and you could see him trembling. I said to him, 'Why don't you do less shows?' And he replied, 'Every time I come on, it gives purpose to my life.' As I think back, I think what he was saying was, 'It's a victory for me every time I come on and do my job.' Like Jimmy V, he found a way to win."

That's what "winners" do. They also bring others along for the ride. It's never easy — and at times can be excruciatingly hard — but hope is the spark, and empathy stokes the flame.

It's easy to wonder what Jimmy would think about that spark continuing to glow in his name. "He would be overwhelmed with joy," said Chris Berman, the renowned ESPN sportscaster, with an air of confidence. "He would be overwhelmed with a sense of accomplishment at the work that everyone's doing, whether they be the doctors, the scientists doing experimental research or those helping families who have someone going through a fight and in need of caregiving. Jimmy would be so overwhelmed by the success of The V Foundation from what it set out to be. He'd say, 'This is in my name? We did this?' That would be Jimmy V."

His humility and passion made that possible.

"For us, the legacy is not going to be cutting down the nets after winning a national title," Dick Vitale added. "Instead, it's about raising over $260 million to fund research into every form of cancer. It's very gratifying to bring somebody an opportunity to survive and move on with their lives through research."

It was an honor for me to host Jim Valvano at the Sertoma sports banquet in Sioux City, Iowa, in April 1991 where he was the keynote speaker. I occasionally stayed in touch with him over the next two years prior to his death. He loved to quote Ralph Waldo Emerson, and did so in that 1991 speech: "Enthusiasm is one of the most powerful engines of success. When you do a thing, do it with all your might. Put your whole soul into it. Nothing great was ever achieved without enthusiasm."

But it was another quote attributed to Emerson that came to mind upon hearing the sad news that Jim Valvano had passed: "A hero is no braver than an ordinary man, but he is brave five minutes longer." Facing his own mortality, Jimmy V somehow found the bravery that was needed to take the stage for that one last and most memorable speech. In doing so, he captured hearts and minds everywhere. The enduring themes from that night continue to inspire, and they have changed the lives of thousands. It concluded with Jimmy telling the audience, "Cancer can take away all my physical abilities. It cannot touch my mind, it cannot touch my heart and it cannot touch my soul. And these three things are going to carry on forever."

The V Foundation is a WINNER for ensuring that Jimmy V's legacy — like his mind, his heart and his soul — truly carries on forever. Robin Roberts said it best: "Jimmy V's legacy is the passion with which he lived his life; the passion which we all now have with this foundation. And just like him, we're not going to give up. We're not going to ever give up until we find a cure."

7.
LESSONS LEARNED

> *"The best classroom in the world is at the feet of an elderly person."*
>
> _____
>
> Andy Rooney, the whimsical contributor to
> CBS-TV's *60 Minutes*

Andy Rooney was well-known for the wit and satirical insights he shared during his end-of-show segments on *60 Minutes* from 1978 to 2011. His advice on the knowledge that can be gleaned from our elders is simple yet profound. In a similar way, some of the best lessons about "winning" can be found in the words of those with wisdom and life experiences to share.

Lesley Visser, a member of the National Sportscasters and Sportswriters Association's Hall of Fame, shared with us what she considers to be the three essential elements to succeeding in business generally and broadcasting specifically: "You need knowledge, passion and stamina. Knowledge is unassailable; passion is what keeps you in it; and stamina because you are going to get knocked down."

That's a good start. But I've compiled a much longer and more diverse list of "winning" elements, representing some of the reflected thoughts and sage advice of folks who've walked the walk. As you read through them, you will discover that "winning" is less about trying to figure out what your limits are and more about realizing you have none.

BUILDING CHARACTER

Suku Radia: "The most critical trait of all is the most important nine-letter word in the English language: integrity. If you don't have integrity, you got nothing."

Ted Koppel: "There's harmony and inner peace to be found in following a moral compass that points in the same direction regardless of fashion or trend."

Paul Rhoads: "Treating people right, reflecting good values and having a kind heart are big — those are the keys."

Jeremy Schaap: "Being a 'winner' starts with integrity, fairness and caring."

Gary Thompson: "Having respect at all times for who you compete against is important. Yes, we compete and winning is the name of the game. But you have to do it in the right way. This beneficial trait from the sports angle carries over into your business. If you're honest and respectful, you have a far greater chance of being successful."

Rich Waller: "Integrity is the bedrock. Do things right and do them right the first time. And do what you say you're going to do."

Bill Knapp: "My father told me, 'You keep your word if it takes your hide, hair and everything that you have.' And so I've always had this deep sense of trying to be honest and faithful. You've got to give your word and you've got to keep your word. … What I've learned in life is that if you keep your word, you don't have to be perfect. You don't have to worry because you know what you stand up for and what you believe in. You can always just be yourself and answer in the way you think is best and reflects the way you want to live."

Gerry Matalon: "'Winners' treat ordinary people extraordinarily and they treat extraordinary people in an ordinary way."

BEING MOTIVATED AND CONFIDENT

John Buccigross: "I think the most important word to go along with 'winner' is motivation. It's almost innate that 'winners' motivate themselves because they're ultra-competitors. Those go hand-in-hand — a competitor and a self-motivator — almost 100 percent of the time. ... There can be different ways to describe a 'winner' but really it just comes down to self-motivation and competitiveness."

Bob Bowlsby: "My high school wrestling coach was Bob Siddens. He had lots of 'Siddensisms' and one of them was, 'Don't ever take a back seat to the other guy.' What that meant was you can go out there and compete and never, ever convince yourself you can't. That's applicable to an awful lot of circumstances in life. I've had the opportunity to compete against people and negotiate against people, and I often recall my former coach saying, 'Don't take a back seat to them.'"

ACCEPTING FAILURE AND EMBRACING ADVERSITY

Bob Iger: "Of all the lessons I learned in my first year running primetime at ABC, the acceptance that creativity isn't a science was the most profound. I became comfortable with failure — not with lack of effort, but with the fact that if you want innovation, you need to grant permission to fail." (From his book, *The Ride of a Lifetime*)

George Bodenheimer: "Failure is a part of winning, and it's a big part. One of my mentors, Tom Murphy, who once ran Cap Cities/ABC, used to say, 'It's okay to make a mistake, so long as it's an honest mistake.' I've lived by that. I've used that line. I've even suggested to people that if you're not trying and swinging for the fences, then you're not doing enough!"

Ben Pyne: "I have a story about George Bodenheimer that may well be the most illustrative of his unique leadership style. At an ESPN strategic planning meeting one day, he played two videos for the assembled group of employees. George showed the first one which highlighted all the successes of the prior year, and then he presented the second one showing all the failures. The room was understandably quiet until George said, 'I am as proud, if not more proud, of the second video with all the failures because at least we tried and we learned.' My God, who does that? Only a very bold and confident leader."

Rece Davis: "There was a mindset that permeated George Bodenheimer's tenure (at ESPN) and still continues to this day. Nobody likes it when you fail, or when you try something and it doesn't work. But there has been a culture at our place that you aren't going to get absolutely shredded if there is a failure. I'm talking about if you have an idea and try to execute a plan to the very best of your ability, and it doesn't work. That happens. Nobody bats a thousand. At our place, those losses are seen as opportunities to learn from. And because of that, I think there's always been a mindset wherein you have the freedom to stretch. That's the only way you're going to achieve a higher level of greatness because if you are complacent — if you don't try to stretch — sooner or later you're going to be passed by as a direct result of that complacency. The failures in many ways are almost necessary in order to achieve the growth that you want. That's been a strong suit and hallmark of ESPN during my 25 years here."

Dan Houston: "I know it sounds cliché when people say, 'No one's ever been successful without making some mistakes.' They might cite Thomas Edison's line, 'I didn't fail 199 times, it just didn't work 199 times.' I would say this: If you make the same mistake over and over, then there might be a serious problem. But otherwise, I think experimentation and openness to new ideas are critical."

Dr. Mehmet Oz: "There's a reason why I often let my kids fail. If you never fail, you will never try as hard as you can. And how are you ever going to know how good you are if you don't fail once in a while? In order to win you have to experience failure along the way."

Daphne Oz: "My dad was very early to the idea of us kids going out and not just failing, but failing often. He's a big sports analogy guy and tried them all out on us to varying degrees of success. One of his favorites was, 'You can't catch the ball if you're not standing on the field.' I don't think my dad ever wanted us to just throw stuff at the wall and see what stuck, but rather to be meditative and precise. I mean, he's a surgeon and his world is very precise. I think in his mind failure would have been never trying, and not about trying and failing."

Jamie Pollard: "Many times with challenges it's not only about who can navigate them, but who can navigate them most efficiently. It's who has the wherewithal, the resiliency, the relentlessness and/or the courage to continue to push. To push when others may be tired or they've given up because they can't see the end. It's not unlike running a marathon. Even the greatest runners will tell you that in their best races there were moments when they thought things were blowing up or going awry. And then, maybe two miles later, they were feeling awesome. It's often about who can push through those moments of adversity. I think that after being an athlete in a sport where I had to do that all the time, I'm just mentally prepared. I feel like I thrive in those moments, and I think that's a common trait of 'winners.'"

Ben Sherwood: "It would be naïve for anyone to believe that life is just about winning. If you pry away all of the press releases and awards and all of that, most 'winners' are people who have experienced a large number of defeats and setbacks and bumps on the road. Those are often brushed aside or easily forgotten. Think, for example, about Michael Jordan, the NBA superstar, who once said: 'I've missed more than 9,000 shots in my career. I've lost almost 300 games. And 26 times, I've been trusted to take the game-winning shot and missed. I've failed over and over and over again in my life.' All too often success stories about 'winners' fail to include all of the missed shots, setbacks and defeats and yet they add so much to the richness of life. It's after you've lost — after you've gotten knocked down or your butt kicked — that's when you can learn the most and have the greatest opportunity to really, really grow."

Jake Tapper: "It's just the idea of working hard, doing your best and showing up every day. Not every pitch you have is gonna get on air. Most of them won't. Not every idea you have is gonna be embraced as a good one. (It's about) just constantly showing up and constantly putting it all out there and trying to figure out how to make it work instead of expecting people to just hand you things … and not taking rejection too seriously, taking rejection too personally, letting rejection really demoralize you — you just can't do that."

Aaron Kampman: "I think when you boil adversity down, it's a kind of binary question. Can you get yourself to a place where you can sacrifice for the higher purpose while also believing that adversity will allow you, with short term pain, to eventually experience long-term success? I remember Coach (Kirk) Ferentz and Coach (Bret) Bielema, my position coach, opening the door for me to switch positions from linebacker to defensive tackle. I said to myself, 'Hey, maybe there's something to explore here.' So anyway, I just went for it … (it was) kind of a leap of faith and it worked out really well. That was the lesson for me: Sometimes seemingly adverse situations that seem like a pain can end up providing a long-term reward."

Gerry Matalon: "I can tell you that every one of the folks that I regard as 'winners' are very human and they're vulnerable. And when they fail, they own it. I used to say, 'If you want to me impress me, show me your accolades; but if you want to impact me, show me your scars.' That's more far more relatable."

Gary Thompson: "In sports as in life, 'winning' is learning how to compete and learning how to take the good with the bad. You have some wins, and you have some big losses at times, too. The biggest thing, and something that I've tried to transfer on to my kids as they were growing up, is trying to do your best at all times. Give your best at all times whether it's in sports, business or your life."

Jay Williams: "My accident and the adversity that followed was such that I could have made the choice to let it define me or I could make the choice to say that this was a part of my journey. I'm going to use it to the best of my ability to grow. I'm going to choose to learn from it. I'm going to choose to let it build me and make me better. When those inevitable setbacks occur, it's up to us to learn from such experiences so we can find ways to navigate them differently the next time. But too often times people get fixated and become so myopic on what they may have lost, that they don't pay attention to what they could have gained."

Rich Waller: "I always had a huge passion for this: own your mistakes. As a leader, everything that happens in an organization is your responsibility. You have to own it. How you respond to those unavoidable failures will inform how your people react in the future. By accepting responsibility and not blaming others for things that go wrong, you will raise morale and engender support across the entire organization. In short, the ability to own and accept mistakes is critical to being an effective leader."

Jon Karl: "I think one of the most important attributes of a 'winner' is to learn the right lessons from loss — to rebound and improve after experiencing disappointment."

DEVELOPING A COMPETITIVE SPIRIT AND STRONG WORK ETHIC

Fred Hoiberg: "I think that everybody in the category of being a 'winner' is there because of their competitive nature. I'm very fortunate in that I was able to play basketball at the highest level for 10 years. A big part of the reason that I made it to the NBA wasn't because of my athleticism, or because I was the fastest or the highest jumper. It had more to do with my competitive nature and work ethic. At the end of the day, I think that's what everyone who is able to make it to the highest level has in common."

Jack Lashier: "Every one of the people I interviewed for the Iowa Hall of Pride— and there were like 350 — had natural gifts. They had something they could do that they were gifted with. It might have been hand-eye coordination. It might have been brains. It might have been science ability. It might have been they were physically strong. They just had these natural gifts. And then they had this crazy work ethic. Not just a moderate work ethic. They worked harder than anybody else. They just worked and worked and worked and practiced. I don't know how those things happen, but I think people are gifted in certain ways. And if they get in tune with their gifts, have this crazy work ethic and then follow through, they're going to be successful people."

John Buccigross: "You've got to be competitive and you've got to have composure. They are the first of the four 'Cs' that are so key: competitiveness keeps you from quitting; composure keeps you from losing your head; concentration gives you the focus to figure things out; and confidence — that finishes it all off."

SHOWING DETERMINATION AND GRIT

Fran Fraschilla: "Grit equals passion plus perseverance. I'm a product of grit. I had it as a coach and wanted my teams to be gritty. I've had a passion for basketball my entire life. It's taught me incredible lessons: teamwork, togetherness, sacrifice, adversity, winning and losing. How to win. How to lose. How to motivate young people by teaching them a work ethic. So I'm a product of grit and grit runs through my veins, because I was not the biggest, strongest, smartest guy on the playground. I had to do everything with passion and perseverance."

Zubin Mehenti: "At the end of the day, even though we're in the business of winning and losing, I think just finishing is super-underrated. For example, if you do something that nobody says you can do for a variety of reasons — and you do it — you kind of win. Everybody is always looking for results in our results-oriented world but finishing is a really big quality that doesn't get enough play."

Bob Bowlsby: "Wrestling in high school taught me a lot. First of all, it's lonely out there when things aren't going your way. There's nobody that's gonna help you, other than perhaps a coach from 25 feet away. The sport is built upon day after day conditioning, and it's hard to get your butt beat one night and then have to get up for a running workout early the next morning. The lessons learned were about self-reliance, resiliency, determination and perseverance."

Ray Cole: "Having grit and demonstrating perseverance is all about the hard work 'winners' do after they're exhausted from doing the hard work they already did."

SEEKING OUT MENTORS

George Bodenheimer: "Nobody does it by themselves … (don't be) toiling away and think you're going to get it figured all out by yourself. The world doesn't work that way. You must seek out and have high-quality mentors. I was fortunate to have mentors along the way, and I hope that I've been able to give back and mentor a number of people in the later years. Mentorship is very important."

Chris Fowler: "There are so many different people you come in contact with, and there are so many different qualities and characteristics of those people that you admire. I was just thinking about John Saunders the other day — posted a video about him. He was a mentor to me and I don't use that word loosely. He was older and wiser and more experienced than I was when I was coming up, and he was generous with his time with me and I learned lots of things from him. (And then there's) Lee Corso in his way — his passion for life, his passion for his job in this world of football. So it's just being around people who care a lot about people, and who have a passion for life and for teaching. They understand that you never stop growing, you never stop improving, you never stop trying to make yourself more whole."

Dan Houston: "I just fundamentally believe you don't go anywhere in life without an incredibly supportive network of personal and professional advisors. End of statement. And then I think to the extent that you never forget where you came from comes the social task of what do you do for the community, and what do you do for mentoring others."

Anne Sweeney: "The first really important moment of leadership that I observed was with Joan Ganz Cooney, who led the Children's Television Workshop (now Sesame Workshop). She would stop into different offices to have conversations with her assistants. Joan had conversations with everyone. She was beautiful, immaculately dressed and so very kind … and running this very successful, very meaningful business. Joan was really my first female role model, a woman who had been part of the team that created Sesame Street. She's someone that I really held in my heart for decades as someone who did something very meaningful. Joan led in a way that was productive, not just for her viewing audience, but for all the people who worked for her."

George Stephanopoulos: "I'd have to start with my father. He really taught me the lessons about balance, connecting with the world and serving your community. I've also been blessed with fascinating, brilliant bosses from Dick Gephardt to Bill Clinton to Bob Iger. Just to have the chance to work with such people and learn from them and watch them lead, it's been an incredible education for me."

Kevin Negandhi: "It was a thrill to work with guys that I had dreamed about and emulated, like the late, great Harry Kalas. I did an internship and worked with him in the booth during Phillies games as a 19- and 20-year old. That's pretty incredible for a young man that had Harry Kalas' voice in his head while playing baseball as a kid."

Jamie Pollard: "I think who we become both professionally and personally is a reflection of those people along the way that had either intentional or unintentional influence on us. Sometimes we like to talk about the intentional ones, but sometimes it's the unintentional things where later you kind of go 'Why did I do what I did' and you reflect back. I can think of numerous people that have had such an influence on me."

BRINGING YOUR "A" GAME

Kevin Negandhi: "I've bumped into a lot of athletes who are 'winners' through the years. Wow, they bring it every day. They're prepared and they understand what's asked of them. It's always fun when you work with someone who's elevating their game, because you know that you're being elevated simply by working with them. And knowing you'd better bring your 'A' game every single day."

Daphne Oz: "Bringing it every single day? My parents, long before it was an actual thing people talked about, were big on FOMO: the 'fear of missing out.' We would go on a trip and immediately be off to the first adventure. There was no 'Let's acclimate for the day' or 'Let's get room service.' That never happened! And the terror they put in us if we bowed out of an opportunity, that we would miss out on the most incredible adventure of our lives, was so real and palpable that to this day I regret it every time I ever have to say no to something."

Jeremy Schaap: "Talent matters. And by that, I don't mean innate talent but rather working on it, trying to prove yourself while enhancing those talents. Trying to hone your talents and working on your craft. My dad (Dick Schaap) was a great writer but he rewrote everything he ever wrote. He was never satisfied with the first draft. The idea that you can always make yourself better is one shared by most people that I've been around at the top of our business. There's a certain level of anxiety about knowing you can't be comfortable. You have to have a certain amount of feeling like, 'I'm doing this for the first time.' 'Winners' find a way to get comfortable but not too comfortable."

Robin Roberts: "Every day when you go to work — if you are working on the smallest game of the week or the largest — act like it's the best day, like you wouldn't want to be anywhere else. Remember in every phase of your career, you are in that moment for a reason and you should be excited about it." (From the article "ESPN's Maria Taylor has a message for women who want to work in sports" by Brittany Loggins, Sept. 27, 2019 on nbcnews.com)

REMAINING CURIOUS

Ben Sherwood: "I've definitely done some things out of order in my career. But the first thing I've always done is follow my curiosity."

Anne Sweeney: "You must have curiosity. Because if you're not constantly asking questions or not constantly curious about how things work or how they could work differently or what you should be doing differently, you won't have growth. 'Winners' are people who continue to grow despite the odds. It's all about growth … growth that is not physical, but emotional growth, intellectual growth and spiritual growth."

Kenny Mayne: "Kids ask me about this or that when they're coming out of school, and what's the way to have the best chance of landing the opportunities they want. The first lesson I always point to is read more in order to write better. It's just a matter of widening your base. If you're into sports stuff, don't just read through sports stuff. Try to be wider than that. One day will come when you'll be in a situation and something will just click. Maybe it's because of that article or book you read, or that podcast you listened to. Be interested in more things and stay curious all the time. I think one of the greatest traits somebody can have is the desire to always learn more and not be content with reinforcing what it is they already know."

Fran Fraschilla: "Many highly successful people that I know and have been around have a growth mindset where it doesn't matter what age they are or what point they are at in their career, they are constantly trying to figure out how to get better. So to me, curiosity is a critical factor in someone's success because as they say: 'It's what you learn after you think you know it all that's really most important!'"

Connor Schell: "Curiosity is something I inherited from my dad: always asking questions and always trying to figure out how to get smarter about something while also trying to be understanding and empathetic with how other people are feeling and what they're going through, and how you can be helpful to them. These are things I try to always think about and traits that I value."

Robin Sproul: "My ultimate career path was driven by just a total, endless curiosity and a need to know. It's curiosity first, and then the absolute dedication to truth and telling people what's going on. It was special for me, throughout my career in Washington, to feel like I was part of a full system of how democracy works. To inform people about what's going on and to help put sunshine on that process was endlessly appealing. I never had a dull day in my 41 years at ABC News. Not a dull day."

Rob Mills: "Most people's so-called 'overnight success' has usually taken years. And that's most likely attributable to having developed good work habits, along with preparedness and being ready. That's really the name of the game. Every 'winner' has a different story but there's so much commonality in each and every one of them. I do think curiosity, drive, hard work, and pride are all qualities that are important to finding success and never, ever go out of style."

Jeremy Schaap: "My dad (Dick Schaap) used to say that journalism is about making connections. But to be a truly great journalist, you can't just know the world of sports. You have to know and be able to draw upon references to history, and literature, and society and politics. To really connect for your audience, you can't have a tunnel vision — you have to have a curiosity about everything."

Ray Cole: "While easily overlooked and undervalued, curiosity is a trait that 'winners' recognize as critical to their success. It can lead to new relationships, help to develop different perceptions and ideas, and serve as the basis to challenge outdated assumptions. Curiosity is oftentimes the fuel source for 'winning' decisions."

SURROUNDING YOURSELF WITH GOOD — AND SMART — PEOPLE

Bill Knapp: "Successful people understand that an 'I, me and my' approach to business — and life for that matter — accomplishes nothing. There's very little you can accomplish alone. It's essential that you hire and surround yourself with good people to help reach your goals. You can't do it on your own. It's true for almost every endeavor in life that little ever gets accomplished unless it's done with a 'we, them and us' philosophy."

Bob Iger: "When hiring, try to surround yourself with people who are 'good' in addition to being good at what they do. Genuine decency — an instinct for fairness and openness and mutual respect — is a rarer commodity in business than it should be, and you should look for it in the people you hire and nurture it in the people who work for you." (From his book, *The Ride of a Lifetime*)

Rob Lowe: "I think it was Alfred Hitchcock who said 90 percent of successful moviemaking is in the casting. The same is true in life. Who you are exposed to, who you choose to surround yourself with, is a unique variable in all our experiences and it is hugely important in making us who we are. Seek out interesting characters, tough adversaries and strong mentors and your life can be rich, textured, highly entertaining and successful, like a Best Picture winner." (From his book, *Love Life*)

Dr. Mehmet Oz: "There are many elements associated with 'winning' and pushing past boundaries. One of the reasons I went into medicine was knowing that I'd never master it. With that comes a humbleness to understanding your approach to complex issues, and a recognition that collaboration can provide an unbelievable power boost for you. Then you have to surround yourself with people you trust, and people that you can trust to challenge you and not tell you what you want to hear."

David Stark: "There are both balcony and basement people in life, and 'winners' surround themselves with the balcony people. Balcony people are those who are always pulling you upward. They're cheering you on, raising you up and supporting you. 'Winners' surround themselves with folks like that. There's too many negatives out there, too many naysayers (and if) you pay attention to them you're going to be brought down by those basement people. You need to connect with the balcony people and I think 'winners' surround themselves with those folks and even seek them out. And they are more successful because of it."

Chris Fowler: "There are so many different people you come in contact with, and there are so many different qualities and characteristics of those people that you admire. It is beneficial just being around those who, by example, share their lessons of excellence. Whether it is tennis colleagues like John McEnroe or Chrissie Evert or Darren Cahill or someone like (college football's) Kirk Herbstreit. I mean, Kirk is younger than I am but I consider him very much a peer. His day-to-day excellence, his level of preparation and unrelenting work ethic are inspiring to me. And there are lots of other people in production that you wouldn't have heard of that do their jobs to a really high standard, and it's contagious."

Rich Waller: "Throw your ego out the door and put the best and brightest beside you who are really good at those things you're not so good at. My mentor and predecessor taught me a lesson that has stuck with me forever: 'You are only as strong and successful as your weakest link.' While it may sound cold, I believed in hiring slow and firing fast. We always made sure to surround ourselves with successful people who were committed to our values."

Rusty Wallace: "We can talk about 'winning' a long time, but you're not gonna win unless you surround yourself with smart people. Surround yourself with people that believe in you, and who are smart 'been there, done that' people. My God, it sure does make life easier. Just surround yourself with passionate, smart people and you're going to be successful."

Bernie Saggau: "If you are going to be a leader, you gotta be around good people. I never hired a person that wasn't better than me. And then, all of a sudden, you watch them grow."

DISPLAYING OPTIMISM AND GRATITUDE

Ted Koppel: "Pessimists calculate the odds. Optimists believe they can overcome them."

Connor Schell: "People are drawn to others who have a smile on their face, who are optimistic and who feel good about what's going on."

Michael J. Fox: "Optimism is really rooted in gratitude. Optimism is sustainable when you keep coming back to gratitude, and what follows from that is acceptance. Accepting that this thing has happened, and you accept it for what it is. It doesn't mean that you can't endeavor to change. It doesn't mean you have to accept it as a punishment or a penance, but just put it in its proper place. Then see how much the rest of your life you have to thrive in, and then you can move on." (From an article in *People* magazine by Kate Coyne and Ally Mauch, November 2020)

Chris Fowler: "For me and for many others, it starts with gratitude. It's simply a recognition that you have a lot to be grateful for and then you make being grateful a part of your daily practice. When you're grateful, I think you can be compassionate. You can be generous with your time and energy and you can look for ways to help because you understand how much you have to be thankful for and how fortunate your position in life is. I think that's a 'winning' trait, if you want to put a label on it. One of the things that people who have been very successful — and not just successful financially but successful in terms of living a life that's worth emulating and admiring — demonstrate is that they are grateful. They understand that with gratitude comes the opportunity to give back and help others that are less fortunate ... others who need help. I just think when you operate from that place of gratitude, feelings like compassion — which lead to giving and generosity — can spring forward."

Bob Woodruff: "Gratitude ... I owe a lot to a lot of people that I could never pay back. I've gotten so much help over the years. I've given back as much as I can, but everybody is always feeling guilty about not giving back enough. So, I would never say that I'm happy about how much I'm thankful for."

Robin Roberts: "Being optimistic is like a muscle that gets stronger with use. Makes it easier when the tough times arrive. You have to change the way you think in order to change the way you feel." (From her book, *Everybody's Got Something*)

Bob Iger: "Optimism emerges from faith in yourself and in the people who work for you. It's not about saying things are good when they're not, and it's not about conveying some blind faith that 'things will work out.' It's about believing in your and others' abilities." (From his book, *The Ride of a Lifetime*)

Bob Bowlsby: "One of the things that struck me about Ray Cole was his remarkable optimism. He was always enthusiastic, and you remember people who always have a smile on their face. He benefited from a level of trust that is rare, and especially rare in a profession that has their share of snake oil salesman. He was solid and you could always take what he said to the bank."

MAINTAINING A GROWTH MINDSET

Fran Fraschilla: "I have a growth mindset in the sense that even now as someone who's been around the game for 50 years, I learn something about basketball every single week. I don't have a know-it-all mindset; I have a growth mindset. How can I get better? How can I learn this game better so that I can teach it better? How do I learn it better so I can teach it to television viewers better?"

Chris Fowler: "Being around people who care a lot about others, and who have a passion for life and for teaching … (they) understand that you never stop growing, you never stop improving, you never stop trying to make yourself more whole while helping other people in different ways."

Rob Mills: "Clichés become clichés for a reason, and there's the one about how success is where opportunity meets preparation. I think that's absolutely true. But it's also about understanding that you always have to keep learning, always have to keep evolving."

Jon Karl: "(It's about) a dedication to self-improvement. You're always trying to push yourself to do a little better than you did before."

Kevin Negandhi: "The advice that I give to every single college student I talk to is about asking questions and seeking answers. I say, 'Don't tell me you know everything or what you think I want to hear.' Many times college kids want to impress you with this is what I'm doing, and this is how I'm doing it. I think they should be saying, 'What else do I need to do? What do you think of my progress?' They're only going to continue to get better by asking the right questions."

George Bodenheimer: "If you want to 'win' and succeed you outwork your competition, whoever that might be, whether they're in your company or another company. That's No. 1. No. 2, I use the expression, 'Every day is a school day.' Never stop learning. You've got to be inquisitive. If you want to grow, you've got to take the initiative to learn and understand. So every day is a school day, and I really took that to heart and tried to constantly be learning about our business. So through hard work and learning and being able to establish relationships with people, I would say those were the keys to my being able to grow over all those years (with ESPN)."

HAVING FUN

Ray Cole: "Do you have fun because you win, or do you win because you're having fun?"

Ben Sherwood: "One of the interesting lessons about Ray is that his journey has taken him to all kinds of places, and he is a person who makes friends and expands his network everywhere he goes. Importantly, one never feels that he is a networker in the negative sense of the word. To the contrary, one feels that he is always making meaningful connections that are first and foremost about friendship — and fun! A lot of people who are networkers are all about work. They're always working, there's always an angle, and/or they're always trying to make a deal. When you get to know Ray, it's about his relationship with you, getting stuff done and having fun. I think it's another one of the secrets of a 'winning' approach to work and life."

George Stephanopoulos: "Thanks so much for being in my corner from the very start. You're a good, loyal — and fun — friend." (In an email to Ray Cole, December 2013)

Chuck Offenburger: "Let's cheer like we did in the '60s: "Yeaaaay RAH! Whole damned team!" (Frequent chant to this very day from a member of the Vanderbilt University Class of '69 and Vanderbilt Student Media Hall of Fame Class of '14 who has never lost his school spirit and youthful exuberance)

Walt Disney: "It's kind of fun to do the impossible."

DISCOVERING WHAT MATTERS AND THE RIGHT BALANCE

Ben Sherwood: "Too often 'winning' is about ratings and revenue and stock prices and accomplishments and awards and inductions into some Hall of Fame. Some of the wisdom that comes from getting knocked down and getting back up again reaffirms that 'winning' is about getting — and keeping — your priorities straight. ... It's about knowing who matters, and who doesn't; it's about knowing what matters, and what doesn't. If you're lucky enough to have a loving family and caring friends, you win."

George Stephanopoulos: "'Winning' is about the kind of fulfillment that comes with all the things I've talked about. Loving family. Good friends. Work that is important to you, and that you can do with integrity. To me, if you are pursuing all those things, and doing it with a sense of balance, that is happiness."

John McWethy: "Never confuse your career with your life." (Words spoken by the longtime ABC News correspondent in a commencement address given at his alma mater, DePauw University, in 2003)

Dr. Jerry Punch: "You find a balance in life that allows you to lay your head on the pillow at night and go to sleep without having to worry about something you've said or something you've done. It's about making 'front row' decisions. Those are decisions based on how they're going to affect the people who are going to be in the front row at your funeral — those are the people who matter. So your life should be about 'front row' decisions. If you live it that way — and you approach it that way — you'll live a very fulfilling life."

Robin Roberts: "Live your life. Let it happen. Enjoy the ride. And whatever you do, do it from the heart." (From her book, *From the Heart - Eight Rules to Live By*)

Diane Sawyer: "If you've got that intersection of your joy and the feeling it's meeting a need of the world, then you're home. That's your whole career."

GIVING BACK

Governor Robert D. Ray: "The happiest people I know are people who are doing nice things for other people."

Susan Braun: "I really do believe the many sage people who have said that what we give comes back to us a hundredfold. I truly feel as though the goodness that comes from giving always showers back on us."

John Skipper: "'Winning' companies usually have a soul. I think it's pretty easy to be a hedge fund and just make money; I think it's much harder to be a big public company that has a place in the community in the way, for example, ESPN does in Bristol. Just making money doesn't help you win. If that's the only thing you care about, you're not going to really win in a profound sense of the word."

Chris Fowler: "There is a real culture of giving back and caring at ESPN which is nice to be a part of ... to see how they embrace and give generously and support others who are doing the passionate work."

Fred Hoiberg: "I think at the end of the day, what's going to define us all is how much goodwill and good work you put back into the community. … When you look past the competition, what have you done to give back? I think that really is the true test of who you are … (to be) seen more for the work you do as a person, not as an athlete or coach."

Sean McDonough: "My primary focus now is on my own foundation which raises awareness for treatments and cures of cardiac amyloidosis. So to me, all of that is more important than anything I've ever done in front of a camera or talking into a microphone. It's about caring for other people."

Ben Pyne: "I am in the camp of people who believe in giving back and feel blessed to have been able to work with so many great people in an industry that is so interesting, diverse and exciting."

Suku Radia: "One of the attributes 'winners' have is a sincere commitment to giving back. It's about 'paying your civic rent' as I like to put it. I'm a very, very big believer in that. It's all about wanting to leave the community a better place than you found it."

Kenny Mayne: "My dad always looked after the little guy and while he wasn't rich, he did it in small ways. It's just a matter of treating the next person the right way, and not worrying about the differences between people."

Paul Rhoads: "Giving back is vital. When you put yourself in a position of success, the opportunity to give back is, first of all, fulfilling. But it can also be essential to keep your circle growing. When you get the chance to do so, it is important that you give back and keep the circle growing."

John Rouse: "Giving back — whether it's money or time or opportunity — is about remembering what others have given to you while keeping in mind that ours is a continuous journey. As you rise and lift others, you will continue to grow as well. It's important to give back in all types of ways."

George Bodenheimer: "By far, the United States is the most charitable country in the world and that's a good thing. We need to continue that, and need leaders to foster that and to keep it going. It doesn't just happen."

Bill Knapp: "It just seemed to me that in everything I wanted to do and accomplish, it was about leaving this world in a better place because I was here. I would be very disappointed in myself if I hadn't done everything I could have to make life better for others before I left."

SUMMARY

In a commencement speech he delivered at Stanford University in 2005, Steve Jobs said, "Your time is limited, so don't waste it living someone else's life. Don't be trapped by dogma — which is living with the results of other people's thinking. Don't let the noise of others' opinions drown out your own inner voice. And, most importantly, have the courage to follow your heart and intuition. They somehow already know what you truly want to become. Everything else is secondary."

Jobs was right. None of the preceding lessons and advice, shared with the best of intentions, should drown out your own inner voice and thinking. It's also important to always remain positive and resilient while following your heart and intuition.

Robin Roberts once made the salient point that your dreams may not quite look like what you thought they would — even if or when they come true. She told me, "I think about how I wanted to originally be a tennis player. That was my life, my love and I would dream about being there at Wimbledon. And I did make it to Wimbledon, but not with a tennis racket in my hand but with a microphone in my hand." Always be ready to adapt and change course when the circumstances call for it.

And finally, while doing the kid of self-reflection that's nearly unavoidable when working on a book of this nature, it occurred to me how important it is to find joy in all the moments we can during life's journey. Allow me elaborate further.

In February 2008, my wife and I had the privilege to attend the 80th Academy Awards. At the Governor's Ball afterward, Bob Iger and Anne Sweeney hosted the Disney tables with special guests Harrison Ford and

Calista Flockhart; Billy Ray, Tish and Miley Cyrus (Miley was the teen idol star of *Hannah Montana* on the Disney Channel at the time); and Kristin Chenoweth, who had performed the Oscar-nominated "That's How You Know" from *Enchanted* during the Oscars broadcast. The next morning we joined Anne, John Rouse and other ABC executives aboard one of The Walt Disney Company's private jets for a flight to New York where Anne was presented the Broadcasters Foundation of America's Golden Mike award that same night. It was an honor to join Barbara Walters, David Westin, Tom Bergeron and Vanessa Williams on the Waldorf Astoria ballroom stage as part of the award ceremony.

In July of that same year, I conducted my last meeting as chairman of the ABC Affiliates Association's board of governors prior to attending the ESPYS with my son, Brandon. And two months later, my wife and I were back in Los Angeles for the 60th Primetime Emmy Awards. The next morning we were at the El Capitan Theatre, home of *Jimmy Kimmel Live!*, for a network presentation fed via satellite to affiliates that kicked off with an opening monologue by Jimmy Kimmel himself.

There is a point to my sharing the above stroll down memory lane. It wasn't until doing some research for this book that I realized just how eventful of a year 2008 truly was. Attending the Oscars, Emmys and ESPYS in the same calendar year was a trifecta that few people ever get to experience! While it was no doubt fun, I'm not sure that I stopped to fully appreciate the collective experiences. Now, more than ever, I better understand the value of a "Live in the Moment" approach to life that avoids getting caught up in the constant drumbeat of minutiae in our day-to-day existences. In fact, I am convinced that realizing our brightest future may well rest on the ability to pay attention to the present.

With the above in mind, the final lesson is this: While we can't wait to ascend the mountain, most of the real growth, personal satisfaction, and genuine happiness occur while we are scaling our way to the top.

"Climb the mountain not to plant your flag, but to embrace the challenge, enjoy the air and behold the view. Climb it so you can see the world, not so the world can see you."

David McCullough, two-time Pulitzer Prize winner and
recipient of the Presidential Medal of Freedom

EPILOGUE
"WINNERS"

"At times our own light goes out and is rekindled by a spark from another person. Each of us has cause to think with deep gratitude of those who have lighted the flame within us."

Albert Schweitzer, humanitarian — philosopher —
1953 Nobel Peace Prize Laureate

There is little doubt that the "spark" or motivation that lead to goal-oriented success of any kind must arise from within each of us. But as Albert Schweitzer implied, learning the variety of lessons shared throughout this book and, especially, in the preceding chapter — while cultivating "winning" traits along the way — can increase the intensity and luminance of the light that guides us. I would like to share some final, insightful thoughts from a few of those who have "lighted the flame" on my journey.

Anne Sweeney shared a deeply touching story about the late Kobe Bryant. She said, "Shortly after announcing I was leaving Disney, I got an email out of the blue one day from Kobe. While I'd seen him play, we had never met. His note said, 'I read about your news, and think we find ourselves on the same emotional page. Are you free for breakfast sometime?' So I wrote him back and we later met up in El Segundo at a coffee shop near the Lakers training facility. We had a long conversation that actually started with Kobe saying to me, 'Do you ever get tired of being the most powerful woman in entertainment?' I said, 'Yes. Do you ever get tired of being legendary basketball player Kobe Bryant?' And he said, 'Yes. Because I am so much more.'"

Now, stop and think about that for a moment. Here was this 18-time NBA All-Star and five-time NBA champion conveying how, despite all his past honors and achievements, he had so much more to accomplish. There's such an important lesson in that anecdote for each and every one of us.

It was fascinating to see the different ways people described what "winning" meant to them. John Rouse told us, "Everybody has their own interpretation of what a 'winner' is. They have a strong work ethic. They're intellectually curious. They're really good listeners and effective communicators. Perhaps most of all, they have a passion for what they do. If you really like what you do, and you have a passion for it, that can only help you excel at it. And then there is what I believe is the secret ingredient: humility. Without that you might not be an effective listener or take the time to fully understand what people around you are thinking and feeling."

Jay Williams was every bit as quick to point out just how subjective the word "winner" is. He said, "It means a lot of different things to different people. What (being a) 'winner' means to you is, first and foremost, the most critical question. I don't think people actually take the time to focus on that. 'Winning' for me means that what I am doing is in the best interest of my family … it's one of those things that I think about. It's about the mindset you have. Is it the mindset to adjust? Is it the mindset to be malleable? Is it the mindset to take one experience, learn from it and let that lead you into the next (one)? What are you looking to gain from an experience? Ultimately, everybody looks at that differently."

Jay and his co-hosts on the *Keyshawn, JDub & Zubin* radio show often look at things from differing points of view. Zubin Mehenti, who once worked for me at WOI-TV in Des Moines, told us how Jay occasionally reacts with an air of contempt and disgust in his voice when athletes are unfairly called out. "We were talking about a certain athlete on our show one day and I said the guy had kind of been a bust," Zubin told us. "Jay stopped me and said, 'Hey, he's still in the top 1% of all athletes everywhere. You know that, right? Don't use that word bust around athletes.' Jay was right because guys in the NFL or NBA have beaten the odds just to get where they are. Too many times it comes down to a zero-sum game. Winner, loser. Huge success, bust. Or as Jay explained it on this occasion, you're either the GOAT (greatest of all time) or a bum." The point is that while we live in a results-oriented world, winning should never be evaluated in a simplistic, binary way. Keep your focus and ignore the noise.

Dr. Jen Ashton boldly told us that she could literally describe "winning" in a one-line quote from her brother, who is also a doctor and a former lacrosse national champion at Princeton. Comparing the first line and second line players on a hockey team, he told Jen, "Second line players will go to their coach and tell them all the things they did right in the last game; first line players will go to their coach and tell them all the things they did wrong."

Having known her for some time now, I can unequivocally state how that is precisely the approach that Dr. Ashton applies to her life. She further reaffirmed this when telling us, "I critique everything I do. With every patient encounter I have and with every line I deliver on television. I don't focus on the good things. Of course I'm happy to see them, but I fixate on the weaknesses so that I can go on a seek-and-destroy mission to improve them and make them better." Dr. Ashton was quick to add that she's always been blessed by having leaders who have made her self-critical approach a safe and productive exercise.

It was also absorbing to consider the view of Rece Davis that sometimes you have to do what's difficult or even uncomfortable in order to achieve personal or team success. "When it comes to 'winning' everybody wants the result, but not everybody wants to walk the path that leads to that result," Rece explained. "Everybody wants the reward, but not everybody is willing to alter their behavior in such a way that gives them the best chance of getting the reward. I think a characteristic that probably exemplifies what a 'winner' is more than anything else is the mindset that sometimes you have to take a path that is more difficult. Maybe inside all of us do, but it's about altering the behavior in such a way that will be most conducive to getting an outcome most favorable for you and for the entire group.

"When I think of the great leaders that I've seen in my career at ESPN, as well as the coaches and players that I have worked with who have been very successful in a variety of fields, all of them have understood that," Rece added. "All of them are driven, all of them want to accomplish (things), and there is a certain inherent selfishness in that that all of us have. But I think the best leaders understand when and how to mitigate that drive with something that will not only benefit them, but will also benefit the entire group. Oftentimes that is not the most comfortable way to proceed. It's not the most convenient way to continue on, but sometimes in order to achieve what you're after you have to do something that's inconvenient or uncomfortable for you in the moment."

I wrote in the prologue about how many of the athletes we interviewed cited the "winning" traits instilled in them by coaches. That appeared to be especially true for those who went on to pursue coaching careers of their own. Ben Jacobson, four-time Missouri Valley Conference Coach of the Year and 2010 ESPYS honoree, couldn't say enough about his college coach: "The head coach at North Dakota was a guy named Rich Glas. He had the traits that so many 'winners' have. Coach Glas worked incredibly hard in terms of preparation for practice, scouting of opponents and games. He wanted success like we all do at a high level and always prepared in a way that gave his teams the best chance to win the game, but that wasn't the most important thing to Coach Glas. What was most important to him was teaching us about the value of having a positive attitude on a daily basis; creating a culture that lent itself to fostering a basketball family; having his players grow as people and prepared for the real world; being respectful and demonstrating humility; winning with dignity and losing with class. Coach Glas was a living example of all those 'winning' traits for us."

As thoughtful as Ben Jacobson was while reflecting back on Coach Glas' influence, he was even more contemplative when talking about the "winning" qualities displayed by one of his University of Northern Iowa players throughout the 2019–20 season. It was anything but your typical anecdote about a star player or a game-winning shot for a championship. Luke McDonnell was a fifth-year senior. He had been an important role player for the Panthers in his redshirt freshman and sophomore seasons. He then moved into a starting position his junior year. Luke started every game and played better and better as the season went on. Then, with a teammate coming off a medical redshirt and with a couple talented freshmen joining the team, he found himself shuffled back on the depth chart for his senior season. Luke was no doubt disappointed, and understandably so.

"When you talk about being a 'winner' outside of the score of a basketball game, Luke was all that," Coach Jacobson said when explaining to us at some length how Luke handled the situation. "He went about his business when it became real clear his role was going to be different: going from a full-time starter to not really being in the rotation. He said to me, 'Coach, I want to do whatever I can.' He would pull a true freshman aside at practice and tell them, 'This is what we're looking for, this is why we do this.' He practiced and competed harder than anyone on the scout team. I could go and on, but to me the way that Luke set aside any personal disappointment to support his team is what 'winning' is all about."

To put all this in perspective, Luke McDonnell saw a total of 15 minutes in playing time during his entire senior season; he played 30 minutes *a game* just one year before. With the character demonstrated by players like Luke, it's obvious that Ben Jacobson is "paying it forward" by instilling in his players the same values and traits he learned from Coach Glas.

The Glas-Jacobson-McDonnell kind of "circle of life" influence that coaches and teachers can have on young people was a subject that Fred Hoiberg touched on as well. Fred had the unique opportunity to play in the NBA for some of the game's great coaches: Larry Brown, Larry Bird, Flip Saunders and Kevin McHale. Fred, now coaching at the University of Nebraska, cited how each of them contributed in different ways to his feel and understanding of the game. "All of them played a part in my coaching style and philosophy," Fred told us.

But in Fred's case, the belief in how coaches can and should impact the lives of their players can be traced all the way back to his grandparents, both of whom coincidentally worked at the University of Nebraska. Fred said, "My Grandpa Hoiberg was a sociology professor and my Grandpa Bush was the basketball coach here for nine years. At the end of the day, it's about what you do to help prepare your students or your players for whatever direction life takes them. I have gotten letters and emails from my grandpa's former players with stories that talk about the impact he had on their lives. That's really cool to hear. I think whether you're a teacher or a coach, which kind of go hand in hand, we help prepare kids for whatever direction life takes them."

Another subject touched on elsewhere in this book is the special relationship that Gerry "GMAT" Matalon enjoyed with the late Stuart Scott. GMAT also mentioned other former colleagues he considered to be in an elite "winner" class.

"Mike Tirico, Rece Davis and Sage Steele come to mind," GMAT said to us. "They all share the same quality of taking a keen interest in others. John Saunders was another special 'winner' and I remember the time when someone had gotten an opportunity that he did not get. He was very, very supportive of that individual, and spoke well of them. I said to him, 'John, that's an incredible quality of yours.' He replied, 'Well, I don't look at other people's success coming at my expense.' I remember sitting there and how it made me stop and think about my life, and how everyone is not your adversary. They can be a friendly rival. John Saunders was a 'winner' with an extraordinary ability to be able to conduct himself in a manner that always embraced others."

GMAT then elaborated further. "Just because someone is a successful player or coach doesn't necessarily make them a successful human being," he said. "I'll give you an example with a guy I highly admire, Herm Edwards. He is easily in the 'Top 10' of most influential men in my life. Herm didn't win a Super Bowl. He got to play in one, but he didn't win one. He didn't win one as a player and didn't win one as a coach. But, oh my, the amount of lives that this man has affected! I don't care about the championships, to me it's how you influence a life positively that is really what being a success is all about. Herm has been in so many different circles throughout his life: the football space as both a player and coach; the media space; and the most important space of all, that of a husband and father. You have to do well by others for them to speak well of you. To me, that is the most important measure of success."

Among the lessons shared in Chapter Seven was one from Kevin Negandhi wherein he talked about the importance of "bringing your 'A' game" each and every day, no matter the job or challenge. Kevin went into much greater detail in our interview with him. "I've bumped into a lot of athletes who are 'winners' through the years," Kevin said. "Wow, they bring it every day. They're prepared and they understand what's asked of them.

"I'm really lucky to work with a variety of different people with what I do on *SportsCenter* and in studio for college football and basketball," Kevin added. "I see guys all the time like Jonathan Velma and Mark Sanchez. I'm impressed with guys like that who played at the highest level in college and then in the pros as first-round picks, and how they always handle themselves. Jonathan is one of the most prepared people I've ever come across. Every day he's bringing something to the table and that carries through to all the guys I've worked with. It's a long list. Louis Riddick is a guy we do NFL stuff with in studio. He played in the league and used to be an executive. He's another guy who's always prepared, and always ready to go no matter what. Dan Orlovsky is a guy whose star is absolutely rising. All of them stand out to me."

Kevin continued, "I'm incredibly lucky to have been surrounded by guys like Mack Brown, who has since returned to the college game as the head coach at the University of North Carolina. He worked our college football studio show on ABC for five or six years. No one was more prepared and better understood what the job was every single week of the season. I sat there and watched one of the greatest college coaches of all time — a college football Hall of Famer — and said to myself, 'Okay, you're going to pick up a thing or two here.'

"When it comes to colleagues like Rece Davis and Chris Fowler, you see those guys prepare every single day. And no matter what the environment is, they always bring it. I worked with Hannah Storm for five years and saw her preparation every single day. It's always fun when you work with someone who's elevating their game, because you know that you're being elevated simply by working with them. And knowing all the while that you'd better bring your 'A' game every single day."

While it was about bringing your "A" game for Kevin Negandhi, it's long been about "quality at-bats" for Lesley Visser. "I was authentically a sports fan," Lesley said while talking about growing up in Boston. "Other kids loved music and poetry but I truly loved sports! I learned to score baseball as in '6 to 4 to 3' when I was 8 years old. My family didn't come from a lot of money, but my brother and I would take the bus to Fenway Park. You know, how blessed was I to be a native Bostonian where it was Ted Williams, Bill Russell, Bobby Orr and then Larry Bird? And the Red Sox were so tragic until they were fantastic. I had that going for me to be born in a city where sports and politics run the city."

In the prologue, we told the story of how Lesley's mother told her 10 year-old daughter that "Sometimes you have to cross when it says don't walk." Lesley shared that anecdote while reflecting on her trailblazing career. "It's a little different (for female sports journalists) now as the landscape is somewhat less demanding, as it should be," said Lesley. "It should be about equality, but back then I just had an attitude of gratitude. I didn't care how hard it was. I just felt like, 'My God, I'm being paid to go cover Wimbledon, the Final Four, the Super Bowl.' I took each first and tried to have every at-bat be a quality at-bat whether it was at a Final Four, World Series or Olympics assignment. Shortly after going to work for CBS, I received a letter from a fan who wrote me to say, 'You know what, I can see how you got where you are because I remember one time you wrote the hell out of badminton!' And that was the attitude I tried to have: Make every at-bat a quality at-bat."

While the use of sports metaphors in business is too often overdone, some do occasionally make perfect sense. For example, a truly poignant one was shared by Iowa State's director of athletics, Jamie Pollard. He said, "You often hear how an athlete who's really good seems to have everything happen in slow motion for them. They never seem helter-skelter, and things appear to be in slow motion for them while everybody else is seeing it in real time. And because they're seeing things in slow motion, they can maneuver so much more strategically through whatever it is they're facing.

"I think about that as an administrator when things are really hectic and seemingly so out of control, and I know on a personal level that's when I thrive. I feel like I'm able to see my way through those adverse situations very strategically, and actually enjoy it. I do think it's a common trait of 'winners' that when everything around them seems chaotic, they find a way to move past the chaos. I think the management challenge, or the game if you will, just slows down for them."

As Jamie pointed out, the ability to remain calm under pressure is a trait many "winners" share. The composure with which the late Peter Jennings was able to anchor coverage of breaking news on ABC, most especially during the events of 9/11, always astounded me. David Westin, president of ABC News at the time, said, "It started Tuesday morning and we were on nonstop until midnight, Friday night (9/14), without a pause, without a commercial break, with no break whatsoever. It was almost a hundred hours, and Peter was on the air for over sixty of those hours."

Peter once said, "The more chaotic things get around me, the calmer I get." John Berman, who toiled for two years as Peter's writer and now works as an anchor himself at CNN, confirmed the essence of Peter's statement with his personal, firsthand observations. John said, "Peter processing breaking news was like Ted Williams seeing the stitches on the ball when he hit." Former *World News Tonight* producer Jon Banner backed that up, saying, "That's 100% true. And Peter reminded all of us who worked with him to do the same. Definitely, a lesson for all of us."

One of the greatest sportscasters of our time, Vin Scully, has said, "Losing feels worse than winning feels good." It was not a surprise that Ben Sherwood, a lifetime Los Angeles Dodgers fan and devoted admirer of Vin Scully, expressed a view that expanded on that sentiment. Ben told us, "I share the same defect with many very competitive people who feel the pain of defeat — of failure — is much greater than any thrill of victory. We hate losing more than we enjoy winning! The misery of losing can be so excruciating and the joy of victory is so often so fleeting. I'd like to think that with some experience and age and plenty of defeats, I've gained a better perspective." Having founded and recently launched a family-oriented app focused on youth sports, Ben's evolving perspective on "winning" will now contribute to the greater good of many.

Ben Sherwood worked closely with John "Skip" Skipper during the time they served together as co-chairs of the Disney Media Networks. Skip's mindset when it comes to "winning" has evolved through the years as well. By his own admission, Skip was a very scrappy and competitive — if not spectacularly skilled — basketball player. For him, it was all about winning and losing. Skip had long subscribed to the "they keep score because it matters, right?" theory of competition. But he told us how his thinking has progressed with experience. Skip said, "I have become a big soccer fan and it took me a while to understand the concept that a draw is not necessarily a bad outcome. That is something I have learned and applied to business. I feel very strongly that it's an enormous mistake when doing business to assume that there has to be a winner and a loser. When you're in business — whether it's your partners, suppliers, marketing firms, advertising outlets or employees — your goal is to have it be a win-win for everybody." Such sensibility and sensitivity to business relationships is all too often undervalued.

John Wildhack, who worked for years with Skip at ESPN, told us, "It's about more than just how many games you win or how many championships you claim. It's about competing the right way, conducting yourself the right way and living your life the right way. I learned at ESPN, but also on my own in terms of collaboration, that those are the keys to being a good leader. I realized pretty quickly when I started producing games that while you may be in charge of the telecast, you're ultimately only as good as the director, camera people, audio operators, graphics people, the talent ... and everybody on the crew. Your job is to get the most out of those people and to make sure that they understand what we're trying to accomplish and why. That experience really, really helped develop the core set of leadership principles that I try to carry and live up to."

It can be cliché to glom on to "The Process" in a way that so many coaches, athletes, and business leaders have in recent years. Books have been written on the subject. Football coaches like Nick Saban at Alabama and Matt Campbell at Iowa State are convinced that team success is, in fact, the direct result of "The Process." Joel Embiid of the NBA's Philadelphia 76ers has even built his entire personal brand around the concept!

The dictionary tells us that a process is a fixed or ordered series of actions or events leading to a result. But practitioners of "The Process" have a cornerstone belief that a culture embracing a commitment to preparing in the right way — and in a methodical fashion — makes all the difference. They believe a "winner" chooses to focus on the constant preparation necessary to reach a goal or achieve a desired result; those who focus on the result itself are doomed to failure and disappointment. Jamie Pollard put a finer point on the importance of having the right focus. He said, "Coach Campbell talks a lot about trusting the process.

It's easy to get motivated by trying to have an outstanding outcome, but too often the outcome gets really shallow. It's working towards the outcome where the reward really is."

The insights embedded in the profiles and the valuable lessons shared by "winners" throughout this book can serve as a guide to nurturing the right habits and routines. They can also help maintain the proper focus on the process necessary to build the traits, qualities and attributes that lead to "winning" outcomes. As we've learned, attempting to define what a "winner" is turns out to be much more subjective and ambiguous than it is quantitative and clear. There is no checklist or secret recipe. That said, treating others with kindness, respect and empathy can be a foundational place to start.

The lasting impression that writing this book has left on me is that what it means to be a WINNER has everything to do with the relentless pursuit of becoming the best version of ourselves; of being the kind of person that you will be happy to live with the rest of your life. It's all about making the most of each and every one of your "winning" qualities by fanning even the smallest sparks of possibility into a bonfire of success.

REFLECTED THOUGHTS
BY ROB GRAY

"While most of us always think of growth as having a trajectory, sometimes it's more linear in nature. I think that's true about the growth people have experienced in the time of this pandemic. People learned things about themselves that they really weren't going to learn any other way. They had to be thrown in to the deep end, and they had to become wildly uncomfortable with their life and the way they ran things. ... I hope a lot of people come out of this time as better people."

Anne Sweeney to Rob Gray (May 4, 2020)

This project changed me. Partly because of the timing of it. Mostly because of the uplifting, yet unsettling subject matter. Conducting the interviews forced me to confront my own paralyzing fears. The words of the people I spoke with challenged my self-limiting beliefs. The confidence Ray Cole showed in me never wavered — even as I struggled to tamp down my own anxiety and sense of despair during the tumultuous 18 months or so that spanned the writing of this book.

A so-called "once in a century" global pandemic raged. A long overdue race-based reckoning roiled our nation. The most contentious presidential election in my lifetime crested and concluded, but not without rancor, unrest and one glaring, appalling incident.

I was hurting. Our nation — and world — was (and is) hurting. Talking to the people I interviewed for this book served as a salve for my shaken soul. I took comfort in the words of many of these "winners," knowing that they were also facing uncertainty, even heartbreak, amid the locked-down turmoil.

We were indeed "all in this together," tethered only by our mobile phone connections and the occasional choppy Zoom-based interaction. But we were still so achingly apart — from each other, from our loved ones, from hugs, kisses, concerts and sporting events.

I found purpose in this chaos. I finally started a meditation practice. Hell, now I've finally written a book along with Ray, something I long planned to do, but never would have gotten around to without his gentle support and generous prodding.

So I'm happy. And scared. That's where this process has put me. Back at square one, but with one critical difference: All of my senses are activated. For that, I'm immensely grateful.

Ray Cole changed my life. He'll change yours, too, through this book (if he hasn't already). Reflecting on all of that sure beats ruminating on everything else.

Oh, and at least three of the people we interviewed for *Hangin' with Winners* came out with excellent books of their own before this one was published:

- ABC News chief Washington correspondent Jon Karl's excellent *Front Row at the Trump Show* hit bookstore shelves three weeks before we interviewed him.
- CNN anchor and best-selling author Jake Tapper released the riveting thriller, *The Devil May Dance*, in May 2021.
- ABC News chief medical correspondent Dr. Jennifer Ashton wrote the powerful and essential book, *The New Normal: A Roadmap to Resilience in the Pandemic Era*, which came out in February 2021.

You should definitely consider reading all three of these, but Dr. Ashton provided us with a preview of sorts during our interview for this book. She shared what for her were the three major takeaways from the COVID-19 pandemic:

"First, it's shown the importance of intellectual honesty and integrity. From the beginning, this was a situation where everyone in medicine and media wanted to make it seem like they had the answer. But no one had the answer because we've never been in this situation before. So it was really important to be able to say, 'We don't know and no one knows' and not try to guess or go out on a limb.

The next thing is along a kind of intellectual diligence road. This has been a time in history when if you're not all in, you can't cover it. You can't cover it in the media, and you can't cover it in medicine, because things change that quickly. You need to have the historical and chronological perspective and context, while also having to know everything or close to everything that's being published and written and reported. That literally requires an around-the-clock kind of dedication to this topic.

Finally, there's the humanity side. It's been scary dealing with this pandemic both as a doctor and as the face of the network (for ABC News). That part of it has been really, really hard. It's hard to see people dying, and sick, and scared, and losing their jobs and be unaffected by that. In fact, it's impossible. But I think that actually being a real doctor has helped me with that aspect of it because it's just human nature, like a defense mechanism, to put up a very stone-faced facade and try to pretend you're so stoic that none of it matters. I don't think that's a good idea."

It's a terrible idea. When confronting a pandemic — or anything in life that involves pain and loss — denying what's happening doesn't change what's true. It all comes back around. Better to feel it all in every moment. That's how we find a path forward. That's how despair dissolves into deeper meaning. Only by moving — and being moved — do we get to the other side.

What is that? Who knows? But I got to the other side of this book; this B-side of "reflected thoughts," as it were. I hope that you, too, reflect on what you've learned from all of the recent events in the world, as well as the jewels of wisdom so many famous and not-so-famous folks shared with us during the course of this work. They can be distilled down to this: Work hard. Then work some more. Love yourself and care for others. If you can't do the first, always do the second. Make a difference in ways both large and small. Your impact on the world can't be objectively measured. "Winning" is a state of being and when done correctly pulls others along with you.

"All of us should be looking out for the next guy or the next gal, the next family, the lady down the block who needs her garbage cans pulled out," said longtime ESPN anchor Kenny Mayne, who has moved on to other lofty and meaningful pursuits. "It's all the little things we can do that are going to be beneficial … and be our salvation during the pandemic."

And as it winds down. So here we are. What now? Who knows. But I'll face it with less fear and more curiosity, because of the journey that began when I met Ray Cole and conducted the 60-plus interviews for this book.

"In some ways, adversity always reveals what's inside," former NFL All-Pro and native Iowan Aaron Kampman told us. "A lot of people are asking questions that are a little deeper than normal right now — and more reflective. They are now asking questions about who and why, rather than about what. It's interesting to observe human behavior, fear, uncertainty and what happens to people when we don't know. We just don't have a bucket for this one."

—Rob Gray, June 30, 2021

A FEW NOTES
ABOUT SOURCES

The content of this book is based overwhelmingly on the more than 60 personal interviews conducted between February 1 and September 30, 2020. It also relies on many of the recollections, conversations and correspondence gathered over the course of Ray's career. Earlier profiles written for the RayColeTV.com website were drawn upon as well.

Additional resources and materials:

Prologue
1. "16 Inspiring Quotes from U.S. Open Tennis Legend Arthur Ashe" Retrieved from Entrepreneuer.com
2. Winfrey, Oprah (January 2007) "Building a Dream" in *The Oprah Magazine*
3. *The Ride of a Lifetime* by Robert Iger (Random House, 2019)
4. (May 20, 2009) "Michael J. Fox to play in Principal Charity Classic" Retrieved from DesMoinesRegister.com
5. "Pat Summitt Quotes" Retrieved from BrainyQuote.com
6. Lenker, Maureen Lee (December 3, 2019) "Jimmy Kimmel proves what's good for the goose is good for the gander with *The Serious Goose*" Retrieved from EW.com

Chapter One

1. *Every Town Is a Sports Town* by George Bodenheimer with Donald T. Phillips (Grand Central Publishing, Hachette Book Group 2015)
2. *The Ride of a Lifetime* by Robert Iger (Random House, 2019)
3. "Walt Disney Quotes" Retrieved from QuoteFancy.com

Chapter Two

1. "Peter Jennings - Wikiquote" Retrieved from Wikiquote.org
2. "Peter Jennings Remembered" Retrieved from ABCNews.com
3. "Nightline: Whitewater: Overplayed Underplayed?" Retrieved from TVNews.Vanderbilt.edu
4. Ryan, Maureen (November 22, 2005) "Ted Koppel signs off '*Nightline*' on Tuesday...with Morrie" Retrieved from ChicagoTribune.com
5. Shales, Tom (November 23, 2005) "An Anchor Who Carried Weight" Retrieved from WashingtonPost.com
6. *Everybody's Got Something* by Robin Roberts & Veronica Chambers (Grand Central Publishing, 2014)
7. Gomez, Patrick (August 23, 2015) "Robin Roberts on Surviving Cancer and the Death of Her Mother: 'I Get Up Every Day and Do What I Can to Be Strong'" Retrieved from People.com
8. *All Too Human: A Political Education* by George Stephanopoulos (Little, Brown & Company, 1999)
9. *Audition: A Memoir* by Barbara Walters (Knopf, 2008)
10. "Oprah Talks to Barbara Walters" Retrieved from Oprah.com
11. Clancy, Martin and Caron, Christina (May 6, 2008) "Audition: Barbara Walters' Journey" Retrieved from ABCNews.go.com
12. *In An Instant: A Family's Journey of Love and Healing* by Lee & Bob Woodruff (Random House, 2007)
13. Barthel, Michael; Gottfried, Jeffrey; and Mitchell, Amy (April 4, 2017) "Most Say Tensions Between Trump Administration and News Media Hinder Access to Political News" Retrieved from PewResearch.org
14. *Front Row at the Trump Show* by Jon Karl (Dutton, 2020)
15. Tani, Maxwell (February 19, 2017) "ABC reporter delivers pointed declaration to Trump: We will 'pursue the truth' even if we must endure your 'wrath'" Retrieved from BusinessInsider.com

Chapter Three

1. Deford, Frank (Aug. 8, 1983) "'I'VE WON. I'VE BEAT THEM.'" Retrieved from SI.com
2. *It's Awesome, Baby* by Dick Vitale with Dick Weiss and Joan Williamson (Ascend Books, 2014)
3. *Life is Not an Accident: A Memoir of Reinvention* by Jay Williams (HarperCollins, 2016)

Chapter Four

1. Romenesko, Jim (August 17, 2011) "WOI-TV: Colbert PAC ad rejection 'a close call'" Retrieved from Poynter.org
2. Eggerton, John (August 31, 2011) "WOI's Super PAC Smackdown" Retrieved from BroadcastingCable.com
3. *Always Looking Up: The Adventures of an Incurable Optimist* by Michael J. Fox (Hyperion Books, 2009)
4. Ellis, Rosemary (October, 2013) "No Complaints, No Excuses" *Good Housekeeping*
5. Hautman, Nicholas (June 6, 2016) "Michael J. Fox on Fighting Parkinson's Disease With Muhammad Ali: We Were 'Part of Something Bigger'" Retrieved from USMagazine.com
6. (February 28, 2017) "Michael J. Fox Leads More Than 200 Parkinson's Disease Advocates on Capitol Hill in Support of Federal Research Funding and Access to Care" Retrieved from MichaelJFox.org
7. Stern, Abby (September 19, 2016) "EXCLUSIVE: Inside Jimmy Kimmel's Celebrity Chef-Studded Emmy Afterparty" Retrieved from People.com
8. Johnson, Zach (May 16, 2017) "Jimmy Kimmel Returning to Host the 2018 Oscars" Retrieved from EOnline.com
9. de Moraes, Lisa (October 8, 2018) "Jimmy Kimmel Heading Back To Brooklyn" Retrieved from Deadline.com
10. Sheckells, Melinda (June 15, 2019) "Jimmy Kimmel Opens Las Vegas Comedy Club, Surprise Lineup Includes Sarah Silverman" Retrieved from HollywoodReporter.com

Chapter Five

1. Noble, Jason and Pfannenstiel, Brianne (May 22, 2017) "Terry Branstad confirmed as U.S. ambassador to China" Retrieved from DesMoinesRegister.com
2. *The Real Deal: The Life of Bill Knapp* by William B. Friedricks (Business Publications Corporation Inc., 2013)
3. Kilen, Mike (May 21, 2015) "70 years later, Bill Knapp tells his story of Okinawa" Retrieved from DesMoinesRegister.com
4. (July 7, 2018) "Robert D. Ray, longtime Iowa Governor, dies at 89" Retrieved from Politico.com
5. *Bernie Saggau & the Iowa Boys* by Chuck Offenburger (Iowa High School Athletic Association, 2005)
6. *Gary Thompson All-American* by Chuck Offenburger (Hexagon Grandhaven Group, 2008)

Chapter Six

1. Parenti, Deborah (August 28, 2017) "The Broadcasters Foundation Is On A Mission" Retrieved from RadioInk.com
2. (May 5, 2010) "Thomases to be honored at ESPYS" Retrieved from ESPN.com
3. Strauss, Chris (July 18, 2013) "Robin Roberts' inspiring speech won the ESPYS" Retrieved from USAToday.com
4. Strauss, Chris (July 17, 2014) "Stuart Scott's ESPYS speech was his finest television moment" Retrieved from USAToday.com
5. Tsuji, Alysha (July 13, 2016) "Craig Sager gives emotional, inspiring speech after receiving the Jimmy V Award for Perseverance" Retrieved from USAToday.com
6. (May 20, 2009) "Michael J. Fox to play in Principal Charity Classic" Retrieved from DesMoinesRegister.com
7. (June 8, 2019) "Jody Reynolds Obituary" Retrieved from Legacy.com
8. *Don't Give Up...Don't Ever Give Up: The Inspiration of Jimmy V* by Justin Spizman and Robyn F. Spizman (Sourcebooks, Inc., 2010)

Epilogue

1. "Albert Schweitzer Quotes" Retrieved from GoodReads.com
2. Berman, John and Banner, Jon (September 26, 2020) [Twitter Posts] Retrieved from John Berman and Jon Banner verified Twitter accounts
3. "40 Famous Vin Scully quotes of All Time" Retrieved from SportyTell.com
4. "For me, there was one…" Interview by Larry King, *Larry King Live*, CNN (April 10, 2002)

INDEX

Page numbers appearing in *italic* type refer to pages that contain photographs.

CPSIA information can be obtained
at www.ICGtesting.com
Printed in the USA
JSHW030221260921
18937JS00004BA/4